Asian Perspectives on the World's Religions after September 11

Asian Perspectives on the World's Religions after September 11

**Arvind Sharma and
Madhu Khanna, Editors**

PRAEGER

AN IMPRINT OF ABC-CLIO, LLC
Santa Barbara, California • Denver, Colorado • Oxford, England

Library of Congress Cataloging-in-Publication Data

Asian perspectives on the world's religions after September 11 / Arvind Sharma and Madhu Khanna, editors.
pages cm
Proceedings of a conference held Sept. 11–15, 2006 in Montreal, Quebec.
Includes index.
ISBN 978-0-313-37896-6 (hardcopy : alk. paper) — ISBN 978-0-313-37897-3 (ebook) 1. Religions—Congresses. 2. September 11 Terrorist Attacks, 2001—Influence—Congresses. 3. Religions—Influence—Congresses. 4. Asia—Congresses. I. Sharma, Arvind. II. Khanna, Madhu.
BL80.3.A85 2013
200—dc23 2012041181

ISBN: 978-0-313-37896-6
EISBN: 978-0-313-37897-3

17 16 15 14 13 1 2 3 4 5

This book is also available on the World Wide Web as an eBook.
Visit www.abc-clio.com for details.

Praeger
An Imprint of ABC-CLIO, LLC

ABC-CLIO, LLC
130 Cremona Drive, P.O. Box 1911
Santa Barbara, California 93116-1911

This book is printed on acid-free paper ∞

Manufactured in the United States of America

Contents

Introduction

Arvind Sharma

I

The events of September 11, 2001, are too well known to need recounting. They are ineffaceable from modern memory. Given their importance, a global conference was held in Montreal from September 11–15, 2006, on the fifth anniversary of the event, to assess its significance in the context of world's religions. This conference, titled *World's Religions after September 11*, was attended by over 2,000 delegates from 84 countries, who participated in presentations and panels on the following eight main themes: (1) religion and human rights; (2) proselytization and religious freedom; (3) religion, dīn, dao, or dharma; (4) religion and science; (5) religion and spirituality; (6) religion and healing; (7) religion and women; and (8) religion and the media. The wide attention the conference attracted led to the inclusion of the following additional themes: (1) religion, children, and youth; (2) religion, conflict, and peace; (3) religion and international diplomacy; (4) religion in the field; (5) religion and war; (6) religion and ethics; and (7) contemporary religious leaders.

Professor Madhu Khanna, a professor at the Centre for the Study of Comparative Religion and Civilizations at the Jamia Millia Islamia in Delhi, also participated in this conference. At the end of the conference, she proposed that the events of September 11, 2001, were of major significance not only for the West, but also for Asia. Therefore, it was highly desirable to hold a sequel to the present conference, in the form of a global congress that viewed the events of September 11 from an Asian perspective. The suggestion was welcomed by everyone with whom she shared it.

Accordingly, a global conference on *World's Religions after September 11—An Asian Perspective* met in New Delhi from January 17–19, 2009, which was inaugurated by His Holiness, the Dalai Lama and which focused on the following themes: (1) religion and civilizational dialogue; (2) religion, conflict, and peace; (3) religion and human rights; (4) religion and the arts; (5) religion and ethics; (6) religion, hermeneutics, and literature; (7) religion and gender; (8) religion and ecology; (9) religion and globalization; and (10) Mahatma Gandhi and conflict resolution.

This book is the precipitate of this conference, as its title indicates.

II

The first chapter, by Madhu Khanna, explores the idea of Asia, and the second chapter, by Anuradha Ghosh, documents the pervasive effect of the events of September 11. Thus, the two together provide the background setting for this book, as each of these two chapters explores one of the two dots that were connected by this conference.

The set of three chapters that follows examines some of the world religions in the context of civilizational dialogue—an issue brought to the forefront by the events of September 11, 2001. The chapter by Ashok Vohra identifies a contribution Jainism could make to this dialogue, while the chapter by Ahmad Sohaib brings a critical lens to bear on the contribution early Buddhism could make to the subject. The chapter by I. H. Azad Faruqi draws attention to the sources available in Islam to deal with the suffering that resulted from the events of September 11.

The next set of four chapters, by Albert Welter, Gerrit De Vylder, Ghulam-Sarwar Yousof, and Malini Saran, deals with examples of mutual influences among religions and cultures in the context of civilizational dialogue in Asia, where religion is not separated from culture the way it is in Western civilization. Welter deals with such interaction at the level of religion, De Vylder at the level of civilization, Yousof at the level of popular culture, and Saran at the level of classical culture.

The impact of the events of September 11 was not limited to religion, but had implications for study of religion as well. This virgin territory is explored by Joseph T. O'Connell and Madhu Khanna. O'Connell examines this point in the context of the study of religion in general, and Khanna examines it in the context of India in particular.

The next set of four chapters shifts the focus of discussion to the interface of religion and human rights, for one way of looking at the events of September 11 would be to consider them as yet another example of the violation of human rights in the name of a world religion. Joseph Prabhu provides a refreshing survey of the evolution of human rights discourse from a cross-cultural perspective, while I examine one such particular right, namely, "religious freedom." Similarly, Tran My-Van documents a specific case of the violation of minority rights from Vietnam, providing valuable data on the point, while Bidisha Kumar and George James indicate how religion can at times obstruct rather than promote the cause of environmental rights.

The last two chapters consist of two case studies from India, which have implications of post–September 11 discourse. The chapter by Radha Madhav Bharadwaj addresses the interface of tribal religions and world religions, highlighting some of its dangers, while the chapter by Rana P. B. Singh harnesses the resources of Hinduism for evolving a global environmental ethic.

The editors hope that these Asian perspectives will enrich the global discourse around the watershed events of September 11, 2001.

The Idea of Asia

Madhu Khanna

While planning for the global congress in India, one question that arose repeatedly was, "Whether there is, or can be, an Asian perspective to the violence and terror in the public sphere that is threatening humanity globally?" In our quest for meaning and insight on that question, the Congress set out to assemble together as many interpretations as possible, and capture different mental maps from the discourses that are going on in the field of religious studies. Undoubtedly, such a proposition was beset with many assumptions and preconceptions, for any attempt to reorient the Orient with the ideal of a universal Pan-Asianism in any defined area is fraught with danger. The idea of Asia today, largely advocated by geopolitical analysts and strategists, conjures up gory images of a dismembered Asia, a zone of violence and terror, border disputes, and nuclear weapons in a civilizationally disparate site. Thus, to link them as one singular entity bound by a common locus of identity smacks of an occidentally constructed Orientalism, where the Eurocentric definition of a romantic and exotic East veils the reality of how Asians perceive themselves. Modern scholarship has brought to light that there is no singular idea of Asia. The buzzword "Asia" is a free-floating term with many contested meanings. The multiple views largely draw upon arguments from economic growth, normative and ideational notions, and civilizational linkages. Thus, there is an "imperialist Asia," "nationalist Asia," "Universalist Asia," "regionalist Asia," and the newly emerging views on "exceptionalist Asia."[1]

The imperialists divided Asia into separate powers, severing the unity of the ocean. Western cartographers further created well-defined frozen borders that were once fluid. The exponents of a "nationalist Asia" were governed by a group of Asian nationalist leaders whose main concern centered on Asia's rejuvenation to decolonize the said countries from Western hegemonic dominance.

Another unitive idea of Asia was in vogue in ancient times and later appropriated by many exponents: namely, the Nobel Laureate Rabindranath Tagore (1861–1941), Okakura Kazuo (1862–1913), and Sister Nivedita (1867–1911), the disciple of Swami Vivekananda. Tagore was undoubtedly a pioneer in spreading the message of Asian Universalism. He traveled to Japan, China, Southeast Asia, Iran, and Iraq in the early part of the 20th century, and advocated a "Universalism with a difference."[2] Tagore was far from supporting political regionalism of states. He believed that there was a "common bond of spiritualism" among Asian people.

As late as 1989, another idea of Asia emerged with its new agenda of regionalism, fostered on the basis of providing support and interdependence among Asian nations. It did not advocate insular isolation of regions but a creative interdependence of regions, based on mutual complementarities. The aim was to harness all-around growth and proactive dynamism that will allow an Asian identity to become more recognizable and prominent.

Alongside these views, by the 1990s, a new vision of an "exceptionalist Asia" was brought into prominence by Asia's power elite. This view puts to rest the negative connotations of Western Orientalists' notion of Asian distinctiveness and subservience. The "exceptionalist Asia" can be read in the emerging discourses on "rising Asia" as a super economic power, a vision centered entirely on spiritual and moral values and cultural traits, rooted in the religious consciousness of the Asian people. It draws its inspiration from the ancient pathways through which religious cultures (Hindu, Buddhist, and Islamic) traveled from India across the seas to Indonesia, Bali, Thailand, Burma, Malaysia, and Cambodia. The great religions of India were not only of Indian origin, but spread out via India. The focus of trade and transmission of the Sanskrit language enabled India to dominate as a center of cultural power.

The role of India as a religious knowledge hub and disseminator of Asian culture and religion in Southeast Asia has gone unchallenged. The dominance of India in the past was triggered by an uninterrupted religious trail. Buddhism spread both eastward and westward via India. As early as the second century, Hindu civilization had left a mark in Vietnam, the Champa, and Funan.

From the ninth century onward, Islam made headway into Southeast Asia not by the sword, but by a band of seaborne traders. Arab Islam was revived as Southeast Asian Islam, modified by local patterns of culture reflecting a more cosmopolitan nature. The cross-fertilization between Hindu,

Buddhist, and Islamic religions that took place in Southeast Asia is reflected in several chapters in this book.

Albert Welter's chapter, while discussing the religious context of Chinese society, argues that modern secular societies like China must embrace a model of secularism that honors the multireligious dimensions of society. Gerrit De Vylder searches for a common ethic based on different potentialities of Asian cultures and Western models. Malini Saran draws up the historical roots of the peaceful, yet dynamic, process of adaptation and integration that took place through the Javanese narration of the Hindu epics, the Rāmāyaṇa and the Mahābhārata. Ghulam-Sarwar Yousof reaffirms the South Asian influences in the Malay theater and the nature of accommodation that has taken place. The multifarious views validate that cross-border ties predate the modern period. Asia and Southeast Asia were culturally knitted together and shared a deep resonance with each other, reemphasizing that both faith and trade played a part in molding their identity.

CONCLUSION

The deliberations at the Congress aim to recover the positive role that the world's religions can play in an era of terror. In the context of emergent views on an "exceptionalist Asia," world religions can play a crucial role to bring about a more collaborative future between cultures.

We have to contend that there is an Asia, and its inhabitants live by their own indigenous worldviews that are rooted in Buddhist, Hindu, Confucian, and Islamic values. There is no reason why a collectivist common ethos cannot reemerge from the indigenous legacy of Asian civilizations where religious ethos blends with perennial human values to alleviate the problems of global terror.

NOTES

1. Amitav Acharya, *Asia Is Not One: Regionalism and the Ideas of Asia* (Singapore: Institute of Southeast Asian Studies, 2011).

2. Sugata Bose, *His Majesty's Opponent: Subhas Chandra Bose and India's Struggle against Empire* (Boston, MA: Harvard University Press, 2011).

Chapter 1

"Civilizational Dialogues" through Popular Frames Post 9/11

Anuradha Ghosh

The "war on terror" post 9/11 was not merely a declaration before a joint session of the U.S. Congress by former U.S. President George W. Bush on September 20, 2001. It was a culmination of popular coinages used by the state in response to the horrific events following the criminal attack on the Twin Towers and the Pentagon in which an estimated 2,976 victims and 19 terrorists died, with another 6,294 people treated in hospitals for injuries. The "Clash of Civilizations," "Crusade against Islam," "Barbarism versus Civilization," and similar descriptive epithets expressed the shock and anger that the United States—and indeed much of the world—felt. Paralyzed in a grip of impotence despite being a superpower and commanding the strongest, well-equipped, and well-trained army with sophisticated internal security networks, it was powerless in preventing the event that was first and foremost a human tragedy.

The asymmetrical nature of "civilizational dialogues" that followed operated on a twin dialectic that, to a large extent, assimilated earlier Eurocentric colonial discourses on the (non-Christian) cultures of West Asian people around a new rallying point that both engaged the specter of terrorism and Islam, and paved the way for a logic of war on civilians who became the mute recipients of "bread and bomb" politics. Attention was first given to the question of barbarism and dictatorship versus democracy in Iraq (as well as the alleged "weapons of mass destruction" or WMDs), and later focus put on Afghanistan. The international sanctions against Iraq, levied by most of the nations of the world, seemed to reify the "Axis of Evil" demarcation by the United States. One of the greatest facilitators to this asymmetrical discourse has been the popular media whose "reality bytes" are little different from the "reel" response in films, literature, and popular arts, in which interstices the subject of this chapter lies. In terms of an ongoing engagement with the theme of violence and terror, it has an all-pervasive influence in the mad circulation of images that surround us with deluge-like intensity today.

9/11 has indeed become such a watershed in the field of popular arts and ideas that in the American context, it has given birth to a distinct genre of literary and cultural representations called the 9/11 genre.[1] If one looks at the video game or comic book industry, one kind of attempt that seems to be emerging is to reassure the young generation that 9/11 was an aberration and that the United States still remains the superpower as it was. The muscle-flexing in West Asia is enough justification for the reiteration of the belief of the invincibility of the Empire. If one takes a look at the dozens of documentaries that were produced around the time—with titles like *Fahrenheit 9/11, 9/11 Mysteries, Terror Storm, Why the Towers Fell?*, and so on and so forth—or movies made like *September 11, 25 Hour, Flight 93, Homeland Security, New York* (interestingly, a Bollywood production), the trend indicates the level of shock generated by the event worldwide. What is further interesting about the production of films, literature, video games, and music albums since 9/11 is that the renderings are not in English alone; other foreign language productions, primarily in Korean and Japanese, had a wide popularity in the context of their origin. In the literary arena, as many as 24 novels and poems have been written on the theme where, at times, the worst kind of stereotyping of the Muslim community is seen. Cashing in on the tragedy and fanning the sentiments of Islamophobia, stereotypes are created to enable what Pankaj Mishra describes, following Don DeLillo's novel *Falling Man,* as "the narcissistic heart of the West"[2] to come to terms with the fact that the dotcom boom was not an answer to the contentions that were spiraling in the world at large. In the Indian context, the release of films like *Aamir, A Wednesday, The Terrorist, Black Friday, Mission Kashmir, Dil Jale,* and *Mumbai Meri Jaan* no longer makes any attempt to address the question of what makes a terrorist. As Gulzar asks in *Maachis,* set against the backdrop of Sikh militancy/terrorism: "*Aatankwaadi kya khet mein ugate hain*? [Do terrorists grow in fields?]."[3]

What emerges as evident from the brief overview of the 9/11 genre is that, like media discourses on the subject of terrorism and violence, as well as those found in popular literary and cultural productions, the principle of populism seems to dominate creating a one-dimensional axis of representation, whereby the distinction between fact and fiction becomes largely blurred. The manner in which television networks sold the "war on terror" in Afghanistan and Iraq, creating a spectacle of power with the grand aura of technological superiority of the American military right up to the capture of the late Saddam Hussein, followed by his death sentence (along with the horrors revealed in Guantanamo Bay and Abu Ghraib prisons), worked in terms of a package that had the façade of neutrality. The perspective of narration was never from the point of view of recipients, the so-called beneficiaries of American benevolence and justice. The notion of neutrality might seem contradictory at the manifest level, but the underlying paradoxical logic on which it operates, or at least in this case has been seen to operate, can be justified in the course of discussing such a fairy tale whose make-believe structures and populist discourses function, embodying only a kind of surface reality, and whose plasticity blunts critical analysis.

It is in this context that one has to see how the "war on terror" followed the "clash of civilization" theory, making civilizational dialogues of any kind more or less a meaningless activity, despite the United States' avowed policy of multiculturalism. The question is why the Bush administration found it fit to follow the clash of civilization theory, originally propounded by Bernard Lewis, an acclaimed scholar in the field of historical studies in Princeton University, in the wake of 9/11 through terms of an "irrational" but surely "historic reaction" of "rivals" against "Judeo-Christian heritage."[4] Lewis's attempt to understand the new global order post Soviet collapse, made popular by Samuel P. Huntington's civilizational conflict paradigm,[5] argues that the source of conflict in the present era would be based on religio-cultural civilizational factors rather than ideological or economic factors. This thesis reveals an interesting shift from the realm of the economic/ideological to that of the religio-cultural civilizational as determining factors, which may threaten to make or mar existence. The earlier territorial nature of conflict as part of colonial expansionist programs, which worked on a certain "civilizing" mission, is displaced with a new enemy that is rather like a bogey; that is to say, the Islam-versus-the-West diametric is a phantasmic construction. The declaration of an inevitable World War III, with a focal alignment of Islamic and Confucian traditions vis-à-vis the West, marks the apocalyptic strain of the discourse of civilizational clash quite in the tradition of scholarship—such scholarship that declared the end of history, the end of ideology, and the end of humans.[6] Although not left unchallenged, this "clash" has received unprecedented attention in recent times, particularly in facilitating the war on terror post 9/11.

In this context, Dr. Hans Koechler's critique of Huntington's "cultural hermeneutics"[7] is interesting. It aims to point out the need of the "other" to define the "self" as it is the "clash of interests"[8] rather than civilizations that propel the wheels of history to rotate. Defining the thesis of civilizational clash as neo-imperialistic in tenor, Koechler goes on to argue that the war on terror conceals "a long-term strategy of re-colonization"[9] in the context of globalization, which "[f]or many in the developing world, has become the keyword for ideological and cultural 'imperialism' of the West."[10] Therefore, it incorporates in its sweep the old rationale of colonialist/imperialist discourse structured on the time-tested "hegemonic scheme of European power politics"[11] of the preceding century. The "us versus them" paradigm, or what is referred to here as "us versus the others,"[12] is the operational dialectic of the "dominationist relationship" that marks the present world order, which is largely unipolar following the fall of the Soviet Union. The need to "construct" the enemy follows the imperatives of dominationist discourses of power for almost a decade. Therefore, the apprehension of an attack on the symbols of American economic and military power seems to have been anticipated, as popular literary and cultural representations indicate; thus 9/11 happens almost like a prophecy. Huntington's thesis only helps in constructing the enemy stereotype, fanning racist as well as religious fundamentalism as an antidote to the politics of Islamic terror.

In the post–Cold War context, the events of 9/11 ironically provided a new oppositional pole for a global alignment of forces, which needs war to "progress," and the best way to replace the rhetoric of Red Menace following the Soviet collapse is to use the upsurge of Islamic fundamentalism.[13] This argument has been reiterated by scholars in the field primarily because American foreign policy seems unable to move beyond the framework of "bloc mentality"[14] of the earlier era to further its strategic interests, particularly in its present phase of financial crisis. This is best described by Fidel Castro in terms of "the casino effect,"[15] which speculative capital interests create. The nature of assimilating old forms to create new stereotypes fomenting Islamophobia has been the leading tendency promoted by what Theodor Adorno called the "culture industry," embedded as it is in the discourse of the ideological dominant. The media constructions of the war on terror on a global scale make it the latest appendage of the culture industry, as it too operates increasingly through mythologies that reproduce a network of images that can sustain the status quo. This catches on the slogan value of the phrases uttered by President Bush when describing the reaction of the United States in response to the devastation of 9/11, while other phrases worked like bylines (as mentioned earlier). The doctrine of the clash of civilizations is incomplete without the construction of the Axis of Evil that operated in the Middle East and Central Asia (including North Korea in its sweep), suspecting the creation of WMD. Meanwhile, countries "beyond the Axis of Evil"[16] included Latin America (primarily Cuba), Syria, and Libya, which justified the war on terror in terms of culmination. All the alternative discourses challenged the United States' proclaimed "war" against a group of people, rather than against a country with a distinct political boundary, as largely an imagined war, which made scholars like Noam Chomsky[17] question and reiterate the outright imperialistic tenor of U.S. foreign policy that brooked no opposition as the world's "leading terrorist state."[18] He added that the popular culture, not the state, was "one of the most extreme religious fundamentalist cultures in the world."[19] Substantiating the accusation that the United States was a murderous terrorist state, Chomsky mentions its role in different countries of Latin America, where direct U.S. interference has been the cause of their spiraling poverty and economic asphyxiation. He cites the example of Sudan in particular, where under the signal of the Clinton administration, the al-Shifa pharmaceutical plant was blown up, destroying the production of life-saving drugs needed particularly in a war-torn country reeling under external attack.[20] The Central Intelligence Agency (CIA)-orchestrated bomb explosions in Beirut on civilian targets and several other instances of "crimes of state"[21] give no moral legitimacy to the "war" against "terror" that it wages.

If, during the Cold War, the communist menace or Red terror was used to justify arbitrary uses of American state power (in particular) to keep the economic regime in place, Islamophobia was constructed after the fall of the Soviet Union, keeping the basic operational schema in place with minor adjustments of terms of reference that could realign it with the cultural political coding necessary to make it plausible. Interestingly, the Islamophobic constructions are of West Asian origin, while the large number of African Muslims and East Asian Muslims are seemingly left out as strategic oil interests and inroads into Asia that need to be created in order to keep the world under Uncle Sam's thumb. But what would happen if Uncle Sam discovered that the game that he is playing on a global scale is much like the game that Charlie Chaplin depicts in the film *Great Dictator?* Originally a commentary on Hitler, Chaplin's character realizes in dismay that what he had thought of as a plaything could be easily deflated, like a prick in a balloon. Leaving conjectures aside, it is important to reiterate that even the attempt to construct the specter of Islamophobia in terms of Islam-versus-the-West is seriously flawed, as one can no longer think in terms of the cultural monoliths that Huntington creates as an ontological normative. As the West cannot be conceived without Islam, Edward Said argues in "The Clash of Ignorance,"

> The altogether more reassuring battle orders (a crusade, good versus evil, freedom against fear, etc.) drawn out of Huntington's alleged opposition between Islam and the West, from which official discourse drew its vocabulary in the first days after the September 11 attacks [fall flat]. There's since been a noticeable de-escalation in

> that discourse, but to judge from the steady amount of hate speech and actions, plus reports of law enforcement efforts directed against Arabs, Muslims and Indians all over the country, the paradigm stays on.
>
> One further reason for its persistence is the increased presence of Muslims all over Europe and the United States. Think of the populations today of France, Italy, Germany, Spain, Britain, America, even Sweden, and you must concede that Islam is no longer on the fringes of the West but at its center.[22]

He further states that the reasons behind Islamophobia can be traced to the deep-rooted anxieties of a collective culture, which has embedded in its memories of the past, the threat Arab-Islamic conquests pose if one cares to go even cursorily through the signposts of European history.

A somewhat similar argument is posed by Oleh Osman Bakar in his keynote address[23] at the *Global Forum on Civilization and Peace* held in Seoul, December 2005, where he traces the fault lines of the discourses of West–Islam cultural divide post 9/11. Refuting the idea of "two monolithic blocks"[24] conceived as "Islam and the West" or "the Islamic world and the West" in perpetual contention with each other, he questions the conceptual tenability of the categories themselves. What the term "Islam" or "the Islamic world" denotes is the first question he raises:

> Do we . . . mean by "the Islamic world" the group comprising of all Muslim majority and Muslim-ruled nation-states? If that is the case, then we have to exclude about 500 million Muslims or a third of world's Muslims from the "Islamic world," because they happen to live as minorities.[25]

Again, with reference to the notion implied in the term "West," he argues that "[i]n recent years, Islam has grown in the West to the point of becoming its second largest religion"[26] and therefore one cannot really be caught in the straitjacket of a discourse that refuses to take into account the mutual influences that the West and the Islamic world have on each other. These are the new realities that the global community, and not the United States alone, faces post 9/11, despite the problems that civilizational dialogues encounter. Taking the definition of the term "Islam" to indicate "the global Muslim community and its civilization" and the term "West" as embracing its Muslim minorities,[27] Osman Bakar foregrounds a peace initiative where the Western world has to engage in a dialogue with the "global Ummah" implying both the "religion and its worldwide community"[28] and therefore asserts that "the West has to dialogue with a part of itself, namely its Muslim minorities."[29] This seems to be like a *khwabnama,*[30] charting not reality, but dream-like aspirations of the secular, liberal, democratic world of the racial other in (and outside) the West, which it needs for furthering its strategic, economic, and political interests. This creates an asymmetrical relation infringing on the sovereignty of nation-states in the name of "war on terror," and at the same time, it tries to adopt a moral and intellectual stance in its rapacious leadership of the world costing not only the U.S. exchequer, but also the lives of people in the battlegrounds they create to maintain their imperial hegemony.

Most peace initiatives post 9/11 attempt civilizational dialogues. Interfaith and intrafaith discourses tend to obliterate ground realities,[31] which need to be evaluated as to what kind of dialogue can be fostered when chemical and phosphorus laden weapons in Palestine target civilians (and not military establishments), and the U.S.-supported Israeli forces do not even spare the UN office there in a spate of attacks in January 2008. The issue of the Kurdish Muslims, caught between a triad of hostile forces in Iraq, has its own tryst with destiny. Films like *Turtles Can Fly*[32] illustrate this with the utmost poignant sensitivity, calling attention to the human dimension of the tragedy, no less than a 9/11. Interestingly, the idea of civilizational dialogues came into existence after the Soviet fall and the end of the Cold War between the socialist and capitalist blocs, which had divided the world into a bipolar axis after the two world wars. The demise of the old confrontational paradigm of international relations paved the way for a new one, as the end of "the age of ideology" ushered in new fault lines that marked the tensions between civilizations, cultures, and religions. Walid M. Abdenasser, in *Dialogue among Civilizations: Dialectics of the Challenge*,[33] draws attention to this new reality, concomitant as it was with the rise of globalization and economic liberalization. Such liberalization did away with the earlier regulatory market modules protecting the interests of nation-states, which now had to follow the dictates of the International Monetary Fund (IMF) and World Banks who caught them in their debt traps, having to allow foreign direct investment to get out of the economic recession, and were part of a eulogy for the triumph of the Western liberal democratic model. As a counter to Huntington's thesis of "clash," which was a response to Francis Fukuyama's *The End of History and the Last Man*,[34] the idea of "dialogue among civilizations" was propounded by the former Iranian president, Mohammad Khatami. As a result of the initiative taken by Iran and supported by Egypt and Italy, among several other countries, the UN General Assembly adopted a resolution in 1998 that declared the year 2001 as the year of dialogue among civilizations. The intention was to orient international relations in the post–Cold War phase in a direction that would not repeat the errors of the past, fraught as it was, in open or tacit global wars. A series of discussions and round tables happened under the aegis of UNESCO and the Organization of Islamic Conference (OIC) until the setback of the 9/11 attacks was dealt to it.

The genesis of the idea of civilizational dialogue can be traced back to the 1893 World's Parliament of Religions held in Chicago, which Swami Vivekananda addressed on the first day, bringing to the forefront a notion of synthesis between the spiritual/mystical traditions of the East and the West. With the centenary year of the global congress being celebrated in Chicago in 1993, followed by the gathering in similar lines at Cape Town in South Africa in 1999, where the issue of AIDS was highlighted on the agenda along with other reform-oriented, humanitarian projects, there seems to be a sustained effort to revive attempts at dialogue between nations and cultures, to foster cooperation and religious tolerance through mutual understanding and regard for the other. The events of 9/11 seem to have turned the flow of the tide in a complete reversal, giving sanction to the idea of "war" rather than that of "dialogue." They are locked in an antithetical play making reality, whether "reel" or "real," as nothing more than a gesture of nations caught in the language game of naming the bogey. In fact, the conjectures around the prophetic proclamation of Swami Vivekananda about threats to human civilizations that fail to incorporate the principle of tolerance made in his Chicago address September 11, 1893, are seen to have been fulfilled 108 years after. 9/11, a mystical number in the calendar of the East, leaves one to wonder whether one is truly living a hyperreal existence, whether the "reel" and the "real" are within the same simulacrum that produces it.

In conclusion, I would like to point out that both the ideas of "clash" and "dialogue," as is evident from the discourses surveyed, seem to be largely the manifestation of the structural logic of a Manichean gesture of imperialist discourses of power, which operate on a phoenix-like twin dialectic, masquerading a generative exterior and concealing the repressive interior through which it necessarily works. In popular literary and cultural representations, narratives of nations and nationalisms reflect the utopic and dystopic dimensions of contemporary existence either through the axis of memory, in terms of recounting the past through which the present is understood, or through the axis of futurism, in terms of imagining what is yet to be, in order to comment on the implications of the present and act accordingly. The 9/11 genre in the American context incorporates both these axes to come to terms with the event, denying in their national memory the "crimes of state" that they had themselves committed as Chomsky's account earlier indicates, and barring the case of Chile when Henry Kissinger organized the coup[35] to upturn the democratically elected government of President Salvador Allende on another September 11, in 1973. As after the nuclear terror attacks in Hiroshima and Nagasaki, American authority could brook no dissidence, particularly of the Red variety—"I don't see why we need to stand by and watch a country go communist due to the irresponsibility of its own people"[36]—and history stands testimony to what happened thereafter. In Iraq, the logic was quite the opposite: establish democracy against the dictatorship of Saddam Hussein, despite the fact that not a single WMD was found. The combined forces of the liberal world rolled into Iraq to fulfill what the British Prime Minister Tony Blair foretold in his address to the Labour Party Conference on October 2, 2001, just four days before their joint forces started their "carpet-bombing" in Afghanistan—a "vision" of the fight against terrorism for which a "far wider struggle for a new world order that would uphold human dignity and social justice from the slums of Gaza to the mountain ranges of Afghanistan"[37] was needed. He was barely able to rid himself of the Churchillian legacy that made him join the cacophony of protests that it was hardly a "war on terror," but rather a "war of terror," if the definition of the term is taken strictly into account. The hysteria that one witnesses after the events of the 9/11 in 2001, particularly as represented in popular literature, culture, and media brings in several similar associations to one's mind when the dates of the events might have been different. But the scale of tragedy in magnitude was far greater as the terrorism of a state power that, like the United States, can in no way be comparable to sporadic efforts of individual networks or organizations, with or without popular support. In *The War on Terror: Reordering the World,* Ninan Koshy refers to John Berger's article "The First Fireball,"[38] arguing that "the US nuclear attack on Hiroshima paved the way for September 11 and its aftermath" by juxtaposing the visual images of the two incidents: September 11, 2001, and August 6, 1945:

> The immediate correspondences between the two events include a fireball descending without warning from a clear sky, both attacks being timed to coincide with the civilians of the targeted city going to work in the morning. . . . A similar reduction to ashes, with bodies flung through the air, becoming debris. A comparable incredulity and chaos provoked by a new weapon of destruction being used for the first time—the A-bomb 60 years ago, and a civil airliner last autumn. Everywhere at the epicentre, on everything and everybody, a thick pall of dust.
>
> The differences of content and scale are of course enormous. In Manhattan the dust was not radioactive. . . . Both attacks, however, were planned as announcements. . . . The bombs dropped on Hiroshima and Nagasaki announced that the US was henceforth the supreme armed power in the world. The attack of September 11 announced that this power was no longer guaranteed invulnerability on its home ground.[39]

Similar to Berger's account is that of Ariel Dorfman, who, in his "The Last September 11," gives a parallel recount of the terror descending from the skies by pitting one against the other. He sees the human dimension of the tragedy, revealing a warped natural sense of justice that is elated in the euphoria of symbols breaking down, threatening to destroy "the symbols of national identity, the Presidential Palace in Santiago, the icons of financial and military power in New York and Washington."[40] In a surreal simulation, one wonders about the thresholds of a reality poised as it is, Janus-faced over the nightmarish grotesqueness and the dream-like fantasy of reveling in riots as Marinetti had once conceived it:

> Except in struggle, there is no more beauty. No work without an aggressive character can be a masterpiece. Poetry must be conceived as a violent attack on unknown forces, to reduce and prostrate them before man . . .
>
> We will glorify war—the world's only hygiene—militarism, patriotism, the destructive gesture of freedom-bringers, beautiful ideas worth dying for, and scorn for woman . . .
>
> We will destroy the museums, libraries, academies of every kind, will fight moralism, feminism, every opportunistic and utilitarian cowardice . . .
>
> We will sing . . . by riot. . . . Injustice strong and sane, will break out radiantly in their eyes. Art, in fact, can be nothing but violence, cruelty, and injustice . . .
>
> Does that amaze you? It should, because you can never remember having lived! Erect on the summit of the world, once again we hurl our defiance at the stars![41]

This replicates the logic of the fascist menace over Europe to a realization gripped in pain that traumatizes those affected, who mutter to themselves in almost a delusive conviction. People like Dorfman, who have lived in both New York and Santiago, observe: "This cannot be happening to us. This sort of excessive violence happens to other people and not to us, we have only known this form of destruction through movies and books and remote photographs. . . . We have lost our innocence. The world will never be the same."[42] The 9/11 genre makes the "monster in the mirror" a reality that no war on terror can contain unless the Manichean gesture through which power works can be wrested from the grooves of a history that perpetuates human misery in its relentless stride. Through a rhetoric of "us versus them" and "ours versus theirs," it moves into a dimension where this binary becomes a mock parody of the past, where all dialogues and clashes are the two poles that perpetuate the structures that lock us in the prison house, not of language games, but games that deprive us of our own humanity in the barbarous tyranny of what civilization is, doomed to survive on the spectral liminality of existences that shadow death in a Faustian intensity.

NOTES

1. See http://en.wikipedia.org/wiki/List_of_cultural_references_to_the_September_11_attacks (accessed Octover 2012) about the 9/11 attacks. The works of art and literature that followed in the wake of the attacks have been termed as the 9/11 genre.

2. Pankaj Mishra, "The End of Innocence," *The Guardian*, May 19, 2007, http://www.guardian.co.uk/books/2007/may/19/fiction.martinamis.

3. See "9/11: And How It Changed the Hindi Film 'Aatankwaadi,'" *Passion For Cinema*, http://passionforcinema.com/9/11-and-how-it-changed-the-hindi-film-aatankwaadi/.

4. See Bernard Lewis, "The Roots of Muslim Rage," *The Atlantic Monthly* 266, no. 3 (September 1990): 47–58.

5. See Samuel P. Huntington, "The Clash of Civilizations?," *Foreign Affairs* 72, no. 3 (Summer 1993): 22, and "If Not Civilizations, What?: Paradigms of the Post-Cold War World," *Foreign Affairs* 72, no. 5 (November/December 1993): 187–89, where he not only puts forward but also defends his thesis in terms of an inevitability and follows it up by a book with the same name in 1996.

6. Interestingly, Jacques Derrida has "nicknamed" this eschatological tradition post Fukuyama as the "apocalyptic tone in philosophy" (pp. 15–16) in Peggy Kamuf, trans., *Specters of Marx: The State of the Debt, the Work of Mourning, and the New International* (London/New York: Routledge, 1994).

7. See Hans Koechler, "After September 11: Clash of Civilizations or Dialogue?" (Lecture, University of Philippines, Manila, March 14, 2002), http://i-p-o.org/Koechler-civilizations-dialogue.pdf.

8. See Engin I. Erdem, "The 'Clash of Civilizations': Revisited after September 11," [online] *Alternatives: Turkish Journal of International Relations* 1, no. 2 (June 2002).

9. Ibid.

10. Ibid.

11. Ibid.

12. Ibid.

13. In the Indian context, post 26/11 (which is our "9/11"), there is a new turn to the notion of terrorism following the coinage by Arnab Goswami while referring to the Maoist upsurge in Chhattisgarh as the assertion of the "Indian Taliban," fusing both the content and the form of two antithetical strains of militancy/insurgency as one in order to homogenize the boundaries that demarcate differences.

14. Erdem, "The 'Clash of Civilizations.'"

15. See Fidel Castro, *The Gigantic Casino: Reflections on the World Financial Crisis* (New Delhi: Left Word Books, 2009). In "Bush's Self-Criticism," September 25, 2008, Fidel Castro questions the "brief 15-minute speech" of President Bush where he describes the economic system of the United States of America as "democratic capitalism" and in line with earlier farcical campaigns of progress, like Kennedy's Punta del Este program in 1961 or Bill Clinton's Free Trade Area for the Americas 1994 and his Pathways to Prosperity in the Americas Initiative in 2008. Fidel Castro "thanks" President Bush in his characteristic tongue-in-cheek humor "for his brilliant contribution to political theory" (p. 41) for trade, which in Castro's analysis, works on "the law of the jungle" (title of his speech on October 11, 2008) and

thereby, he asks "What kind of progress can imperialism guarantee . . . with its atomic weapons, its arms industry, its escorted fleets of nuclear aircraft carriers, its wars of conquest, its unequal exchange and permanent pillaging of other peoples?" (p. 41), reinforcing thereby in a different vein what Noam Chomsky terms America as "the leading terrorist state" (p. 43) in an interview to David Barsamian on September 21, 2001. See Noam Chomsky, *9-11: An Open Media Book* (New Delhi: Rpt. Natraj Publishers, 2002), first Indian edition.

16. See Ninan Koshy, *The War on Terror: Reordering the World* (New Delhi: Left Word Books, 2003). Koshy quotes from the speech of the U.S. Under-Secretary of State John Bolton on May 7, 2002, where the link between terror-states in Asia and other parts of the world were put together on one platform apart from the series of justifications given by the Bush administration to justify the notion of "war" as it met with stiff opposition.

17. See Chomsky, *9-11*.

18. Ibid., p. 23.

19. Ibid., p. 21. Chomsky also refers to the 1986 condemnation of the United States "by the World Court for 'unlawful use of force' (international terrorism)," and for the violent assault on Nicaragua in the 1980s that led to the death of "tens of thousands" accompanied by "a devastating economic war" precipitated when its government did not respond by counter attack, but appealed for justice in the World Court and the Security Council.

20. Ibid., p. 48.

21. Ibid., p. 39.

22. Edward W. Said, "The Clash of Ignorance," *The Nation*, October 22, 2001, http://www.thenation.com/article/clash-ignorance.

23. Oleh: Osman Bakar, "Dialogues of Civilisations after 9/11 with Specific Reference to the West-Islam Cultural Divide: Promises and Obstacles," *KATHA—The Official Journal of the Centre for Civilisational Dialogue* 3 (2007): 1–12.

24. Ibid., 3.

25. Ibid., 4.

26. Ibid.

27. Ibid., 5.

28. Ibid.

29. Ibid., 6.

30. The term literally means "a charter of dreams."

31. This needs qualification as although larger challenges with which human civilisations necessarily contend like ecological hazards and diseases like AIDS become part of the agenda and foreign policy, issues pertaining to inter-nation rivalry or economic concerns regarding self-sustaining growth and poverty do not become substantive as agenda.

32. *Lakposhtha Parvaz Mikonand* (English title: *Turtles Can Fly*) was made by the Kurdish Iranian filmmaker Bahman Ghobadi in 2004, critiquing the reign of Saddam Hussain and in a way endorsing the "Operation Iraqi Freedom" as an aftermath of 9/11. Although the film has won several accolades, it has been critiqued for not being vocal about what happened to the Kurds after the fall of Saddam Hussain.

33. For a comprehensive understanding of the connections he draws between the idea of civilizational dialogues and the context of globalization, see Walid M.

Abdenasser, *Dialogue among Civilisations and the Challenge of Globalization* (Cairo: Al Ahram Center for Strategic and Political Studies, 2006).

34. Francis Fukuyama, *The End of History and the Last Man* (New York: Avon Books, 1992).

35. See Pilar Aguillera and Ricardo Fredes, eds., *Chile: The Other September 11* (New Delhi: Left Word Books, 2008), Indian reprint. In fact, on March 25, 1970, in a meeting of the White House "Committee of 40," Henry Kissinger, in charge of U.S. plans to thwart Allende's ascendancy to presidency, approved $125,000 for a "spoiling operation" in Chile (p. 5). It was followed by President Nixon's instructions to the CIA Director Richard Helms on similar lines to organize the military coup that came to be known as Track 11 on September 15, 1970 (p. 25). This indicates the level of interference that the U.S. state can go into and then couple it with economic embargos, which can even lead to that denial of relief during disasters resulting from natural calamities like the 1971 earthquake in Chile, for the crimes of the people who voted Allende to power on October 24, 1970, despite their best efforts in halting it.

36. Ibid., p. 10.

37. As quoted in Koshy, *The War on Terror,* p. 181.

38. John Berger, as quoted in "Terrorism: Theirs and Ours" in Koshy, *The War on Terror,* pp. 36, 37.

39. Ariel Dorfman, "The Last September 11" in Aguillera and Fredes, *Chile: The Other September 11.*

40. Ibid., p. 2.

41. From the 1909 "Manifesto on Futurism" as presented by Fillippo Tommaso Marinetti (1876–1944) in the Paris newspaper *Le Figaro,* which steeped in a vocabulary of blood, violence, and the fumes of war declares an open revolt against all received traditions of knowledge as a dead weight of the past to usher in beauty and speed in creativity through outright aggression foregrounding an aesthetics of violence that is necessary as a midwife to historical transformation. See his essay in Vassilika Kolokotroni, Jane Goldman, and Olga Taxidou, eds., *Modernism: An Anthology of Sources and Documents* (Edinburgh: Edinburgh University Press, 1998), pp. 251–53.

42. Ariel Dorfman, *Other Septembers, Many Americas: Selected Provocations, 1980–2004* (New York: Seven Stories Press, 2004), pp. 40, 41.

Chapter 2

Jainism: The Way to Lasting Peace through Pluralistic Understanding[1]

Ashok Vohra

In the Jaina text *Bhagvatīsūtra* 9.386,[2] Mahāvīra replies to Gautama's question, "What is the nature of the soul?" by saying: "The nature of the soul is equanimity." Hearing this answer, Gautama further asks: "What is the ultimate goal of the soul?" To this question also Mahāvīra replies: "The ultimate goal of the soul is also equanimity." That equanimity is the foundation of Jaina philosophy and ethics is also supported by Acarya Kundkunda in his text *Samayasāra*. He uses the term *samaya* or *samayasāra* for the soul (*ātman*). According to Sagar Mal Jain, Acarya Kundakunda "has purposely used this word for *ātman* . . . (because) the term *samaya* appears to be the Prakrit form of the Sanskrit words *samaé* + *yaé*, meaning one who has the quality of equanimity, i.e., *samatva*, one who has *samatva* as his essential nature is called *samayasāra*."[3]

My purpose in this chapter is to show how the Jainas, through their metaphysics and epistemology, develop, justify, and teach the supreme value of equanimity—a mind-set that results in the peaceful coexistence of different religions and their subsects.

Let me begin with the notion of substance. *Tattvārthasūtra* 5.29 and 5.30, while explaining the notion of substance, assert that "*sad dravyalakṣṇam*" (existence is the character of a substance). Additionally, the characteristic of *sat* is "*utpāda-vyaya-dhrauvya-yuktam sat*" (origination, cessation, and persistence constitute existence). A substance, *dravya*, according to the Jainas, is that which is eternal and unchanging, and which has a number of essential and accidental characteristics. The essential characteristics are called *guṇas* (qualities), and the accidental characteristics are called *paryāyas* (modes). While *guṇas* of a substance are its permanent features and the substance is what it is because of them, the *paryāyas* are its ever changing features that a substance may possess at one moment and may not possess at the consequent moment. In other words, the *guṇas* account for the being of a substance, and the *paryāyas* account for becoming. Therefore, the substance is both eternal and unchanging as well as in a state of constant flux. This can be explained with the help of two examples. The first is the example of gold, whose essential *guṇa* is that it is malleable and ductile. However, the accidental *paryāya* is the form of the ornament into which it is shaped at a given time. The shape of the ornament can be changed at any time, but the qualities of malleability and ductility of gold are its permanent features. If these characteristics are missing, then it cannot be called gold at all.

The second illustration is the soul. The essential characteristic or *guṇa* of the soul is its consciousness. However, its accidental properties or *paryāyas* are the pain and pleasure with which we may associate it, or describe it as possessing, at a given time. A soul ceases to be a soul the moment it loses its consciousness, because consciousness is the defining attribute of a soul. But pain and pleasure represent the changing state in which a soul may be at a given time. It may be in a happy state at one moment and in a sad state at another moment. These states are impermanent and cannot be the defining attributes of a soul. S.N. Dasgupta says, while explaining the relationship between qualities, modes, and substance: "Experience shows that in all changes there are three elements: (1) that some collocations of qualities appear to remain unchanged; (2) that some new qualities are generated; (3) that some old qualities are destroyed. It is true that qualities of things are changing every minute, but all qualities are not changing."[4]

In *Tattvārthasūtra* 5.37, Umāsvāti defines substance as *guṇa-paryāyavad-dravyam*—that which possesses qualities and modes. In the Jaina account, therefore, an existent thing must be seen on three levels: (1) at the level of the modes, which last only a moment and belong to the qualities; (2) at the level of the qualities, which undergo changes and yet inhere forever in their substances; and (3) at the level of the substance, which remains the abiding common ground of support for the qualities and their modes. A substance is individuated and identified on the basis of its qualities.

Substances are classified into two types on the basis of extension: (1) those which are extended in space and (2) those which are not extended in space. Souls (*jīvas*), matter (*pudgala*), space (*ākāśa*), and media of motion and rest (*dharma* and *adharma*) are substances that are extended in space. Time (*kāla*) is the only substance that is not extended in space. According to another classification based on consciousness, all existents are classified into three following categories:

1. Those who are animate or sentient
2. Those who are inanimate or material
3. Those who are neither sentient nor material

To the first category belong the *jīvas* or souls. Consciousness is the defining attribute of all the *jīvas*. To the second category belong the *ajīvas* with form, color, taste, smell, and palpability. Matter or *pudgala* fall in this category. To the third category belong the existents that have neither form nor consciousness. They are called *arūpīa-jīvas*. They include space (*ākāśa*), the principle of motion and rest (*dharma* and *adharma dravyas*), and time (*kāla*). The *jīvas* are further classified into those that are liberated (*mukta*) and those which are bound (*saṁsārī* or *baddha*). The *saṁsārī-jīvas* are classified into those that are mobile (*trasa*) and those that are immobile (*sthāvara*). While the immobile *jīvas* have just one sense organ, the sense organs in the mobile *jīvas* vary from two to five. These six substances constitute the world—*saṁsāra*. Since each one of them has the characteristic of being as well as becoming, *saṁsāra* too is both constantly changing and permanent.

A substance has innumerable qualities and infinite modes of presentation. It has manifold aspects (*anekānta*). It is impossible for an ordinary being to know each one of them, and the whole substance in its entirety, because these *guṇas* and *paryāyas* of the substance are not just in the present, but are also there from the beginningless past (*anādi*) to endless future (*ananta*). "At a single moment he can be aware either of the persisting unity (*ekatva*) of the substance or the transient multiplicity (*anekatava*) of its modes. This complexity of the existent—its simultaneous unity and multiplicity, eternity and transience—finds expression in the Jaina term *anekānta*, manifold aspects, which purports to fully describe the existents nature."[5] The finite observer can only apprehend a few of the qualities and modes and have limited knowledge of the aspects of the substance. This fact about our knowledge gives rise to the Jaina doctrine of *anekāntavāda* (the doctrine of nonabsolutism) or the principle of relative pluralism, as opposed to the doctrine of *ekāntavāda* (absolutism). However, an omniscient being (a *kevalin*) knows the object in its entirety. He knows all *guṇas* and *paryāyas* of a substance.

The doctrine of *anekānta* is explained by Lord Mahāvīra in three words (*tripadī*). These are *uppannei va, vigamei va,* and *dhuvei va* (it arises, it ceases, and it persists). It is called *anekānta* because reality is conceived here as a manifold entity having many characteristics (*aneka*) such as persistence and cessation (*dhruvatva* and *vigama*), being and nonbeing (*bhava* and *abhāva*), permanence and impermanence (*nityatva* and *anityatva*), unity and plurality (*ekatva* and *anekatva*), and similar pairs of opposite attributes. This conception is apparently based of the relation of identity-*cum*-difference between a substance, which is permanent, and its modes (including qualities), which are undergoing a change without a pause.[6]

The principle of *anekāntavāda* is a unique contribution of the Jaina thinkers. Literally, the term "*anekāntavāda*" means "the theory of non-one-sidedness" or, to be more specific, "the theory of the many-sided nature of reality." *Anekāntavāda* can therefore be said to be an epistemological doctrine that synthesizes the knowledge of metaphysics and ontology. In the Jaina tradition, this doctrine is known by several names. Some of them are *saṁhāravāda* (the philosophy of integration), *sarva-vastu-śabalavāda* (the theory of manifoldness of every real entity), *ākulavāda* (the philosophy of "that" and "not that" or a position where conflicting views are harmonized together), and *saṁkīrṇavāda* (the philosophy of intermixture). From the above descriptions, it follows that *anekāntavāda* is the doctrine of bringing together the conflicting views. It is an attempt to resolve conflicts by admitting that there are infinite ways of knowing and recognizing the fact that any viewpoint is just one of several.

The most appropriate illustration of *anekāntavāda* can be seen in the reply and reply's justification that Mahāvīra gives to the questions, "Is the world eternal or noneternal?" and "Is the soul eternal or noneternal?" To both the questions, Mahāvīra replies that world, as well as the soul, is eternal as well as noneternal. It is eternal because "it did not cease to exist at any time and it will not cease to exist at any time. It was, it is and it will be. It is constant, permanent, eternal, imperishable, indestructible, always existent."[7] He goes on to say that the world is noneternal because "it becomes progressive (in time cycle) after being regressive. And it becomes regressive after becoming progressive."[8] He justifies his answer by saying: "The world is infinite from the point of view of its substance, finite (i.e. measurable) from the point of view of its area, but infinite from the point of view of time (duration) and also infinite (unaccountable) from the point of view of its modifications."[9] The same argument is advanced by him in the context of the soul or the *jīva*.

It may be noted that the use of the expression "point of view" is very significant in the doctrine of *anekāntavāda*. One of the direct implications in admitting that there are infinite number of qualities and *paryāyas* of a substance—and that the ones that we can apprehend at any given point of time depends upon the context in which we are situated at that particular time—shows that the Jainas demonstrated tolerance of others' views. This is because the views upheld by others can, in principle, be justified from some point of view—the number of points of view being infinite. It also shows that they did not believe in any final or conclusive knowledge of finite beings. The second advantage of upholding the doctrine of *anekāntavāda* is that it results in the rejection of skepticism and agnosticism, with respect to the existence of objects or our knowledge of them, by saying that all the alternate views each had some truth and that complete truth lay in understanding the value of the perspectives. For example, when I place my hand first in a bowl of hot water marked "A" and then in bowl of warm water marked "B," the water in bowl B appears to be cool. But is it cool, warm, or hot? I do not and cannot know whether the water in the bowl B is cool, warm, or hot, as these are conditional statements that possess no absolute qualities. In this sense, my assessment results in skepticism and agnosticism. Following the Jaina doctrine of *anekāntavāda,* however, if I say that it is cool, warm, and hot but from different standpoints, I shall not end up as a skeptic or as an agnostic.

It can be concluded from the above discussion that the Jainas admit, ontologically speaking, that there are infinite characteristics in a substance and that we, as knower, can apprehend only a few of them. What we apprehend at a given time depends upon the vantage point from which we are observing the object. What we observe or apprehend has to be articulated in language in the form of a judgment for our own as well as for the benefit of the others. When we articulate our observance, it has to be made clear at the outset that the judgment we are making is only from a definitive perspective. In order to be true to ourselves, what one says or observes has to be admitted as true from our own observance. However, the right method of a debate in philosophy or in other discourses does not imply that we do not emphasize our position or argue for it vehemently with all the force of known facts and logic at our command. In the right method, while emphasizing one aspect or standpoint, we should not lose sight of the fact that this is but only one out of many equally viable standpoints—this method is one of inclusiveness. Nevertheless, when we emphasize only one standpoint by excluding all others, we employ an incorrect philosophical method. The aim of *anekānta* is to expose an incorrect method of debate and discussion that leads to strife and disharmony, and to identify the right method that leads to harmony, peace, tolerance, and cooperation without compromising the truth. It helps us develop a mind-set that upholds that every theory is partially true, but not exclusively—there is no such thing as a perfect theory. This mind-set believes that the perfect theory is one which recognizes that our theory is one of the many theories that are equally (partially) true. In this sense, *anekāntavāda* advocates a sort of relativistic approach and denies supremacy to any one view. In short, *anekāntavāda* is that method of philosophy that recognizes all the philosophical theories to be the partially true expressions of reality.[10]

To highlight this fact, the Jainas apply the device of using the expression "*syāt*" before a judgment. The indeclinable term "*syāt*" in its optative sense means "might be." But using it in that sense would imply that "there is some doubt about the assertion" or the judgment is dubitable, but the Jainas specify that the term "*syāt*" is used in the sense "in some respect." The term "*syāt*" means really "it would like to be" and expresses the relativity of judgment. It stands thus for *kiṁcit* as Jainas say this can be rendered somewhat by "in certain sense."[11] Bimal Krishna Matilal thus states: "*Syāt* means, in the Jaina use, a conditional YES. It is like saying, 'in a certain sense yes.' It amounts to a conditional approval. The particle *syāt,* in fact, acts as an operator on the sentence in which it is used. It turns a categorical: 'A is B' into a conditional: 'if p then A is B.' "[12] This doctrine, which emphasizes that each judgment is made and is true in some respect, is called *syādavāda.* It is also known as *saptabhaṅgī* (the sevenfold prediction) or *nayavāda* (the doctrine of standpoints). According to the doctrine of *syādavāda,* we can logically make the following assertions about our knowledge:

1. *Syād asti*—From one point of view, "something is": e.g., in a certain sense, in a specific context, there is a pot or the pot exists.
2. *Syād nāsti*—From another point of view, "something is not": e.g., in a certain sense, there is no pot, or the pot has a determinate nonexistence. Therefore, the first two collectively show that there is neither absolute being nor absolute nonbeing.
3. *Syād asti nāsti ca*—From a third point of view, "something is and is not": e.g., in a certain sense, there is a pot and there is no pot. This shows the equipollence of existence and nonexistence of what we regard as real.
4. *Syād avaktavyam*—From the fourth point of view, "something is indescribable": e.g., in a certain sense, the pot is inexpressible. It "gives a glimpse of the real as unique synthesis which transcends the equipollence. This character of a real cannot be grasped by a definite concept and so is not expressible by a definite symbol."
5. *Syād asti ca avaktvyam*—From the fifth point of view, "something is and is indescribable": e.g., in a certain sense, the pot both exists and is inexpressible. The jar is inexpressible *qua* a synthetic unity, but nonetheless expressible *qua* existent.
6. *Syād nāsti ca avaktvyam*—From the sixth point of view, "something is not and is indescribable": e.g., in a certain sense, the pot does not exist and is inexpressible. The opposite of the fourth point of view stated above.
7. *Syād asti ca nāsti ca avaktvyam*—From the seventh point of view, "something is and is not and also is indescribable": e.g., in a certain sense, the pot exists, does not exist, and is also inexpressible. This reveals the double character of the fourth predicate stated above.

The above seven are only illustrative predicates with respect to existence and nonexistence. They are equally applicable to the pairs of characteristics like unity and plurality, permanence and impermanence, etc.

The doctrine of *syadavāda* is the logical implication of the doctrine of *anekāntavada.* "The *anekānta* doctrine," according to Matilal, "to be sure, is neither a doctrine of doubt (or even uncertainty) nor a doctrine of probability."[13] Many Jaina thinkers argue that the two in essence are identical. They are known by two different names. One of the important outcomes of the doctrine of *syādavāda*[14] is that it highlights the fact that all our knowledge can only be incomplete, in the sense that each of the claims of knowledge is made from a certain standpoint. Consequentially, all our judgments logically can be only partial. Jainas therefore call all our judgments as *nayas.* According to Dasgupta, "the different standpoints from which things (though possessed of infinite determinations) can be spoken of as possessing this or that quality or as appearing in relation to this or that, are technically called *naya.*"[15] From the fact that each object has infinite number of characteristics, it follows that there are infinite number of *nayas.* The *nayas* on the basis of the characteristic of "existence" have been categorized into seven types. They exhaust all the logical possibilities. These are as follows:

All affirmations are true in some sense.
All affirmations are false in some sense.
All affirmations are inexpressible.
All affirmations are true as well as false in some sense.
All affirmations are true as well as inexpressible.
All affirmations are false as well as inexpressible.
All affirmations are true, false, and inexpressible.

For the purpose of this chapter, we need not go into further details of the doctrine of *syādavāda* as well as *nayas.* The discussion so far is sufficient to establish that the Jainas outrightly reject absolute, dogmatic, unconditional, and exclusive claims of knowledge and truth of judgments. They argue that the ignorance of the doctrine of *syādavāda* invariably leads to vehement but futile arguments and disputes concerning nature of reality, which in turn gives rise to egoism, conflict, hostility, disharmony, and antipathy. The doctrine of *syādavāda* makes one conscious of the fact that he or she, like the proverbial blind men, knows only one aspect of the elephant, which removes the ego—the cause of all conflict. Philosophies and religious doctrines that claim absolute and unconditional truth are therefore taught by Jainism that in all our knowledge there is an essential element of incompleteness; all our knowledge is necessarily partial and relates to a particular aspect of the object of knowledge. The dawning of the relative aspect of knowledge makes us accept the alternative viewpoints, even conflicting viewpoints, as acceptable and as authentic as our own. The doctrine of *anekāntavāda* or *syādavāda* or *nayavāda* does not merely say to the opponent's thesis "let it be so but. . . ." On the contrary, it enters into a dialogue with him by initially conceding the opponent's thesis in order to blunt the sharpness of his attack and disagreement, by reassuring him that his thesis may be right from a particular standpoint. At the same time, it is calculated to persuade the opponent to see another point of view or carefully consider the other side of the case, which for the opponent, it has both a "disarming effect" and implicitly "contains a persuasive force." It "helps us in cultivating the attitude of toleration towards the views of our adversaries. It does not stop there but takes a step forward by making us investigate as to how and why they hold a different view and how the seeming contradictories can be reconciled to evolve harmony. It is thus an attempt towards syncretism."[16] In doing so, Matilal says *anekāntavāda* proves to be "a philosophy of synthesis and reconciliation since it tries to establish rapprochement between seemingly disagreeing philosophical schools."[17] The mind-set cultivated in this manner in both the proponent and the opponent leaves no space for religious, social, and political conflict in the society.

NOTES

1. Parts of this chapter have been published previously by the author in "Why Jainism Matters," *The Pioneer,* March 10, 2012, http://www.dailypioneer.com/sunday-edition/sundayagenda/spirituality-agenda/48683-why-jainism-matters.html.
2. Quoted in Bimal Krishna Matilal, *The Central Philosophy of Jainism (Anekanta-vāda)* (Ahmedabad: L.D. Institute of Indology, 1981).
3. Sagar Mal Jain, "The Jaina Spirit and Spirituality" in Krishna Sivaraman, ed., *Hindu Spirituality: Vedas through Vedanta* (New York: Crossroad, 1989), p. 156.
4. Surendranath Dasugupta, *A History of Indian Philosophy, Volume I* (Delhi: Motilal Banarsidass, reprint 2006), p. 174.
5. Matilal, *The Central Philosophy of Jainism (Anekanta-vāda),* p. 41.
6. Ibid., p. 32.
7. Matilal, *Bhagvatīsūtra,* 9.38., p. 19.
8. Ibid.
9. Ibid., p. 21.
10. Ibid.
11. Helmuth von Glasenapp, *Jainism: An Indian Religion of Salvation* (Delhi: Motilal Banarsidass, 1999), p. 172.
12. Matilal, *The Central Philosophy of Jainism (Anekanta-vāda),* p. 52.
13. Ibid., p. 60.
14. Ibid., p. 52.
15. Ibid., p. 176.
16. Hiralal Rasikdas Kapadia, "Introduction" in Haribhadra Sūri, *Anekantajayapataka* (Baroda: Oriental Institute, 1940), p. cxiv.
17. Matilal, *The Central Philosophy of Jainism (Anekanta-vāda),* p. 61.

Chapter 3

Tolerance in Early Buddhism: Ideation, Praxis, and Fault Lines

Ahmad Sohaib

> Brethren, if outsiders should speak against me, or against the Doctrine, or against the Order, you should not on that account either bear malice, or suffer heart burning, or feel ill will.[1]

At the conclusion of a debate with the Buddha, Upāli, the *gahapati* (master of the house), requests an instantaneous avowal or approbation as an *upāsaka* (lay follower), whereupon the Buddha states:

> Now . . . for a long time, householder, your family has been a wellspring to the Jains. You will bethink you to give alms to those that approach you.[2]

The early Buddhist standpoint on tolerance toward their contemporary adversaries has often been studied and appreciated in the light of such instructions spread throughout the Pāli *Nikāyas*. Arguing for a tolerant early Buddhist attitude toward their religious antagonists, scholars have almost unanimously remarked that tolerance is both integral and fundamental to the Buddhist character—notwithstanding the actuality that, as a virtue, it is nowhere directly mentioned by the Buddha. However, a virtue repeatedly stressed in the Pāli Canon is "patience" (*kṣānti*)—inculcation of which fosters other noble traits of character (viz., forbearance, mercy, forgiveness, endurance, compassion, etc.), which in the aggregate is reckoned to embody the trait of "tolerance."

Setting aside this lack of textual evidence for a parallel Pāli word for "tolerance," certain themes recurrently appear in studies[3] on Buddhist tolerance, which could be laid out as follows:

> The spirit of tolerance in (early) Buddhism is derived from the Eightfold Path and is a product of the perfection of patience (*kṣānti*)—it is embedded in its religious guidance.
>
> An apparent complementarity and equivalence of "patience" with "tolerance."[4] Tolerance, in Buddhism, is of a unique kind: neither compromised nor knuckled under pressure to False Views (*micchādiṭṭhi*). Neither did it fanatically condemn other *dhammas* or philosophies, nor forced Truth into reluctant ears and mind.

In a broader time-frame and context, we would be happy to walk with this part. Yet, we have reservations and difficulties regarding an all-pervading spirit of tolerance in "early Buddhism."[5] It is our submission that certain pieces of evidence from the *Nikāyas*[6] appear a trifle incongruous, ambivalent, and inconsistent with the bulk of those often cited for espousing the ideation of tolerance in Buddhism—not the slightest suggestion is made regarding early Buddhism as an intolerant faith, or that its tolerance was of a mitigated character. Our mere suggestion is that the evidence—at least a few pieces of it from the *Nikāyas*—do not add up to an unquestioned and all-pervading tolerance toward the "others."

WHAT IS MEANT BY TOLERANCE?

Let us begin by asking: "How has tolerance in the study of religion been defined and interpreted?" Khantipalo defines tolerance as

> allowing others to hold opinion on religious, political and other matters differing from oneself or from whatever the dominant authority, and allowing their free expression in speech or by bodily acts, provided that these do not cause harm to others in any way either mentally or physically.[7]

In the narrower context of a religious attitude, Francis Story defines it as "the ability to live with others who hold divergent views, and perhaps follow different ways of life that arise from such views, without interfering with them or attempting to force one's own ideas and ways on them."[8] Stated simply, it is the practice and attitude of noninterference. Quite remarkably, such definitions do not profess that one should amalgamate, appropriate, or embrace the beliefs, practices, and doctrines of other faiths,[9] nor does it state that one should force one's own religio-philosophical beliefs, etc., on those belonging to other religion.

On the other hand, patience—closely allied to tolerance—has been defined as "the quality of equanimity and steadily bearing with ourselves and others, even in the face of intense provocation which interferes with one's beliefs, speech or body."[10] Thus, while tolerance is more or less restricted to the intellectual sphere—"ideas, doctrines, and institutions established upon these"[11]—patience is more a practical attitude related to the personal afflictions of body and mind.

In modern times, the contours of liberal toleration[12] based themselves on the Protestant conceptualization of religion as a voluntary and private matter of conscience. This to an extent informed early (liberalism's) ideation of religious toleration. Distinction needs to be made between the two operative zones of tolerance—internal and external. Internal toleration has been understood as providing a fair degree of latitude to the "believers" or adherents to follow religion according to their conscience, not to be purely and entirely dictated by the sacred texts. Besides, being crucially linked to the design of individual "autonomy," it is premised on the base that those tolerated have a common general concept of the faith—irrespective of internal differences of opinion and details. An internally tolerant religious ideology allows its members forsaking of the faith[13] *sans* posing the threat of retribution—albeit this was not clearly the case with the early Buddhists. External toleration "allows other groups to live by their religious practices,"[14] doctrines, beliefs, etc.; individual "autonomy" has marginal or no role in such toleration.

EVIDENCE FOR EARLY BUDDHIST TOLERANCE

It would be apt to begin with the striking passage from the *Brahmajāla Sutta* (*Dīgha Nikāya*) cited at the beginning. It alludes to the Buddha's instruction to *bhikkhus* (monks) and is occasioned by the itinerant ascetic Suppiya's disparaging remarks and malicious talk regarding the Buddha and his *dhamma,* and Suppiya's pupil Brahmadatta's eloquent praise to the contrary. The Buddha cautions his disciples that in case the "outsiders"[15] speak against the Buddha, the *dhamma,* and the *saṅgha* (monastic order), then on that account, they should not bear anger, malice, or animosity toward them. Illustrating external tolerance, he instead instructs the monks to "judge how far that speech of theirs is well said, or ill."[16]

What is noteworthy is that the Buddha is calling for restraint of anger, malice, and hatred (by the monks)—exhortation is thus primarily against particular inclinations that he patently considered deleterious and not conducive for reaching the status of an Arahant (saint). As Story aptly puts: "[I]t was against anger that he was giving this warning, for anger is an unwholesome state of mind."[17] Rather than reflecting anything exclusively tolerant, the passage pleads for restrained behavior and ethical and moral conduct.[18] Richard Gombrich remarks that "some aspects of restrained behaviour such as self-control in the face of provocation we would consider moral, many others we would consider morally neutral matters of decorum."[19]

The other passages cited to prop up the case of the Buddha's encouragement of tolerance toward "others" are the instructions to Upāli and Sīha—both followers of Nigaṇṭha Nātaputta. After admitting Upāli (a famous and wealthy Jaina layman) as an *upāsaka* (lay follower) into his *dhamma,*[20] the Buddha asked him to continue to support and revere his former preceptor—similar injunction occurs in the case of the Licchavi general Sīha, in a passage of the *Aṅguttara.* Together, these have been taken as unmistakable and clinching evidence for the Buddha's tolerant attitude toward the "other" faiths. But these injunctions, when placed alongside another one, bare the Buddha's "tolerant" attitude toward giving alms to "others." Upon being asked by the wanderer Vacchagotta, whether the Buddha speaks thus: "[A]lms should be given to me, not to others; to my followers, not to another's followers,"[21] the latter denounces it to be utter falsehood and a misrepresentation of his teachings.[22] While categorically stating that giving alms always accrues merit—irrespective of the creed of the recipient—as a parting shot he adds the condition that only the gift (*dāna*) given to virtuous ones are worthy of fruition, and not those given to the wicked ones.[23] By "virtuous" here is meant those who have abandoned the five hindrances[24] and cultivated the qualities[25] essential for *nibbāna.* Quite noticeably, the above instructions are covertly tantamount to an exhortation that alms should be preferably given only to the Buddhist renunciants, for ipso facto only they (Buddhist *bhikkhus*) were expected to be virtuous in the above manner.

Remarkably, in both the instances, that the Buddha allows the protraction or continuance of giving alms to their previous preceptors, the recipient happens to be the Nigaṇṭha. Should we take it as a mere coincidence? Or, should we construe it as emanating from a certain commonality between the Nigaṇṭhas and the Buddhists? We are inclined to believe that the latter was the case.[26] We wonder whether the Buddha would have similarly instructed, had the converts Upāli and Sīha been followers of Pūrana Kassapa or Makkhali Gosāla?—whom he severely reproached and denigrated. We are not in a position to answer this with any degree of certitude.[27]

Scholars have also sought to explain the above episode—giving of alms—in the light of Buddhism's nonattachment to material things and willful surrender of these to those who needed them most.[28] But we regard the instructions to Upāli and Sīha as illustrative of broad-minded compassion, benevolence, and magnanimity that results from the enlightenment of a personality like the Buddha. Often such benevolent attitude of the Buddha tends to be contrasted with the religious exclusiveness found in others creeds, in order to construe a tolerant attitude for the Buddhists.[29] We plead to take these noble traits of personal character on their own terms and not to equate them with tolerance or attempt to establish its veracity.

Patience (*kṣānti*) and its perfection (*pāramitā*) has often been extolled in the Pāli Canon. Khantipalo, taking note of this, argues for an attitude of tolerance on the part of Buddhists. We do not basically dispute his construction, yet in spite of numerous references to "patience" in the Pāli Canon, one fails to find mention of it as one of the perfections to be fulfilled by aspirants to Buddhahood. Quite remarkably, Khantipalo comments that "patience is a passive quality . . . is indispensable to those who would truly be tolerant."[30] Hence, besides patience, he considers the related virtues of forgiveness, forbearance, and endurance as sure foundation of tolerance. However, we need to ask at this juncture: Did it really lead to a tolerant attitude among the rank and file of the early Buddhists?—who were not as enlightened as the Buddha himself, for whom it was easier to practice, master, and adhere to these virtues.

The weight and meaning of patience is clearly illustrated by a passage of the *Majjhima Nikāya*.[31] Here, three types of endurance (patience) are mentioned, and that are expected of a devout monastic follower. First comes the exterior conditions of the environment; second comes the endurance of others' speech—harsh, sarcastic, abusive, full of hatred, etc.; and third is the endurance of personal states of bodily feelings that are painful and unpleasant. Of these three, only the second points to any sort of restraint in behavior compatible with the Buddhist ethical code and comes close to what has officially been designated as Buddhist tolerance.[32]

Exhortation to maintain patience and endure painful sensations—experienced either from within or without—by a monk is found in two identical passages of the *Majjhima*.[33] These have been cited as an evidence for early Buddhist tolerance, though we do not quite concur on this. In the second passage, Sāriputta, addressing the monks, uses the simile of a saw "to show that the body, being of a nature to experience painful sensations, should not react to them with hatred but with patience."[34] This appears to be a profound advocacy of tolerance—we have no qualms about it. Besides being unsure about its practical adherence by the laity, our submission is that it is basically against the fallacious identification of body (*rūpa*) with the "self" that caution is laid out here. Besides, we wonder how far this theoretical injunction was followed by the monks—instances are not lacking of monks' indulgence in strife.

The other instance of perfect tolerance and exemplary patience enjoined by the Buddha or his chief monks is found in a statement as the following: "wherefore, monks, even if others should revile, abuse, annoy you, there should be in you no resentment, distress, dissatisfaction on mind concerning them."[35] Elsewhere, as cited before,[36] the Buddha advises his followers to remain calm in the face of provocation by the "outsiders."

FAULT LINES—INCONGRUOUS EVIDENCE

The *positive* evidence for the popular notion of "pervasive" tolerance seems to be a tad offset through culling instances of what may be called *negative* evidence spread out in the *Nikāyas*—moderately, these may be construed as *occasional* lapses into *atypical* intolerance. Illustrated here are some outstanding incongruities, which impel us to suggest that the early Buddhist attitude of tolerance—so far as the first four *Nikayas* are concerned—exhibit a certain degree of discrepancy between precept and praxis. There are apparent divergences from ideation and of the doctrinal from actuality.

The anomalous behavior of Upāli,[37] after his conversion to a Buddhist *upāsaka,* is illustrative of such negative evidence. Upāli is enjoined that his benefaction to the Jainas should not cease on account of his conversion to the Buddha's fold, yet he instructs his doorkeeper not to admit Jainas to his presence.[38] Nevertheless, he instructs his doorkeeper that in case they need food, it should be given to them. We have here a clear case of a Buddhist disregarding the ethos of tolerance that the Buddha passionately tried to inculcate—albeit by way of charity, he is willing to give alms to the Nigaṇṭhas.

Another deviant conduct exposing the fissure between theory and praxis comes from a passage of the *Dīgha Nikāya.* We are informed by the Buddha that Pasenadi, the King of Kosala, does not allow the *brāhmaṇa* (priest) Pokkharasādī to enter in his presence and speaks to him from behind a curtain.[39] We are at loss to explain this queer behavior of Pasenadi—by now converted to the fold of the Buddha[40]—who in fact was once the benefactor of Pokkharasādī. Apparently, Pasenadi's reluctance to grant a direct audience to Pokkharasādī reflects the tension between *kṣriyas* (warriors) and *brāhmaṇas* (priests). Nevertheless, it does not mitigate the strange behavior of Pasenadi, and rather points to a certain degree of inconsistency.

Let us now turn our attention to the evidence cited earlier: the Buddha was in principle not opposed to lay people (especially Buddhists) giving alms to the virtuous ones, irrespective of their religious affiliations. However, this appears to run counter to a passage of the *Aṅguttara.* Here, the Buddha categorizes a layman pursuing the following five things as an outcast, and likens him to a *cāṇḍāla.* These five things are as described in the passage below:

> [H]e is without faith, without morals, is a diviner by curious ceremonies, he believes in luck, and not deeds, he seeks outside (the Order) for a gift-worthy person and there first offers service.[41]

We have no doubt that the layman referred to here is a Buddhist *upāsaka* and it does not describe the untouchable outcaste of *cāṇḍāla*.[42] An analogy seems to be drawn here between an aberrant Buddhist *upāsaka* who pursues the five "forbidden" things and a *cāṇḍāla*.[43] But, most remarkable is the last mentioned pursuance, i.e., he seeks recluses *outside the Order* (emphasis added) to bestow gifts, and actually gives them preference. The Buddha is critical of it, so much so that those indulging in such a practice are clubbed with outcastes. We are inquisitive if the Buddha was implying that there were no worthy ones outside the (Buddhist) Order to receive such gifts from laymen. But, it certainly appears that implicitly the Buddha asked gifts and alms to be preferably given to Buddhist renunciates. Likewise, a passage of the *Aṅguttara* lists seven activities that hasten the decline of the *upāsakas*—three significant ones are failing to look after monks, seeking faults with the *dhamma* with a critical mind, and searching for a gift-worthy person outside the *saṅgha* and serving him first.[44] These run counter to other instances of the Buddha's magnanimity, but sound reasonable when seen against a background of competition between different sects for cornering material benefits.

In the case of early Buddhism, the clash over "competing conceptions" of Truth should be seen as central to tolerance versus intolerance of the "others." The issue of tolerance further gets muddled with the Buddha's acknowledgement of individual autonomy to choose faith together with his insistence on rationally examining doctrine before accepting it—discourse given to the Kālāmas[45] hypostatizing it—and his repeated criticism of all those religions that he condemned to be either entirety or partially false and debauched. The stress on individual intellect, reason, and conscience for uncovering the "true" religious path is beset with a fundamental impasse: Can anyone at all determine with certainty the "correct" path to salvation? Probably, the Buddha did realize this quandary and therefore, throughout the Buddhist texts, we find a pragmatic replication of a solution—a triumphant proclamation and insistence that the Buddha's *dhamma* was the only "true" path capable of leading to salvation.

True that the Buddha did not wrangle about whether other teachers had or had not realized truth,[46] but he certainly did hold his *dhamma* aloof from other welter of creeds, and unequivocally roared that his *dhamma* was indeed the only "true way." All other *dhammas* not proceeding from the Buddha were held either entirely or partly incorrect, or false, in some respect or the other. They were labeled *micchā-diṭṭhis* (wrong views). The Buddha's teachings cannot be diluted with "others" having different goals, as according to the Buddha there is only "one way"—the path shown by the Buddha. This is confirmed by his remarks in two identical passages.[47] Phra Khantipalo thinks that the "one way" does not refer to a doctrine, but refers to the method through which *nibbāna* could be achieved, and specifically, it refers to the methodical cultivation of mindfulness.[48] However, in our opinion, it refers to the fact that the Buddhadhamma is the only way to liberation.[49] Even accepting Khantipalo's explanation does not either substantially alter our suggestion or preclude the Buddha's claim to exclusivity vis-à-vis the way to salvation—not found to be technically perfected and systematically developed in the teachings of other heretical teachers.

Often when this exclusiveness to salvation is perpetuated and forcefully articulated, then the question of tolerating other religions, which are considered as necessarily evil or wrong, seldom arise. Francis Story remarks: "[F]rom such a viewpoint as this, tolerance could never be seen as a virtue, but only as a reprehensible weakness of faith or a disregard for the welfare of the others."[50] It is precisely due to this altruistic and philanthropic attitude that in such religions, there is no space for tolerating those belonging to other deficient religions, who do not have the supposed key to salvation. The more steadfastly such a belief is held and perpetuated, the less possibility exists for magnanimous toleration. True, early Buddhism deemed humans to be the master and contriver of their own destiny, yet it also made the "initial error" of claiming that there is but one way to the final cessation of sufferings—the way of release from the passions as exhorted by the Buddha.[51]

Theologies that believe in one "strait and narrow gate"[52] to salvation often lay it out that as the conscientious duty of the rightful believer, to use any conceivable means in his power to drive the infidels through this "golden gate," in order to bring them round the sanctuary of true faith.[53] To attain this end, they should be first exhorted and implored and then if necessary coerced. In a perceptive article, Syrkin[54] brings to our notice one such modus operandi employed by the Buddha in the course of his evangelic career, to bring the nonbelievers to his fold of dhamma. Here the Buddha is seen issuing an open threat to his opponent regarding the incurring of physical impairment or damage, if he fails to satisfactorily answer him. In the *Ambaṭṭa Sutta,* arguing with the young *brāhmaṇa,* Ambaṭṭa (who places the *brāhmaṇas* above the *khattiyas* in the social hierarchy), the Buddha threatens him: "If you do not give a clear reply or go off upon another issue, or remain silent, then your head will split into pieces on the spot."[55] Ambaṭṭa is unable to offer an explanation and the Buddha, demanding an answer, renews his threat, adding that such a punishment is befitting and reserved for those who fail to "answer a reasonable question put up by a Tathāgata"[56] thrice. Thereupon, as a visual embodiment of the potential threat, a *yakkha* (godly spirit) appears in the sky, bearing a thunderbolt and ready to split asunder Ambaṭṭa's skull, who is seemingly "terrified, startled, and agitated"[57] and seeks protection from the Buddha, acknowledging him to be right. Syrkin remarks that the "subsequent repetition and justification of this threat by the Buddha, together with the apparition of the menacing *yakkha* evidently makes this idiom not so harmless."[58] Noticeably, Ambaṭṭa escapes the peril of perishing only because he repents at the appropriate time: "What would have been his fate had he with dogged determination held on to his belief?" The answer to it could be very conjectural and thus we refrain from assessing its ramifications with any degree of certitude. Syrkin relates this intimidation to another significant religious phenomenon—the process of "descent" (or humanization). Here, the (divine) religious teacher undertakes the role of a "savior"—this prevents him "from indifference towards human values, since by virtue of his aim he cannot disregard them."[59] He further argues that the Buddha's threat has to be "understood in the context of the pragmatic behaviour which marks the beneficial salutary function of the teacher."[60] Irrespective of their alleged therapeutic value, it does not prevent us from suggesting that these devices functioned as intimidations to bring the recalcitrant and nonbeliever to the fold of the Buddha's *dhamma*. Such coercive strategy is incongruous with the Buddha's tolerance, patience, and advice given elsewhere to the Kālāmas as well as his doctrines.[61]

We conclude this section on the Buddha's threat by stating that the physical threats are not the only ones found in the *Nikāyas*. We also find the Buddha holding out threats in the spiritual domain when he thunders: "Monks, for him who has perverted view, of two destinies, one may be expected—rebirth in Purgatory or in the womb of an animal."[62] The caveat and stern admonition—albeit an implicit one—warns those adhering to *micchā-diṭṭhi* (false views) to give it up or else they are doomed.

Criticism and faultfinding are often linked closely to intolerance and impatience. In the Pāli Canon, we find a sizeable portion of it concerned with criticizing the wrong views of the other *dhammas*. For instance, in the *Brahmajāla Sutta*, the Buddha disapproves of the 62 *micchā-diṭṭhis*. He criticizes and systematically demolishes these,[63] besides counteracting all religious speculations and dogmatic assertions. In the *Mahāparinibbāna Sutta* too, an implicit criticism of other *dhammas* is found, when the Buddha says that in whatsoever doctrine the Eightfold Path is not found, there the four type of (true) recluses are not be found either.[64] The implication quite clearly is that, while holy men could be found in other religions, one finds "wise" men who have gained insight and wisdom only in the Buddha's *dhamma*.

Buddhist scholars—Khantipalo and Story—faced with such paradoxical situations have attempted a neat balancing act. They have sought to explain these acrimonies and anomalies in terms of the uniqueness of the early Buddhist tolerance. While not compromising or yielding to false views, it did not condemn other false teachings either irrationally or on account of antipathy, i.e., the early Buddhist's condemnation or reproach of other *dhammas* was legitimate and with sufficient raison d'être. In other words, the Buddha's criticisms were philanthropic—rectifying the wrong or false methods of other sects—and motivated out of the overarching concern and compassion for the multitude of suffering humanity.

If tolerance is taken to construe that one does not sting anyone's religious (or otherwise) sensibilities and susceptibilities, in anyway whatsoever, then it does not appear that the Buddha interpreted it in this way. Perhaps, the strongest term of reproach that the Buddha used was "foolish men." In umpteen references in the *Nikāyas,* the Buddha calls those belonging to other *dhammas* as "foolish men," besides censuring their beliefs as one of "fools." In the *Majjhima,* while dealing with the misleading and erroneous heretical view of the permanent and unchanging soul, there is a forceful or vehement criticism of it made through a rather acrimonious expression "absolute complete folly."[65] In several *suttas,* the Buddha can be seen openly attacking the *brāhmaṇas,* who may have smarted under these censures, and even ridiculing their certain beliefs, rites, and claims.[66]

Among the most-striking incongruous pieces of evidence is the one that comes from the *Aṅguttara.* Here, in two identical passages, the Buddha heavily comes down upon the doctrine of one of his contemporaries and perhaps a fierce adversary, Makkhali Gosāla. He refers to two kinds of persons born in the world—one who is a savior and is born for the benefaction and welfare of the mankind, and the other who is born to the detriment of mankind. The Buddha puts Gosāla in the latter category and passes a strongly worded uncharitable remark: "Monks, I know not of any other single person fraught with . . . such loss, discomfort and sorrow to *devas* and mankind, as Makkhali, that infatuated man."[67] This most certainly points to the fact that the Buddha was not very charitable toward him and also goes against the usual references to the criticism of "other" sects by the Buddha. We would like to round off this discussion by citing certain instances of atypical behavior[68] among the early Buddhists—more precisely within the Buddhist *saṅgha.* Very early, we come across instances of factionalism, centrifugality, and personality clash within the *saṅgha.* We have examples[69] of monks leaving the *saṅgha* due to doctrinal differences,[70] as many of them had their own individual views[71] on different issues or because of personal ambitions. However, the most significant of the revolts was that of Devadatta, who was perhaps opposed to the lenient rules in the Order and pleaded for a more stringent life for the monks. The Buddha, however, refused to accept the suggestion of Devadatta. The latter, thereupon, deserted the *saṅgha* along with a company of 500 monks.[72]

RECAPITULATION AND REMARKS

What is apparent from the foregoing discussion is that the character of Buddhadhamma—with pronounced emphasis on *ahiṁsā, karuṇā,* and *kṣānti* (patience)—is largely bound up (on numerous occasions) with traits like reason, restraint, forbearance, rationality, etc., which commanded the projection of an attitude of tolerance in early Buddhism. Secondly, high-flown theories and ideas are difficult to translate into practice—gap creeps in between norms and praxis and between precept and observance. Noticeably, in the *Nikāyas* too, such anomalies exist—instances of paradigmatic patience/forbearance and rationality giving way to those of irrationality or aberrant behavior are not uncommon. Early Buddhism certainly could not have afforded to be a passive and meek player, ready to appease all and sundry—not to forget that it was competing against a welter of religio-philosophical views and could have hardly afforded to remain passive and deferentially docile. Some amount of aggression—albeit a controlled one—was called for and inevitably imperative.

Thirdly, there is no such term as "tolerance" in the Pāli Canon and the virtues that are stressed are compassion, patience, and endurance. Even within these supposedly exemplary instances, instances of contradictions and atypical irrational behavior are neither hidden nor can they be overlooked, although scholars have tended to do exactly that. On the practical plane, there appears to be considerable tension between religious toleration and individual autonomy. An internally tolerant faith (like Buddhism) may as well insist upon conformity, if not uniformity, of beliefs and practices—any deviation from this is not usually tolerated and is frowned upon. It is this split between faith, ideation, and praxis that makes the concept of toleration an awkward fit—when speaking of early Buddhism—and exposes the fault lines.

Categories like external and internal tolerances are used with reluctance but purposefully to lay bare the romanticized, historic, and celebrated "invented" tolerance apparently typified by Indian religions like Buddhism, Hinduism, etc. Such tolerance, if any, was narrow and inflated. It neither translated to autonomy for members within the community, nor conferred much latitude to nonbelievers.

Finally, we mark the existence of "parallel views" within the "practical" modern Buddhism of all shades and schools. On the one hand, there is the lay population mostly concerned with following the essential spirit and core precepts of Buddhism, while on the other, are the monastics of the *saṅgha,* relentlessly involved in power struggles and rancorous-discordant relationship both within and without the *saṅgha.* In the ancient past, we have the outstanding example of Devadatta's revolt, and later, the instance of arch rivalry between the monasteries of Mahāvihāra and Abhayagiri in Sri Lanka.[73] To cap it all, notwithstanding the overarching firmament of tolerance in early Buddhism, there remains enough outstanding incongruous evidence exposing the fault lines that stare at us and question the praxis of an ideation.

NOTES

1. Brahmajāla Sutta, *Dīgha Nikāya,* Sutta No. 1 in T.W. Rhys Davids, trans., *Dialogues of the Buddha,* Vol. I (London: Luzac & Co., 1956), p. 3.

2. Upāli Sutta, *Majjhima Nikāya,* Sutta No. 56 in I.B. Horner, trans., *The Collection of Middle Length Sayings,* Vol. II (London: Luzac & Co., 1957), p. 44. A similar advice is rendered by the Buddha to Sīha, the Licchavi general, when he likewise wished an on-the-spot recognition as an *upāsaka,* after hearing a Dhamma talk. See F.L. Woodward, trans., *The Book of Gradual Sayings,* Vol. IV (London: Luzac & Co., 1961), p. 127.

3. See Phra Khantipalo, *Tolerance: A Study from Buddhist Sources* (London: Rider & Co., 1964).

4. It has been argued that with the cultivation of patience, other noble traits of character appear: endurance, forbearance, friendliness, and forgiveness, which may all be summed up under the quality of tolerance. Ibid., p. 19.

5. "Early Buddhism" generally refers to Buddhism as it had crystallized by the time the Pāli Canon—or at least most of it—had been composed. Hence, it would cover a time frame from the time of the Buddha to the fixation of the *Nikāyas,* which could be extended to the reign of Aśoka.

6. The picture that we are attempting to unfold is entirely from the standpoint of the first four *Nikāyas* under scrutiny, and hence precludes hopping to any generalization for the entire corpus of the Buddhist sacred texts.

7. Khantipalo, *Tolerance,* p. 81.

8. Francis Story, *The Buddhist, Outlook: Collected Writings,* Vol. 1 (Kandy: Buddhist Publication Society, 1973), p. 233.

9. In practice, we often notice that people often in enthusiasm carry the spirit of tolerance to the extreme of trying to incorporate into their beliefs those of others—which the early Buddhists seldom indulged in. However, in other cases, it is the inability to tolerate others views and condemn it as false. Ibid.

10. Khantipalo, *Tolerance,* p. 81, emphasis added.

11. Ibid.

12. For a discussion of religious toleration in the liberal tradition, see Jeff Spinner-Haley, "Hinduism, Christianity, and Liberal Religious Toleration," *Political Theory* 33, no. 1 (February 2005): 28–57.

13. Ibid., 38.

14. Ibid., 37.

15. The Pall equivalent for "outsiders" mentioned in this passage from the Digha Nikāya is *pare* (singular: para). According to the Pāli English Dictionary, in a special sense, *pare* means "others," i.e., "outsider or those alien to the religion of the Buddha," in other words, the opponents. See T.W. Rhys Davids and William Stede, eds., *The Pali Text Society's Pali-English Dictionary* (London: Luzac & Co., 1921), p. 418.

16. Rhys Davids, *Dialogues of the Buddha,* Vol. I, p. 3.

17. Story, *The Buddhist, Outlook,* p. 236.

18. For a detailed list of abstentions that conform to moral conduct, see *Dīgha Nikāya,* Sutta No. 1, p. 62. Here follows the whole of the *sīlas* (paragraphs on morality) in the words already translated at Brahmajāla Sutta, see Rhys Davids, *Dialogues of the Buddha,* Vol. 1, pp. 3 and 26. For "the recluse Gotama," read the *bhikkhus,* and alter in each case the words of refrain accordingly.

19. Richard. F. Gombrich, "Notes on the Brahmanical Background to Buddhist Ethics" in Gatave Dhammapala et al., eds., *Buddhist Studies in Honour of Hammalava Saddhatissa* (Nugegoda: Buddhist Research Library Trust, 1984), p. 93.

20. See Horner, *The Collection of Middle Length Sayings,* p. 44.

21. See Woodward, *The Book of Gradual Sayings,* p. 43.

22. "Those who say so, Vaccha are not of my way of thinking. Moreover, such misrepresent me by stating what is not true but falsehood," quoted in ibid., p. 144.

23. "Nevertheless, I say, Vaccha, that a gift in the case of virtuous is of great fruit, not those given in the case of the wicked," quoted in ibid.

24. The five hindrances are malevolence, sloth-and-torpor, excitement and flurry, doubt and wavering, and sensual desires.

25. The five qualities are the constituents of morality, of concentration, of insight, of emancipation, and of release by knowledge and vision.

26. The system of the *Nigaṇṭhas* was not considered wholly evil or a false view, and hence, the Buddha's attitude toward these teachings—ethically and morally upright, notwithstanding the metaphysical differences—was fundamentally different from those philosophies and religions that either denied moral responsibility or disregarded moral values. Morality of the Jains contained essential similarities and elements of the Buddhist moral code and while it was not wholly capable of leading to final *nibbāna,* it at least safeguarded those who observed it from falling into deeper states of woe, i.e., being born into animal or *preta* world, etc.

27. Story, however, concludes quite confidently that "it is safe to say that the Buddha would not have encouraged the support to the Nigaṇṭhas if their doctrine had permitted violation of any of the five Precepts," quoted in Story, *The Buddhist, Outlook,* p. 245. If this were to be true, then it reflects an intolerant attitude on the part of the Buddha.

28. Francis Story believes that the narrative of Sīha (and, of course, of Upāli) exemplifies "the Buddha's requesting his convert to continue his material support of a sect with whose doctrine he did not agree," quoted in ibid..

29. See ibid., p. 240.

30. Ibid., p. 82.

31. "And what monks, are the cankers to be got rid of by endurance? In this teaching, monks, a monk wisely reflective, is one who bears cold, heat, hunger, thirst, the touch of gadfly, mosquito, wind and sun, creeping things, ways of speech that are irksome, unwelcome; he is of a character to bear bodily feelings, which arising are painful, acute, sharp shooting; disagreeable, miserable, deadly." Sabbasava Sutta, Sutta No. 2 in Horner, *The Collection of Middle Length Sayings,* Vol. I, p. 14.

32. Endurance of the first and the third types is very personal and does not concern others, and thus obviously cannot be taken as conclusive evidence for tolerance of the early Buddhists.

33. (1) Once when the monk Moliya Phagguna was closely associating with the nuns, the other monks criticized these nuns and he became angry. This was

reported to the Buddha who admonished him as following: "Phagguna, even if anyone . . . speak dispraise of those nuns, even so should you . . . train yourself thus: 'Neither, will my mind become perverted, nor will I utter an evil speech, but kindly and compassionate will I dwell with a mind of friendliness, and void of hatred,' " quoted in ibid., p. 160. In another passage of the same sutta, the venerable Sāriputta tells the monks that even if thieves were to sever their limbs, they should not set mind on enmity, for whosoever does that is not a believer of Buddhadhamma.

34. Khantipalo, *Tolerance*, p. 84.

35. See *Majjhima Nikāya*, Sutta No. 22 in Horner, *The Collection of Middle Length Sayings*, Vol. I, p. 180.

36. See Brahmajāla Sutta, *Digha Nikāya*, Sutta No. 1.

37. This Upāli is to be distinguished from Upāli there who received the Vināya Pitaka at the First Buddhist Council. The former lived at Nalanda and was a follower of Nāṭaputta.

38. "Today, good doorkeeper, I am closing the door to men and women Jains; but the door is open to the Lord's monks nuns and women lay-disciples," quoted in Horner, *The Collection of Middle Length Sayings*, Vol. II, p. 45. As a matter of fact, he even refuses to meet the Dighatapassin, who seeks an audience to confirm the news that the former had indeed gone over to the Buddha's fold. However, when Nigaṇṭha Naṭaputta (Mahāvīra) himself visits him, Upāli is courteous enough to meet him.

39. And the *brāhmaṇa* Pokkharasādī is in the enjoyment of grant from Pasenadi, the King of Kosala. But the king does not allow him to come into his presence. When he consults with him, he speaks to him only from behind a curtain. See Rhys Davids, *Dialogues of the Buddha*, Vol. I, p. 128.

40. Pasenadi was a contemporary of the Buddha, and quite early in his career, he became a follower of the Buddha. The first meeting of Pasenadi with the Buddha and his subsequent conversion is recorded at Dahara Sutta, *Saṁyutta Nikāya*, 1, p. 69. At their first meeting, we find Pasenadi referring to the Buddha as being very young in years. We are not exactly assured, but we believe that perhaps Pasenadi's reluctance to admit Pokkharasādī in his presence must have come at a time after his conversion to the Buddha's *dhamma*. Conversion to a different fold hardly led people shedding their caste prejudices.

41. Woodward, *The Book of Gradual Sayings*, Vol. II, pp. 151–52, emphasis mine.

42. Y. Krishan states that the above stated description is of a *cāṇḍāla*, who was considered to be an outcaste. See Y. Krishan, "Buddhism and Caste System," *Journal of the International Association of Buddhist Studies* 9, no. 1 (1986): 77. Disagreeing with him, we think that it refers more to a deviant Buddhist *upāsaka*. If we carefully examine the passages, it divulges the fact that out of the five things that he is seen pursuing, the first four are such that the Buddha held in abhorrence—not expected to be present in a Buddhist (monk or layman) and hence those found to be in such a state were unreservedly categorized as an outcast.

43. Perhaps, it was owing to these five moral and religious deficiencies that such a layman is called an "outcast," and is likened to a *cāṇḍāla*, who is an outcast and probably lived in similar moral and religious abyss.

44. *Saṁyutta Nikāya*, IV, p. 25.

45. The context of the discourse delivered to the Kālāmas is that the Buddha outlines the 10 ways of claiming knowledge, on the basis of some kind of authority or reason, which are unsatisfactory. It is thus a discourse on the right or wrong ways of knowledge, and the criterion for its acceptance reflects more a spirit of rationalism than tolerance or anything else. See Kālāma Sutta, in Woodward, *The Book of Gradual Sayings,* Vol. I, p. 172 and Vol. II, p. 200; *Saṁyutta Nikāya,* II, p. 219.

46. See the Buddha's answer to Subhadda's query in the *Mahāparinibbana Sutta* in Rhys Davids, *Dialogues of the Buddha,* Vol. II, p. 165.

47. "There is this one way, monks, for the purification of beings for the overcoming of sorrows and griefs . . . for winning the right path, for realising *nibbāna,* that is to say the four applications of mindfulness," quoted in Satipaṭṭhāna Sutta, *Majjhima Nikāya,* Sutta No. 10 in Horner, *The Collection of Middle Length Sayings,* Vol. I, p. 71, emphasis mine. A similar but more emphatic declaration occurs in Rhys Davids, *Dialogues of the Buddha,* Vol. II, p. 327.

48. Khantipalo, *Tolerance,* p. 114. He bases his argument on the text following the quote, where the Buddha explains the way in which *nibbāna* could be achieved.

49. In the *Nikāyas,* we come across several passages where either direct or indirect claim for exclusive path to liberation is found. For instance, in a passage of the *Saṁyutta,* in reply to a wanderer, the monk Sāriputta contends that the path to *nibbāna* is the Eightfold Path (*Kindred Sayings,* IV, p. 170). Besides, several indirect claims are made by stating that different false views (*micchā-diṭṭhi*) are incapable of leading to liberation. See Horner, *The Collection of Middle Length Sayings,* Vol. I, pp. 11, 12 and Vol. II, p. 103; *Kindred Sayings,* II, p. 66; *Kindred Sayings,* III, p. 39; Woodward, *The Book of Gradual Sayings,* Vol. I, p. 8.

50. Story, *The Buddhist, Outlook,* p. 229, emphasis mine.

51. The point we wish to make is that the attitude of Buddhism with respect to salvation was fundamentally no different than the Semitic or other faiths—merely the emphasis shifted from the will of a God, or the intercession of a priest, or the surrender of one's reason to dogmas, to solely ones personal actions as obtained by the path shown by the Buddha.

52. Story, *The Buddhist, Outlook,* p. 229.

53. In early Buddhism, often the liberation by insight is figuratively spoken of as "crossing-over to the sanctuary."

54. A. Syrkin, "Notes on the Buddha's Threats in the Digha Nikāya," *Journal of the International Association of Buddhist Studies* 7, no. 1 (1984): 147–58.

55. Ambaṭṭha Sutta, *Digha Nikāya,* Sutta No. 3, in Rhys Davids, *Dialogues of the Buddha,* Vol. II, p. 116. Analogous expressions of Buddha's threats are found in the passages from Kutadanta Sutta, *Digha Nikāya, Sutta* No. 5, in Rhys Davids, *Dialogues of the Buddha,* Vol. I, p. 181. Another extremely curious threat occurs in a passage of the *Aṅguttara,* where upon being asked by a certain *brāhmaṇa* why the Buddha does not salute, pay respect, or rise off the seat in the presence of the aged *brāhmaṇas,* the Buddha says that he sees no one who is deserving such treatment from him. Furthermore he adds: "If the *brāhmaṇa* whom the Tathagata should salute rise up . . . verily his head would split into two," quoted in Woodward, *The Book of Gradual Sayings,* Vol. IV, p. 118.

56. Rhys Davids, *Dialogues of the Buddha,* Vol. I, p. 117.

57. Ibid.

58. Syrkin, "Notes on the Buddha's Threats," 148.

59. Ibid., 153. Furthermore, Syrkin remarks: "Descending to a layman's level . . . the Buddha, the Upanishadic sage, etc.—must adopt a definite strategy of behaviour, a certain pragmatism. Therefore, such devices which seem to him appropriate for the final success, as threats, curses, humiliations, etc.," quoted in ibid.

60. Ibid., 155.

61. Syrkin too acknowledges these devices to be inconsistent with the Buddha's own doctrines. But he bases his observation on the fact that the Buddha is resorting to miracles—manifested in the appearance of *yakkha*—which he clearly denounced. See *Dīgha Nikāya,* Sutta Nos. 2 and 24.

62. Woodward, *The Book of Gradual Sayings,* Vol. I, p. 55. Similar "threats" are recorded in Rhys Davids, *Dialogues of the Buddha,* Vol. I, p. 291.

63. A wealth of other *suttas* also harp on similar criticisms. See *Digha Nikāya,* Sutta Nos. 1, 15, 23, 24, and 28; *Majjhima Nikāya,* Sutta Nos. 1, 2, 10–12, 25, 60, 63, 72, 76, 101, 102, 110, etc; and *Saṁyutta Nikāya,* Sutta No. 21.

64. *Aṅguttara Vikāya,* II, p. 16; III, p. 61; X, p. 93; etc. in Rhys Davids, *Dialogues of the Buddha,* Vol. II, p. 166. The four types of recluses are the stream-winner, the once-returner, the no-returner, and the arahant. See *Aṅguttara Nikāya,* II, pp. 86–90 and Woodward, *The Book of Gradual Sayings,* Vol. II, pp. 242–244.

65. Paripura-bala-dhamma, in Horner, *The Collection of Middle Length Sayings,* Vol. I, p. 177. The *Pali English Dictionary* describes *bāla* as originally meaning young and unable to speak, hence like a child. However, it gives "ignorant" as another meaning. This "ignorance" is often with reference to the moral ignorance of the common people. It also gives "foolish" as yet another rendering.

66. In the *Kūṭadanta Sutta,* the Buddha ridicules or criticizes the Brahmanical method of performing sacrifices (Rhys Davids, *Dialogues of the Buddha,* Vol. I, p. 173). In the Ambaṭṭa Sutta, Madhura Sutta, Assalāyana Sutta, etc., he derides the Brahmanical claim for caste superiority of the *brāhmaṇa.* In *Aṅguttara,* the Buddha goes on to suggest that today the *brāhmaṇas* are even worse than dogs (*Aṅguttara Nikāya,* III, p. 220). He likewise denigrates the *brāhmaṇas* in the *Saṁyutta Nikāya* (IV, pp. 117–20).

67. Woodward, *The Book of Gradual Sayings,* Vol. I, p. 29. A similar reference occurs at pp. 265 and 266 as well.

68. Phara Khantipalo, in an endeavor to give an unbiased account, does try to give instances of these atypical behaviors among the Buddhists. However, he appears to be more concerned with the perception of modern Buddhists regarding other schools of Buddhism, which they condemn as heretical. He also analyzes the biases creeping into the writings of scholars who are Buddhists by faith. For details, see Khantipalo, 1964, pp. 104–12.

69. We shall not be much concerned with these instances of dissent, factionalism, and schism within the *saṅgha* as bulk of the evidence is confined to the *Vinaya Pitaka,* which is outside the purview of our study. However, instances of personality clashes and monks reviling the *dhamma* and leaving the *saṅgha* as well as indulging in strife are not uncommon or altogether lacking in the *Nikāyas.*

70. Monks like Sāti and others are mentioned as those who misunderstood and misrepresented the *dhamma* and very often causing trouble to the Buddha. Some left the *saṅgha,* while some were subjected to suspension by the Order for refusal to renounce a sinful doctrine.

71. See S.N. Dube, *Cross Currents in Early Buddhism* (New Delhi: Manohar, 1980), p. 37. It elucidates the controversies presented in Kathāvatthu in the light of the development of Buddhist thought.

72. Tradition has it that Devadatta, burning with an ambition to head the *saṅgha,* asked the Buddha to relinquish the leadership of the *saṅgha.* When the latter refused to oblige, Devadatta tried to have the Buddha assassinated. Having failed in his bids, he tried to bring a schism in the *saṅgha* with the help of some influential monks, and finally left the Order with a large following of dissident monks. For details, see G.P. Malalasekera, *Dictionary of Pali Proper Names,* Vol. 1 (London: Pali Text Society, 1960), pp. 1106–18.

73. Tradition has it that after a protracted period of rivalry (which goes back to 4th century), between the two monastic establishments, in the 12th century, the monks of Mahāvihāra finally succeeded in instigating the ruling king who seized the Abhayagiri *vihāra,* and worse, he went on to burn the Abhayagiri books, which were described as heretical by their opponents. For modern Buddhism and the essential discussion of the dialectical relations or symbiosis and mutuality between the Buddhist *saṅgha* and the Thai polity, see S.J. Tambiah, *World Conqueror and World Renouncer: A Study of Buddhism and Polity in Thailand against a Historical Background* (Cambridge: Cambridge University Press, 1976); for Myanmar/Burma, see Melford E. Spiro, *Buddhism and Society: A Great Tradition and Its Burmese Vicissitudes* (London: George Allen & Unwin Ltd., 1971); and for Sri Lanka, see Richard F. Gombrich, *Theravāda Buddhism: From Ancient Benaras to Modern Colombo* (London: Routledge, 1988).

Chapter 4

Suffering as a Catalyst for Spiritual Development: The Islamic Perspective

I. H. Azad Faruqi

Suffering, in its different varieties, has been a challenge as well as a riddle for humankind since its earliest days. As they continued to attain self-consciousness and became worthy of being called human, their realization of their predicament in this mundane existence—which is "imperfect, impermanent and devoid of any permanent basis" (to express it in Buddhist terms)—also increased. The pain, anguish, and suffering and its undesirability are encountered by humans on various levels: physical, mental, and spiritual. This is one of those fundamental facts of life that is shared by the whole of humankind without exception. However, simultaneously, from the earliest times along, with the experience of suffering, there began a search for its eradication, or its sublimation into a bearable phenomenon. In fact, the whole cultural and civilizational history of humankind can be said to be a history of inventions and adaptation of ways and means to eliminate suffering or to attain what is its opposite—that is, pleasure.

The Holy Qur'ān, which is the basic source of Islamic religion and culture, attempts to provide guidance for the whole of mankind in various walks of life, and also deals with suffering. However, in this regard, its fundamental approach is realistic and down to earth rather than being intellectual and philosophical. It directly addresses the heart and soul of man rather than draw logical conclusions from a hypothesis. The heart and soul of man is extremely impressionable to the influence of the words, which were not used to illustrate abstract ideas and conjectural concepts. It is, perhaps, due to this fact that the imagery, similes, and parables the Holy Qur'ān has used to impart its teachings have been drawn mostly from the environment with which the Arabs were fairly familiar. The tough and weather-beaten population of Arabia, mostly a barren land in its early stage of cultural development, was divided into bigger or smaller tribal groups that were continually at war with each other. At the time of the revelation of the Qur'ān, the Arabs were well aware of various kinds of sufferings, privations, adversities, and miseries. It is thus that the Qur'ān takes a serious note of suffering in its various forms as part of the lot of normal human existence. For instance, referring to some of the common types of suffering at that time in Arabia—though their nature is universal and the attitude recommended by the Qur'ān in face of such adversities is eternal—the Qur'ān says:

> Be sure we shall test you with something of fear and hunger, some loss in goods, lives, and the fruits (of your toil), but give glad tidings to those who patiently persevere, who say, when afflicted with calamity, "To Allah we Belong, and to Him is our return."[1]

It should be kept in view that the Holy Qur'ān, inviting a belief in a strictly monotheistic concept of God, emphasizes the Divine omnipotence and complete sovereignty over the whole gamut of existence almost only next to its most central theme, the oneness of God (*tauheed*). The phrase at the close of chapter 5 verse 19, "And Allah hath power over all things," can be said to be one of the most frequently repeated themes in its slightly varying forms in verses throughout the Holy Qur'ān. But, although from the basic Qur'ānic viewpoint, Allah is the Ultimate Cause of everything, a difference can still be seen in various secondary or immediate causes and purpose of the sufferings.

There are adversities and sufferings that occur due to changes in the natural course taking place through the working of the laws put in the physical realm by God Himself. Such sufferings are to be borne equally by all humans, irrespective of the fact whether they are believers or nonbelievers, pious or sinners. These undesirable situations or happenings are just part of the imperfect worldly existence. The examples of such calamities can be seen in the verses quoted earlier (Q.II:155–156) or in verses like Q.III:140 that are about the war of survival between a small group of companions of the Prophet Muhammad (pbuh) and the non-believers of Mecca:

> If a wound hath touched you, be sure a similar wound has touched the Others. Such days (of varying fortunes) we give to men and men by turns: That Allah may know those that believe, and that He may take to Himself From your Ranks martyr-witness (to Truth). And Allah loveth not those That do wrong.

The universality of this kind of suffering is such that even prophets and saints are not considered exempt from these laws, built in the very structure and design of the universe. All are equally subject to these natural forces:

> How many of the Prophets fought (in Allah's way) and with them (fought) large bands of Godly men?
> But they never lost heart if they met with disaster in Allah's way, nor did They weaken (in will) nor give in.
> And Allah loves those who are firm and steadfast.[2]

Sometimes, man or communities are afflicted by calamities or adversities in the course of their life due to their transgression against the moral laws, put in the universe by God and termed by the Qur'ān as *Sunnatul-Lah*. Such calamities are a direct result of a human's own actions and they should regard only themselves responsible for these.[3]

Similar is the case of such sufferings, according to the Qur'ān, which are willed by God with the purpose to serve as a warning or chastisement to provide man an opportunity to improve and reform himself as stated in the following verse: "And Indeed We will make them taste the lighter chastisement before the greater chastisement in order that they may (repent) and return."[4]

These provide situations where humans or communities are afflicted by miseries or sufferings because they went against the Divine laws regarding the ethical realm, or their conscious transgression against the Divine commands. Sufferings of these kinds provide man an opportunity to reform and purify himself and thus make peace with God. The proper attitude for humans, according to the Qur'ān in such situations, is that of repentance with a firm resolve never to repeat the same mistakes again. They are also required to be patient and adopt an attitude of resignation to the Divine will. This making peace with God or turning to Him as the ultimate refuge in face of the insurmountable adversities is an example where, according to the Qur'ān, suffering can be a catalyst for spiritual development. Failing in this, however, and perpetuation in their transgressions by humans or communities, in spite of warnings from God, is ultimately to invite Divine wrath and the irreversible retribution and punishment, as repeatedly described in the Holy Qur'ān:

> If the people of the towns had but believed and feared Allah, We should indeed have opened out to them (all kinds of) blessings from heaven and earth; But they rejected (the truth), and We brought them to book for their misdeeds . . . did they then feel secure against Allah's devising but no one can feel secure From the Plan of Allah, except those (doomed) to ruin.[5]

From what we can gather from the description of these various kinds of sufferings and the condition of those who are afflicted by these, in the view of the Qur'ān, is that it is not that all kinds of suffering can be a catalyst for spiritual development. In fact, it is suffering accompanied by faith, or at least with a potential for reform and readiness to learn, which is required for this purpose.

The second source of Islamic law and theology is *Hadith,* the reports about sayings, deeds, and approval of the actions by the Prophet (pbuh). There are a number of *Ahadith* (plural of *Hadith*) that establish a relationship between a person's piety or spiritual exaltation and suffering. A *Hadith* from the *Musnad* (a *Hadith* collection) of Imam Ahmad-ibn-Hanbal narrates that being asked by a senior companion of the Prophet (pbuh), Hazrat Sa'd bin Waqqa (may God be pleased by him), as who among men are most afflicted by the calamities, the Prophet (pbuh) replied:

> The prophets, then the pious, everyone according to the degree of his piety. A man is afflicted according to his faith (*din*); if his faith is durable, his affliction is accordingly increased, and if his faith is weak [literally thin], his affliction is made lighter. Afflictions continue to oppress the worshipful servant (*'abd*) until they leave him walking on the face of the earth without any sin cleaving to him.[6]

According to another *Hadith:*

> The greatness of the reward [of the man of faith] is proportionate with the greatness of his afflictions. For, if God loves a people, He visits them with afflictions. He who is content [that is, with God's will], with him God be pleased, and he who is wrathful, divine wrath will he have.[7]

These excerpts sufficiently establish the relationship of suffering and religious life in Islam. However, these excerpts also make it clear that the miseries and calamities, or suffering of any kind, can truly be a catalyst for spiritual exaltation and greater closeness to God only when these are accompanied by the recommended attitudes of patience and contentment.

By contentment (*raza*), here is intended complete resignation and acceptance of whatever befalls a person, happiness or suffering, as it is through the Divine will that everything happens.

There are groups and subtraditions within the Islamic culture that have paid special attention toward making suffering a means for spiritual advancement. Particular subsections in Islam have even institutionalized it as a major source of religious merit and means of salvation. I am referring specifically to the Sufis and the Shi'ahs.

Sufism, as the case is with other mystical traditions across religions, stands at the spiritual core of the Islamic religion. They are the specialists who have consciously cultivated and actualized the spiritual vision of Islam and the values related with it. What other Muslims believe as part of their tradition or accept intellectually, the Sufis experience it directly or, at least, they aim for it. They are considered more advanced than other Muslims, in their faith in God and in the realization of values that result from such a staunch faith. Hazrat "Ali bin Uthman al Hujwiri (who died between 1072–1076 CE and is buried in Lahore) was one such Sufi shaikh [spiritual master]. In his famous work on Tasawwuf (*Kashful Mahjub*), which is considered the oldest Persian treatise on Sufism, in the section dealing with the phraseology and metaphorical terms of the Sufis, he writes that the Sufis consider *bala*" (affection) as a test or probation of God of his friends through diverse troubles, sicknesses, and tribulations. He adds: "The more severely a man is afflicted the nearer does he approach unto God, for affliction is the vesture of the saints and the cradle of the pure and nourishment of the prophets?"[8] He quotes two *Ahadith* similar in content. In the second one, the Prophet (pbuh) says: "The prophets are the most afflicted of mankind, then the saints, and then other men, according to their respective ranks."[9]

The approved and the recommended attitude in the face of calamities and afflictions, as practiced by the Sufis, have been further explained by Hazrat Ali al-Hujwiri elsewhere in the book:

> Commander of the Faithful Husain ibn Ali (may God be pleased with him) was asked about the saying of Hazrat Abu Zarr Ghifari (may God be pleased with him): "I love poverty better than riches and sickness better than health." (Imam) Husain replied: "God have mercy on Abu Dharr! But I say that whoever surveys the excellent choice made by God for him does not desire anything except what God has chosen for him. When a man sees God's choice and abandons his own choice, he is delivered from all sorrow."[10]

As far as the Shi'ahs are concerned, at least in the Athna Ash'ari tradition among them, a religious stance can be observed in which the sufferings of the *ahle-bait* (the family of the Prophet [pbuh]) and particularly those borne by Imam Husain (may God be pleased with him), the grandsons of the Prophet (pbuh) and his martyrdom, play a central role. This utilization of suffering for its redemptive effects has been conceived in Shi'ah theology, and more so in the beliefs and practices of the common people in this tradition, in various respects. First of all, there is the concept of the purifying effects of suffering itself. This has been described to be the case with the *ahle-bait* even during the lifetime of the Prophet (pbuh), due to various kinds of deprivations. After his lifetime, things became more oppressive. Hazrat Ali was dispossessed of his legitimate right to become a successor. The *ahle-bait* continued to face prejudice and discrimination from the ruling caliphs of various dynasties, except during the times and in the areas where they were able to establish Shi'ah dynasties.

Now apart form the religious merit acquired by the *ahle-bait* in general through their patient tolerance of all types of miseries heaped upon them, the fact that these calamities were being borne by such a spiritually exalted group of people as the house of the Prophet (pbuh) and particularly Imam Husain (may God be pleased with him), who was specially a victim of all kinds of afflictions, raises the level of the religious merit of the *ahle-bait.* According to Shi'ah belief and practice, the faithful can and do share this religious merit by participating in the sorrows of the *ahle-bait.* Furthermore, due to their particular attachment with the *ahle-bait* and with the *imam,* they hope to attain their intercession on the Day of Judgment. Some of these special, traditionally approved concepts and practices to express this sharing of the sorrows of the *ahle-bait* are limited to particular times in the year, like the tradition of 'Izadari or Ta'ziah Dari. It is linked with the month of *Muharram* in the Islamic calendar, the month of the martyrdom of Imam Husain (may God be pleased with him). *Majlis* (congregation) can take place whenever required. The *zyarat* or the visit of the faithful to the shrines and tombs of the *imams* and other members of *alhe-bait* is also another practice considered meritorious by the Shi'ahs.

NOTES

1. Q.II:155–156. All translations of the Qur'anic verses are from Abdullah Yusuf'Ali, trans., *The Holy Qur'an: English Translation of the Meanings and Commentary* (al-Madinah al-Munawarah: King Fahd Holy Qur'ān Printing Complex, 1410 H).
2. Q.III:146.
3. Q.III:165 and Q.VII:96.
4. Q.XXXII:21.

5. Q.VII:99.

6. Ahmad ibn Muhammad ibn Hanbal, *Musnad,* 1st ed. (Beirut: al-Maktab al-Islāmī, 1966), pp. 173, 174 as quoted in Ayoub Mahmoud, *Redemptive Suffering in Islam* (Hague: Mouton Publishers, 1978), p. 25.

7. Ibid., H.4226. See also Abu 'Isa ibn Muhammad ibn 'Isa ibn Sawrah al-Tirmidhi, *Sunan al-Tirmidhi,* 1st ed., ed. 'Izzat 'Ubayd al-Da''as (Hums: Matabi' al-Fajr al-Hadithah, 1387/1967), p. 316.

8. R.A. Nicholson, trans., "Hazrat 'Ali bin Uthman al Hujwiri," *Tasawwuf (Kashful Mahjub)* (New Delhi: Zia-ul-Quran Publications, 1989), pp. 388, 389.

9. Ibid.

10. Ibid., pp. 177, 178.

Chapter 5

From the *Cakravartin* Ideal to Realpolitik: Buddhism and Confucianism in the Premodern Chinese Context and Its Implications for Contemporary Chinese Secular Policy toward Religion

Albert Welter

Since September 11, many governments around the world have used the event as a pretext to target religious-based protest. This issue is keenly felt in the People's Republic of China, a nation that retains strong socialist leanings with implicitly negative attitudes toward religion and religious activity. Yet, many Chinese citizens harbor a deep and growing attraction to religion. This is attributable to two general factors: (1) the government's relaxation of antireligious policies and more tolerant approach to religious institutions and activities and (2) the declining influence of socialist ideology among the people, paving the way for renewed interest in alternate belief systems. Given China's strong secularist orientations and the multireligious context of Chinese society—which includes significant numbers of adherents not only to indigenous Confucianism and Taoism, and indigenized Buddhism, but also to non-Han forms of Buddhism (Southeast Asian Theravāda and Tibetan/Mongolian Vajrāyāna), Islam (Uighur and Hui), Christianity (Protestant and Catholic), and various forms of Chinese folk religious practices—the issue of religious accommodation is a decisive one for China's future.

This chapter explores Chinese perspectives on religious accommodation. While I frame the issue broadly, looking at both the range of theoretical possibilities and the spectrum of actual policies implemented, my focus is on the concrete experience of the state management of Buddhism during a time of great transition in the premodern period, when the legitimacy of Buddhism in the Chinese context was coming under increasing scrutiny from secular (i.e., Confucian) authorities. My presentation reviews both positive and negative examples of issues relating to religious accommodation drawn from Chinese history, in an attempt to set the current issues China faces in historical context. In effect, my suggestion is that as China faces a multireligious, multi-ideological future, it will be well advised to revisit the history of its multireligious, multi-ideological past.

BUDDHISM AND CONFUCIAN CIVILIZATION: MODELS AND MOTIVES FOR GOVERNMENT ACCOMMODATION AND REPUDIATION

The notion of a multireligious, multi-ideological society based on a secular model has deep precedence in China. Historically, the triumph of monotheism in the West and Middle East rendered the notion of a multireligious society, not to mention secularism, an unattractive and ultimately untenable option. The faiths of others may (or may not) be tolerated; all were bound to ultimately recognize the orthodox creed of the one true God. In India, where the reality of multireligious societies prevailed, such reality was not accompanied by secular systems of authority, at least not to the extent that was the case in China. In China and throughout East Asia, Confucianism provided a secular-style framework for the administration of Chinese society, including its multireligious, multi-ideological dimensions. Although Confucianism, too, had marked religious and ideological dimensions, these may be regarded as little different from the implicit religious and ideological dimensions of many modern secularisms. With regard to the administration of religions, secular regimes in traditional China followed patterns familiar to modern observers of relations between secular governments and religious ideologies in the modern context. In the modern context, one sees three distinct types of models for religious accommodation: (1) theocratic type models that are not only sympathetic to religion, but also espouse religious doctrine as inseparable from state ideology; (2) secular models that follow a Marxist inspired agenda, are generally unsympathetic to religion, and view religion as a threat to state policy and an impediment to true social amity; and (3) constitutional or "liberal" democracies that espouse the separation of religion and the state, and generally restrict religion to the private sphere, circumscribing its activities in the public realm.

These three models have parallels to the way religions were administered in China in the premodern period, but with an important distinction: The Chinese emperor was, by definition, the ruler of a secular state with theocratic type responsibilities. As political head of state, the emperor administered the government through bureaucratic agencies. But the Chinese emperor was also a quasireligious figure, the Son of Heaven, who ruled and derived his legitimacy from Heaven's mandate. An important part of the emperor's religious duties involved rituals that acknowledged the emperor's relationship with Heaven and the incumbent duties that accompanied it.

The presence of other religious ideologies in China added further complications to China's secular-based theocracy. For the most part, these other religious ideologies were restricted to non-Han ethnic groups and, however widespread, did not threaten the fundamental orientations of Han-based Confucianism. Indeed, a mark of Sinification among non-Han ethnic groups was their adoption of Confucian values and principles, not unlike the processes of Westernization (often accompanied by secularization) that takes place among modern non-Western immigrant groups to Western countries or in the process of the adoption or adaptation of Western values in non-Western countries.

The exceptions to this Confucianization process in China were Taoism and Han, or Chinese Buddhism. As an indigenous tradition with roots roughly as old as Confucianism, Taoism was integrated and accommodated, if not compromised, by the dominant Confucian tradition. Buddhism in China, however, was quite another matter. The advance of Buddhism among the populace and secular elite, in particular, "muddied the water," so to speak, and challenged the theological orientations of China's Confucian-based secularism. While there are different species of Buddhism in China—Theravada among Chinese ethnic communities bordering on Southeast Asian countries and Vajrayana among Tibetan and Mongolian communities—it was Han Chinese Mahayana that traditionally provided the greatest threat to Confucian hegemony.

The presence of Buddhism in China posed, for example, a number of challenging questions. What, for example, was the emperor's relationship with the Buddha, and what was the proper way for an emperor, a semidivine figure, to acknowledge the Buddha's existence? Several options were available, but in principle, these can be reduced to three possibilities:

(1) the emperor could acknowledge the Buddha's spiritual superiority and pay homage, albeit as a high-level practitioner, a kind of Bodhisattva-in-waiting; (2) the emperor could regard the Buddha in his own right while making no claims regarding his own superiority or inferiority, in a kind of "separate but equal" fashion; or (3) the emperor could regard the Buddha as a masquerading imposter, who had no business on Chinese soil, a figment of some foreign fantasy that had a debilitating effect on the national spirit and native (i.e., Confucian) values.

In a word, the emperor could be pro-Buddhist, neutral, or anti-Buddhist. It goes without saying there are varying degrees of each, and the history of China is rich with examples of emperors who followed combinations of all three, depending on the specific circumstances of his reign. Even within each category, there is room for variance. A pro-Buddhist emperor might, for example, patronize Buddhism purely for political expediency, to appease domestic or international interests, as well as for reasons of deep faith and sympathy with Buddhist teaching. An anti-Buddhist emperor, by the same token, may adopt minor policies aimed at curbing mild Buddhist excesses, or he may mount a full-scale campaign of suppression aiming at exterminating the Buddhist presence in China. At any rate, the imperial relationship with Buddhism in China, given the ideological–theological differences, was always potentially tempestuous. As Neo-Confucianism resurfaced in China, these differences became a central feature of the Neo-Confucian ideological platform espousing anti-Buddhist policies.

When we examine the motives behind imperial implementations of Buddhist policies, be they pro, neutral, or anti, we can make the following general observations. Pro-Buddhist policies are inspired by piety, but the inspiration for such piety may come from varied sources. Emperors may come from pious Buddhist families, and their pro-Buddhist policies may be seen as an extension of this piety. In other cases, individual emperors may identify with the Buddhist message for personal reasons, perhaps owing to some traumatic personal event, like a bout with illness, and promote Buddhism as an extension of his own personal spiritual quest. In other instances, emperors may seek solace in Buddhism for redemption from past misdeeds, especially in the case of brutalities committed in the quest for power. In this case, the emperor's pro-Buddhist policies stem from his quest for atonement.

Neutral-Buddhist policies are formed out of feelings of indifference toward Buddhism. In this case, policies often reflect a continuation of the status quo, an affirmation of existing, expedient attitudes toward Buddhism that confirm the utility of Buddhist beliefs and institutions in the exercise of secular authority. In this case, policies toward Buddhism are formed from the perspective of realpolitik recognition of the advantages and disadvantages that Buddhism holds for the state. Buddhism may be useful, for example, in international initiatives with pro-Buddhist states, and may play a positive role in diplomatic missions with such states. Buddhism may also prove useful in efforts aimed at domestic pacification, to temper aggressive tendencies, and curb immoral conduct. Yet, even while acknowledging the positive effects that Buddhism may have for international and domestic policies, the emperor and secular officials may exercise caution in their promotion of Buddhism for its inherent unconformity to Confucian principles.

Antigovernment policies are formed out of resentment and suspicion toward Buddhism. In this case, Buddhist faith is viewed as conflicting with national allegiance, and Buddhist influence over the populace is feared as a potential threat to secular authority. In the Chinese context, suspicion regarding Buddhism was inflamed by Confucian polemics against it. Neo-Confucian critiques of Buddhism from the Song dynasty onward sounded a common refrain built around a similar litany of complaints based on moral, social, economic, and political criteria. The domestication of Buddhism in the Chinese context may be read as a concentrated effort to adapt Buddhism to Confucian principles. As successful as Buddhist adaptation was, in the eyes of many, namely Neo-Confucians, it was doomed to failure.

With its emphasis on monasticism, Buddhism allegedly disrupted family relations and filial behavior. Sons and daughters who chose celibacy over marriage could not fulfill the mandatory Confucian obligations of looking after parents in old age, preserve the family lineage through (male) offspring, or perform the required rites for honoring ancestors. Moreover, the Buddhist goal of a personal, otherworldly nirvāṇa conflicted with Confucian notions regarding the proper exercise of one's mandate through positive social activity. One way of looking at the differences between Confucian and Buddhist aims is a comparison between the Buddhist Noble Eightfold Path and the Neo-Confucian agenda outlined in the *Great Learning*. While both agendas are predicated on acquiring wisdom or knowledge and place a premium on moral development, they diverge regarding the public versus private dimension of their activity. Because Buddhists focus on internal mental cultivation aimed at producing advanced stages of consciousness and ultimately the extinction of consciousness itself in nirvāṇa, Confucians criticize them as self-obsessed (and selfish) pursuers of a fantasy existence. Confucians never question the reality of this world. The samsāric existence of Buddhism is for them the only possible arena for human endeavor. It is only through human effort in this world that it may be rendered a humane and harmonious place to live. This is the true human pursuit, not the passive retreat that Buddhists advocate.

Confucians also criticized Buddhists for economic and political reasons. From a Confucian perspective, monastic Buddhism created an unproductive class that produced added strains on the economy. In addition, the monastic institution was seen as hoarding national wealth through its elaborate buildings, gilded halls, and use of precious metals and other valuable materials for making and adorning Buddha images and other utensils used in Buddhist rituals. As a result of these concerns, government proscriptions against Buddhism often called for monks to be laicized, i.e., returned to productive labor, and for statues to be scrapped and melted down to recover the precious metal they were made of for "more useful" purposes.

Buddhist monastery lands, or estates, enjoyed tax-free status and were thus viewed as a strain on the economy. In times of economic crises, in particular, Buddhist monasteries were singled out as major sources of the problem, with effective remedies proposed, ranging from the closure of monasteries to the confiscation of land and valuable materials in their possession, to restrictions on numbers of monks allowed at individual institutions, and to the forced return of monks to lay life. From a political standpoint, Buddhist monasteries were viewed as havens for criminal elements and licentious behavior. Monastery residents enjoyed freedom from military service and the forced labor duties accompanying government works. Confucians resented the private, individualized reasons that led people to opt for the monastic lifestyle, a way to avoid public, civic duties. To counter this, Confucians often accused monastery residents of unsavory activities and licentious behaviors. Undoubtedly, there was some truth to Confucian accusations, as monasteries could hardly be free of transgressions, but these were largely propagandistic claims to sway public (in this case, imperial) opinion against Buddhism.

BUDDHIST AND CONFUCIAN APPROACHES: THE *CAKRAVARTIN* IDEAL VERSUS REALPOLITIK

I now turn to an examination of two approaches for ruling monarchs: one inspired by Buddhism, in the interests of spreading Buddhist ideals, and the other based on secular Confucian values that treat Buddhism as a commodity in the exercise of state policy. In the first case, the ruler espouses Buddhist ideals and sees his regime as an extension of them, and is known as a *cakravartin*.[1] In the other case, the ruler implements Buddhist policies from nonideological, practical concerns, according to realpolitik.[2] As Buddhism reemerges as a potent force across economically burgeoning Asian regions, the question of what role it will assume, both in domestic and international affairs, in increasing significance.

My focus here is on the *cakravartin* versus realpolitik approach to accommodating Buddhism in China, concentrating on case studies involving two historic figures: the Buddhist scholastic monk Yongming Yanshou 永明延壽 (904–975) and the literati monk Zanning 贊寧 (919–1001). Natives of the same Chinese region (Wuyue 吳越) and separated by only a generation, the circumstances of these two Buddhists differed dramatically and resulted in dissimilar recommendations regarding the Buddhist role in state and government affairs. This suggests that circumstance plays a leading role in determining the possibilities open to Buddhism as an active player in secular affairs. While Yanshou's approach typifies that found in pro-Buddhist regimes whose identities are framed around Buddhist ideals (the *cakravartin* model), Zanning faced potentially hostile anti-Buddhist sentiments that caused him to recommend Buddhism for its practical utility, devoid of ideological concerns (the realpolitik model). In this regard, Zanning's approach may be beneficial to those seeking modest accommodations for Buddhism as a practical measure, and exposing the pitfalls of dealing with those in power reluctant to acknowledge Buddhist legitimacy.

THE CONFUCIAN REVIVAL AND THE BUDDHIST REVIVAL IN THE WUYUE KINGDOM

The origins of the *cakravartin* model in Wuyue lie in the complicated legacy of Buddhism from the end of the Tang 唐 (618–906) to the Wudai 五代 or Five Dynasties period (907–959). Often heralded as the "golden age" of Buddhism in China, the Tang legacy is complicated by rising anti-Buddhist sentiments that culminated in a major suppression of Buddhism during the Huichang 會昌 era (841–846). While many Tang emperors favored Buddhism and saw in its teachings a force for good that could pacify the realm, others viewed it as a threat and attempted to curb its influence.[3] From the mid-Tang period, central authority suffered a serious blow when the military warlord governor (*jiedu shi* 節度使) An Lushan 安禄山, charged with guarding the northern frontier, usurped his authority and marched his loyal troops into the capital of Chang'an 長安 (contemporary Xi'an 西安) in 755. Emperor Xuanzong 宣宗 and his court were forced to flee, and although the rebellion was suppressed, the fortunes of the dynasty never recovered. Successive attempts to restore dynastic unity and the power of central authority resulted in excessive tax burdens on the peasantry, and eventually to growing patterns of disorder and banditry, and garrison insurrections. The final decades of Tang rule saw a popular rebellion of great magnitude and the central government reduced to surrendering large areas of its domain to independent and quasi-independent military warlord rulers.[4]

The declining state of Tang society, political authority, and the economy brought forth calls for reform. Among the strident critics of this period was Han Yu 韓愈 (768–824), whose spirited anti-Buddhist rhetoric helped spawn a Confucian revival.[5] While it is not the case that Confucianism during the Tang was as lethargic as often supposed,[6] many of the brightest minds of the period were captivated by Buddhism and spent their careers enraptured by the rarified air that Buddhism led them to. The message of Confucianism was uninspiring for many, and seemed to have little to offer on fundamental questions of human nature and the human condition. Implicated in the fall of the Eastern Han dynasty (25–220), confidence in Confucianism as a sole pretext for ruling authority had been seriously undermined, and successive generations of Chinese elites were reluctant to rely on it exclusively. Instead, they preferred to acknowledge its utility as a social ethic but circumscribe its authority to the realm of practical affairs, relying on Buddhism (or Taoism) for serious matters relating to metaphysics and epistemology. All of this began to change with Han Yu, who launched a broadside against Buddhism as an alien, non-Chinese religion, based on evil, socially damaging superstitions subversive of public morality and "true" Chinese (i.e., Confucian) values.[7]

Through Han Yu, the Confucian-trained Chinese elite began to awaken to the possibilities of renewing China as a "Confucian" state. The teachings of Confucius 孔子 and Mencius 孟子, previously subordinated to the "old" canon of the five Confucian authoritative texts (*Li ji* 禮記 or Book of Rites, *Shu jing* 書經 or Book of Documents, *Shi jing* 詩經 or Book of Poetry, *Yi jing* 易經 or Book of Changes, and *Chunqiu* 春秋 or Spring and Autumn [Annals]), were elevated to the new status of "classics." Their words, previously relegated to secondary status, acquired new meaning and a new sense of relevancy, pointing to a direct and penetrating insight into the workings of the way as applied to pressing moral, social, and political issues. As Han Yu breathed new life into Confucius and Mencius's words, he created a new model of the sage as active participant in the affairs of the world for Chinese literati to follow. As Confucian confidence in this new approach grew, Confucian scholars began to challenge the assumptions that pervaded Buddhist teaching.

While Zanning was forced to confront this new, virulent form of Confucianism head-on in the Song, Yanshou was shielded from it by the dictates of state policy in Wuyue. As the Tang deteriorated, the southern principality of Wuyue was able to carve out an independent, politically stable and economically vibrant regime centered in the regional capital of Qiantang 錢塘 (which became the Southern Song capital of Hangzhou, as it is known today). Like other southern-based regimes of the late Tang and Five Dynasties periods (e.g., Southern Tang, Min, and Southern Han), Wuyue was built on the promise of a Buddhist revival, as a revision of the glories of the previous Tang, Buddhist-based society and culture.

The ruler who carved out an independent regime for Wuyue, Qian Liu 錢鏐 (893–932), showed his support for Buddhism by beginning a campaign to construct temples throughout the region.[8] Monks from various regions sought refuge under the protection of the Buddhist temples that Qian Liu supported, including representatives of Northern and Southern Faction Chan.[9] The campaign to revive Buddhism in Wuyue culminated in the personal connection and political fortunes of Tiantai Deshao 天台德韶 (891–972) and Qian Chu 錢俶 (r. 948–978). Nearly 40 years his junior, Qian Chu naturally relied on Deshao for advice, practicing Buddhism under him in a manner more akin to a master–disciple relationship than the natural pattern pertaining between a ruler and his spiritual advisor. Deshao's stature in the region was such that he was praised as the reembodiment of the famous Tiantai prelate, Zhiyi 智顗.[10] His influence over Qian Chu resulted in favored treatment for Deshao's students in Wuyue, many of whom studied alongside Qian Chu in Deshao's congregation.[11] Most prominent among them were Zanning, who succeeded Deshao in the role of Wuyue political advisor, and Yongming Yanshou (904–975), who assumed the role of spiritual leader in Wuyue. Yanshou's career culminated as abbot at the Yongming monastery, a newly established institution in the Wuyue capital that symbolized the central role of Buddhism in the region.

YONGMING YANSHOU AND THE *CAKRAVARTIN* MODEL IN WUYUE

Generally speaking, the Buddhist revival in Wuyue was a reaction against the chaos of the late Tang and Five Dynasties. In addition to its strictly spiritual role, Buddhism in Wuyue was linked to social and political stability. Through the promotion of Buddhism, Wuyue rulers envisioned a revival of the old glory of the Tang, where Buddhism served as a central feature in the definition of civilization and culture. Of all the regions of the south, Wuyue was economically and politically the strongest during the Five Dynasties period. It also provided the strongest support for Buddhism, and Buddhism served as the cornerstone of Wuyue cultural policy. Its support for Buddhism was driven by conservative forces, which sought in Buddhism the recovery of a former glory. While Wuyue Buddhism was embodied largely through support for Chan masters and institutions, it sought to weld these to precedents founded in the doctrinal traditions of Buddhist scholasticism. As a result, although the Wuyue Buddhist revival was carried out largely under the Chan banner, Chan in Wuyue had its own distinct character. Wuyue Chan was identified with older Tang Buddhist traditions, and this identification with the larger Buddhist tradition became a standard feature of Wuyue Chan. The major protagonist of Wuyue Chan was Yongming Yanshou, whose Chan syncretism redefined the contributions of the doctrinal schools of Buddhism and their textual traditions in terms of Chan principles. Yanshou's notion of *zong* 宗 is articulated extensively in his major work on Chan scholasticism, the *Zongjing lu* 宗鏡錄 (Records of the Source-Mirror).

Rather than an architect of the Wuyue *cakravartin* model, Yanshou's writings reflect prevailing assumptions regarding orthodox Buddhism in Wuyue. Although Yanshou identifies himself in his writings as a Chan master, his brand of Chan should not be confused with Linji faction teachings that became dominant in the Song.[12] Yanshou is quite critical of the leading tenets associated with Linji Chan (Rinzai Zen) teaching, whether it be the rejection of Buddhist scripture as a meaningful guide or the dismissal of Buddhist piety, seated meditation, and other conventional Buddhist practices as impediments to direct apprehension and sudden awakening (*wu* 悟). Yanshou's Chan, true to the orientation toward Buddhism prevalent in Wuyue, reflects broad assumptions in Chinese Mahayana teaching and incorporates the full range of practices that this teaching offers. While Yanshou agrees that these teachings are preparatory, in some sense, and do not reflect the complete awakening experience that Chan affords, these teachings are also part and parcel of true *bodhisattva* practice and no true Buddhist would reject them. The myriad good deeds (*wanshan* 萬善) that Yanshou advocates in his *Wanshan tonggui ji* 萬善同歸集 (Collected Writings on the Common End of Myriad Good Deeds) are thus a reflection of the pan-Mahayana universalism promoted by Wuyue policy.[13]

The architects of Wuyue policy were the aforementioned ruler Qian Chu and his spiritual and political advisor the Buddhist monk Tiantai Deshao. Qian Chu was a self-espoused *cakravartin*. Although the revival of Mt. Tiantai as a spiritual center in Wuyue, at Deshao's urgings, was a strong priority, as a ruler, Qian Chu identified with the *stūpa* (commemorative mound or tumulus) reliquary on Mt. Ayuwang (King Aśoka). According to Buddhist traditions in China, when the famed pro-Buddhist Indian monarch dictated that *stūpas* containing relics of Śākyamuni be erected throughout his kingdom, some—like the one on Mt. Ayuwang in Wuyue—were erected in China. It is, of course, illogical to regard this as literally true, no matter how much the rulers of Wuyue were inclined to think so. The presumption that Aśoka's *stūpas* were erected in China should be read as the symbolic inclusion of China in the larger pan-Asian Buddhist world.

Yet, the Aśokan model in Wuyue was more than symbolic. In imitation of Aśoka's pro-Buddhist regime, Qian Chu mounted a massive construction campaign aimed at physically imprinting Buddhism on the Wuyue landscape. The number and scale of construction activities carried out by Wuyue monarchs has been well documented.[14] Indicative of this activity was the aforementioned reconstruction of Mt. Tiantai—its numerous monasteries, temples, and shrines—as a spiritual center, and the affirmation of the Śākyamuni Stūpa on Mt. Ayuwang as a symbol of the Wuyue Buddhist state. In addition, countless Buddhist monasteries, temples, and shrines were either constructed or refurbished throughout the Wuyue region. This was particularly true in the capital, Qiantang. Yanshou, for example, received his first posting, at the request of Qian Chu, to assume abbotship of the newly refurbished Lingyin Chan monastery 靈隱禪寺 located on the outskirts of the capital. After a brief tenure there, Yanshou was again asked by Qian Chu to assume abbotship of a large, newly constructed Yongming monastery 永明寺 on the southern shores of the famed West Lake. Yongming monastery functioned as a leading Buddhist institution in Wuyue, the center from which Wuyue's leading spiritual advisor Yanshou disseminated authorized Buddhist teaching throughout the region. In addition, Qian Chu erected a number of pagodas (*ta* 塔) throughout Wuyue in obvious emulation of Aśoka, many of which survived, at least as relics, into the modern period.[15]

ZANNING AND BUDDHIST REALPOLITIK IN THE SONG

While Zanning was raised in the same pro-Buddhist environment in Wuyue as Yanshou, the circumstances of his career took a drastically different turn. When Wuyue was amalgamated with the recently formed Song dynasty in 978, two years after Yanshou's death, Zanning accompanied Qian Chu to the Song capital to oversee the tense transfer of power. With the transfer, a specter of uncertainty surrounded Zanning and the fate of Buddhism in the new regime.

The relationship between the Buddha and the Chinese emperor, the status of the Buddhist clergy vis-à-vis Chinese secular authority, had been an issue in China since the introduction of Buddhism. Prior to the Song, major campaigns were mounted by the imperial government to curb and restrict Buddhist influence on Chinese society. Yet, Buddhists were constantly able to reclaim their independence and intellectual superiority in ways that garnered a measure of respect, if not outright support. At the beginning of the Song dynasty (circa 960), questions regarding the proper role of Buddhism were raised again, and the resolutions arrived at became key features of Song Neo-Buddhism. In theoretical terms, the question was simple: How would the emperor be regarded vis-à-vis the Buddha? Zanning's attempts to influence imperial policy are vividly represented in two episodes regarding him and the emperor's relationship with the Buddha.

The first episode reads as follows:

> The monk Zanning accompanied the prince of Wuyue [i.e., Qian Chu] to the [Song] court. The [Song] Emperor [Taizong] conferred on him (Zanning) the honorific title "Great Master, Expert in Wisdom," ordered him to dwell at the Tianshou Monastery 天壽寺 in the Eastern Precincts [of the capital], and commanded him to write a history of the Sangha 僧史.The following year, [the emperor] ordered Zanning to go as an official courier to the [*stūpa* containing] relics (*śarīra* 舍利) of the true body of Śākyamuni Buddha on Mt. Ayuwang 阿育王山 (King Aśoka) in Mingzhou. He entered the inner sanctum, made offerings, and obtained a portion of the relics [and returned to

> the capital]. With these, an eleven-storied pagoda was built on a site at the northwest tower of Kaibao Temple 開寶寺, at the base of which was built an imperial shrine (*tiangong* 天宮) to inter the relics.[16]

As we have seen, the Śākyamuni Stūpa on Mt. Ayuwang in Mingzhou, reputedly containing the Buddha's own relics, served as the center of Aśoka emulation in Wuyue and the symbol of how Buddhist state relations were intertwined in a common goal framed by a Buddhist agenda. In this instance, we see Zanning invoking the Aśokan model of Buddhist kingship, and suggesting its adoption by Song emperor Taizong. In this context, the relics offered by Zanning at the court of Song Emperor Taizong can be construed as Zanning's attempt to establish the Wuyue model of Buddhist state relations for the Song ruler, at the ruler's request.

Buddhist records attempt to validate this strategy by claiming the emperor specifically built an 11-storied pagoda on the site of Kaibao Temple, with an imperial tomb at the base to house the relics (as above). In point of fact, the early Song emperors, like Taizong, were interested in promoting Buddhism as part of an effort to build a dynasty based on *wen* 文 (culture or letters) as opposed to *wu* 武 (military power). For the Song emperors, these were practical concerns. For nearly two centuries, dynasties and central governments in China had suffered from lack of sound authority and a mandate for effective rule. The Song—which, like its predecessors, relied on military means to seize power—reversed course and called for a new basis (in these times) for their mandate, *wen* instead of *wu*. This proved an effective strategy, and in the early decades of the Song, Buddhism proved to be a beneficiary of the new Song policy.

As concrete manifestation of early Song commitment to Buddhism, one can point to two developments. Early Song emperors invested heavily in the translation and publication of Buddhist texts as an integral part of the literary learning that they strove to establish.[17] Zanning also underscored the significance of the resumption of Buddhist translation bureaus under imperial sponsorship, noting that no translations of Buddhist texts had been completed in China for 160 years.[18] In addition to translation bureaus, early Song emperors called for the compiling of Buddhist histories and biographies as part of their overall campaign to mark the Song as a regime of letters.

There is also indication that early Song emperors were committed to promoting Buddhist institutions through building projects.[19] The large, 21-meter bronze statue of Guanyin 觀音 (Avalokiteśvāra) at Longxing monastery 隆興寺 in Zhenzhou 真州 (contemporary Zhending, Hebei Province), for example, was erected during the *kaibao* 開寶 era (963–976). While the original building housing the Guanyin statue, the Pavilion of Great Mercy (*Dabei ge* 大悲閣), does not exist, the existing one is a massive structure over 30 meters in height, reputedly built on the Song model. Local records detail the seven-stage process in the construction of the image, a testament to contemporary artistry, and the hundreds of workers commissioned for the project.

The building of such large statues and structures and the commitment to the translation and publication of Buddhist texts exhibit the early Song commitment to Buddhism. In this context, one can easily imagine that Zanning held out some hope, in spite of other indicators to the contrary, that Song emperors could be persuaded to adopt the Aśokan model of *cakravartin.* In actual fact, Song emperors were interested in Buddhism, but for markedly different reasons than Wuyue rulers had been. Taizong had no illusions about creating a state validated by Buddhist principles. Rather, he was interested in appeasing Buddhist interests in an attempt to minimize factionalism at the Song court.

The second episode, a story related about Zanning's recommendation on how the emperor regards the Buddha, suggests how complicated the situation was for Buddhism at the Song court. The story involves an imperial procession to Xiangguo Temple 相國寺 (monastery for assisting the country) to worship the Buddha. When the emperor went before the image of the Buddha to burn incense, he asked Zanning, "Should I perform prostrations or not?" to which Zanning responded, "The Buddha of the present need not perform prostrations to the Buddhas of the past." Zanning being widely learned, eloquent, and unsurpassed in rhetorical skill, the source tells us, the emperor concurred with his opinion, and with a smile nodded in agreement. As a result, it became the policy of the Song government from then on to offer incense but not perform prostrations (to the Buddha).[20]

This story of the emperor worshipping the Buddha dramatizes a markedly different role for Buddhism in the Song. Reemerging interest in Confucianism at the Song court provoked a reevaluation of the role that Buddhism should play in government affairs. One of the areas most affected was government participation in Buddhist rituals. Zanning, as the leading official at the Song court in charge of Buddhist affairs, was caught in the middle of this reevaluation. The issue was the Buddhist role in government ritual. The question was what role Zanning advocated: one in which the status of the emperor was acknowledged as equal to that of the Buddha, or one in which the superiority of the Buddha's status was openly accepted. This story represents Zanning's full acquiescence in the realities of Song politics. The only road open to Buddhism, Zanning admits in the story told here, is compromise and acceptance of the emperor's status vis-à-vis Buddhism.

Zanning's proposals for Song policy toward Buddhism reflect emerging realities facing Buddhism at the Song court, particularly the hostility expressed toward it by increasingly vocal anti-Buddhist officials. Zanning's response to this situation is couched in his own idea of harmony between the three teachings in China: –Buddhism, Taoism, and Confucianism. While three teachings syncretism in China is hardly new (it was a staple in Buddhist treatises promoting integration), previous proponents championed models that presumed the superiority of Buddhist teaching while acknowledging Confucian and Taoist contributions. Zanning invoked the three teachings model for different effect, one that recognized the new realities for Buddhism in the Song.

Zanning compares his plan for the Buddhist role in China to a three-legged sacrificial *ding* 鼎 vessel, a vessel commonly used in ancestral sacrifices. Each leg represents one of the three teachings (*sanjiao* 三教): Confucianism, Taoism, and Buddhism. If one leg is missing, the vessel will fall over. Zanning's position is summarized in his conclusion to the *Seng shilue* 僧史略, where he speaks of the "grand strategy (*dayou*) of the three teachings" 三教大猷. The "grand strategy" is Zanning's own way of speaking about the "great plan" (*hongfan* 弘範), a euphemism for the emperor's stratagem for governing the empire. Zanning's grand strategy, based on the aim of assuring a role for Buddhism in China, can be summarized in four propositions:[21]

(1) The emperor, as the undisputed head of the Chinese state and leader of Chinese society, is the legitimate supervisor of the Buddhist religion.
(2) Buddhism is useful to the emperor for conducting affairs of state.
(3) Each of China's three teachings—Buddhism, Confucianism, and Taoism—have a legitimate position in the function of the state.
(4) It is the duty of the emperor to supervise the activities of the three teachings, and direct them in accordance with the aims of the state.

The first proposition is an admission of the reality that Buddhism faced in the Song. The survival of Buddhism depended on imperial sanction and support for its activities. The second proposition is a reminder of the stronghold that Buddhist concepts have over the populace. This influence is a strong tool in the imperial arsenal. The third proposition is a cornerstone of Zaning's proposal for the role of Buddhism. For Zanning, the three teachings represent three aspects of a single imperial ideology. Zanning's concept places the emperor alone at the top as the sole authority, with the three teachings in tripod-like harmony underneath. Within this ideology, each teaching occupies a legitimate place acknowledged by the others. As a result, the fourth proposition assumes that the emperor has sole authority over the three aspects (i.e., teachings) of his imperial ideology. The three teachings are the emperor's implements: he may direct them as best suits his "grand strategy." In this manner, Zanning likens the three teachings to the possessions of a single family, the Chinese nation, with the emperor as the head of this family. While conceding the emperor's authority over Buddhism, as one of the three teachings, Zanning asserts that Buddhism, as a member of the Chinese family, has a legitimate place in Chinese society.

CONCLUDING REMARKS

What do these two models of Buddhist rule, *cakravartin* and realpolitik, tell us? Do they offer any insight for the role that Buddhism might assume in modern secular states? With rare exception, the era of unadulterated Buddhist kingship (*cakravartin* model) is over, no matter how much it might be invoked by contemporary monarchs with Buddhist sympathies as an inspiration for pro-Buddhist policies. In my opinion, Zanning's realpolitik model invites closer scrutiny from the perspective of policies toward Buddhism enacted by modern secular states. The *cakravartin* model, in other words, may be suitable for self-styled Buddhocracies, but can function as little more than nostalgia for states acquiring the apparatuses of modern secular rule.

The Song dynasty defined early Chinese modernism and provides a model for the role of Buddhism in the contemporary world. In spite of its theocratic dimensions (the emperor as Son of Heaven with religious as well as political responsibilities), Confucianism in Song China defined a kind of secularism, and affairs of state were conducted in accordance with secular ideological norms and principles. Secular states, especially of the Song Chinese variety, are not ideologically neutral, but are predicated on a secular ideology rarely free of religious overtones. The Buddhist response to the emerging form of Confucian secularism in Song China thus represents a case study that may inform the present.

What is interesting about Zanning's response is that it is couched in terms of contemporary Song ideological rhetoric. Rather than parade the well-worn arguments based on Buddhism's intellectual and philosophical sophistication (and which assume Buddhist superiority) stemming from the *cakravartin* model in a manner like Yanshou, Zanning assumes the vantage point of Confucian secularists and argues from premises that they accept. As such, Zanning proposes that Buddhism be adopted and implemented in China for cultural, rather than ideological or religious reasons.

Zanning's proposal that Buddhism be accepted as part of China's cultural heritage was based on a perspective on Chinese traditions as dynamic and evolving. Rather than accept some hypothetical "golden age" that located China's core values in remote antiquity, Zanning argued that Chinese culture was dynamic and its values evolved over time. No single age held exclusive access to the truth; truth advances along with the changing dynamics of history and civilization, as viewed through the lens of contemporary perspective. As Zanning observed:

> [The meaning of] things differs according to the group [determining it], and [the meaning of] events changes in accordance with the times. The one who regards the sage-kings of antiquity [as his model] (i.e., the current emperor) does not overlook the deceptions of the past. The one who controls myriad lands (i.e., the current emperor) has the prerogative to reinterpret the meaning [of the model].[22]

In societies based on secular ideologies, the formation of a society based solely on religious or spiritual principles is an idle fancy. This does not mean, however, that religious and spiritual principles cannot have influence in secular societies. Clearly, they may. In order to do so, they must coincide, and not conflict, with state policy governed by national self-interest. To determine how Buddhist interests coincide with national self-interest, Buddhists must ask themselves how Buddhism contributes to national self-interest. Equally, they must understand how Buddhism might be considered a threat or dangerous to national self-interest. This raises further questions as to when and how Buddhism should contest state policy as anathema to Buddhist principles, and when it should support state policy as an ally to its own cause. Yet, as Zanning implies, it is necessary for Buddhism to be granted legitimacy within the broader government structure if it is to influence state policy. In his recognition of the realities facing Buddhism in the Song dynasty, Zanning suggested ways for the inclusion of Buddhism within Chinese culture (i.e., not as a foreign religion) and ways in which Buddhism could be considered an asset to the emperor and secular establishment in their conduct of state policy.

POSTSCRIPT: REFLECTIONS ON CHINA'S ACCOMMODATION OF RELIGION IN THE 21ST CENTURY

In spite of the ultimate failure of Zanning's multi-ideological Song model, I believe it offers potential for the administration of China's multireligious and multi-ideological future. Modern China is no longer a country of three teachings, but five: Confucianism, Taoism, Buddhism, Islam, and Christianity. As a result, nearly all the world's leading traditions (with the exception of Judaism and Hinduism) have strong representation in contemporary China, giving it opportunities to forge a new consensus on how to harmonize disparate teachings through shared aims and purposes. In this regard, preserving the preeminent position of a Chinese secularism, however defined, is the key.

Adapting Zanning's model, where the three teachings created a tripod-like harmony supporting the emperor, suggests a five teachings model supporting a secular ideology. The downfall of Zanning's earlier proposal rested, in part, on the natural alliance between Confucianism and the imperial institution. Since China's inception as a Confucian civilization, the position of the emperor and the authority of Confucian teaching have been intertwined. As a result, Confucianism assumed dominance that over time and in most instances rendered opposition ideologies impotent.

This raises questions regarding the role of Confucianism in China's future. The assumption of a privileged position by Confucianism, or any other ideology, will not only threaten the balance among China's five teachings, but, more importantly, will also jeopardize the role of a religiously neutral secularism itself as the leading force governing China's modern tradition.

The effect of increasing bureaucratization in the Song dynasty led to the primacy of Confucianism as an ideology underpinning notions of Chinese culture. As China revisits its ideological underpinnings in the 21st century, we must ask what role Confucianism might assume in China's future, and what hope there is in preserving the integrity of China's various religious traditions within a Chinese cultural framework. As China moves from a totalitarian- to an authoritarian-governing structure, the status of independent religious and ideological systems remain in jeopardy. Without independent status, other traditions are always susceptible to the whims of government authority and the ideology, whether Communism or Confucianism, it espouses. This may be fine when the government feels comfortable and magnanimous, but the threat of suppression always looms. A mature secularism, of whatever ilk, will strive to accommodate religious and ideological rivals in a harmonious fashion that honors their integrity as independent traditions and encourages their participation for the greater good of the nation as a whole.

PRIMARY SOURCES (BY TITLE)

Fozu tongji 佛祖統紀, Zhipan 志磐, T 49-2035.

Guitian lu 歸田錄, Ouyang Xiu 歐陽修, *Sibu jiyao* 四部紀要, ed.

Seng shilue 僧史略, Zanning 贊寧, T 54-2126.

Shiguo qunchiu 十國春秋, Wu Renchen 吳任臣, 1983, Zhonghua shuju, Beijing.

Shimen zhengtong 釋門正統, Zongjian 宗鑑, *Xuzang jing*, Vol. 130.

*Song Gaoseng zhuan*宋高僧傳, Zanning 贊寧, T 50-2061.

Taishō shinshū daizōkyō 大正新脩大藏經, edited by Takakusu Junjirō 高楠順次郎, 85 volumes, 1922–1933, Daizō shuppan kai, Tokyo.

Xuzang jing 續藏經, Reprint of *Dainihon zokuzōkyō*, 1968–1970, Xinwenfeng, Taibei.

Zongjing lu 宗鏡録, Yongming Yanshou 永明延寿, T 48-2016.

NOTES

1. The term "*cakravartin*" refers to the ancient Indian conception of the world ruler, derived from the Sanskrit words *cakra* meaning "wheel" and *vartin* "one who turns." Thus, a *cakravartin* may be understood as a ruler "whose chariot wheels roll everywhere" or "whose movements are unobstructed." In Buddhism, the *cakravartin* ideal embodied the principles of ideal rulership based on Buddhist notions of righteousness, wisdom, compassion, etc. See Lindsay Jones, Mircea Eliade, and Charles J Adams, *Encyclopedia of Religion* (Detroit, MI: Macmillan Reference USA, 2001–2006).

2. The term "realpolitik" refers to politics based on practical objectives rather than on ideals, a politics of adaptation to things as they are rather than on moral or ethical criteria. Realpolitik thus suggests a pragmatic, no-nonsense view and a disregard for ethical considerations. In diplomacy, it is often associated with relentless, though realistic, pursuit of the national interest.

3. Stanley Weinstein, *Buddhism in the T'ang* (New York: Cambridge University Press, 1987).

4. Robert M. Somers, "The End of the T'ang" in Denis Twitchett, ed., *The Cambridge History of China, Volume 3: Sui and T'ang China, 589–906* (Cambridge: Cambridge University Press, 1992).

5. Charles Hartman, *Han Yu and the T'ang Search for Unity* (Princeton, NJ: Princeton University Press, 1986).

6. On this, see David McMullen, *State and Scholars in T'ang China* (Cambridge: Cambridge University Press, 1988).

7. William Theodore De Bary et al., eds., *Sources of Chinese Tradition*, 2nd ed. (New York: Columbia University Press, 1999), pp. 583–85.

8. Hatanaka Jōen 畑中浄園, "Goetsu no bukkyō—toku ni Tendai Tokushō to sono shi Eimei Enju ni tsuite" 呉越の仏教—特に天台徳韶とその嗣永明延寿について(Buddhism in Wuyue: With Special Reference to Tiantai Deshao and His Heir, Yongming Yanshou), *Ōtani daigaku kenkyu nenpō* 大谷大学けん研究年報 7 (1954): 305–65.

9. Abe Jôichi 阿部肇, *Chūgoku zenshūshi no kenkyū* 中国禅宗史の研究 (*A History of Chinese Zen*), revised edition (Tokyo: Seishin shobō, 1987), pp. 129–74.

10. Wu Renchen, *Shiguo qunchiu*, p. 89.4b.

11. For a discussion and list of the monks supported by Qian Chu (Prince Zhongyi), see Jôichi, *Chūgoku zenshūshi no kenkyū*, pp. 186–210. A list of the important monks who studied with Qian Chu under Deshao and whose biographies appear in fascicle 26 of the *Jingde Chuandeng lu* (Jingde Era Record of the Transmission of the Lamp) is given in Ishii Shūdō 石井修道, *Sōdai zenshūshi no kenkyū* 宋代禅宗史の研究 (*A History of Zen in the Song Dynasty*) (Tokyo: Daito Shuppansha, 1987), pp. 82, 83.

12. Albert Welter, "The Problem with Orthodoxy in Zen Buddhism: Yongming Yanshou's Notion of *Zong* in the *Zongjing lu*" (Records of the Source Mirror), *Studies in Religion/Sciences Religieuses* 31, no. 1 (2002): 3–18.

13. Albert Welter, *The Meaning of Myriad Good Deeds: A Study of Yung-ming Yen-shou and the Wan-shan t'ung-kuei chi* (New York: Peter Lang, 1993).

14. Jôichi, *Chūgoku zenshūshi no kenkyū.*

15. Edouard Chavannes, "Le Royaume de Wou et de Yue," *T'oung Pao* 17 (1916): 129–264.

16. Ibid.

17. According to Tansen Sen ("The Revival and Failure of Buddhist Translations during the Song Dynasty," *T'oung Pao* 88, no. 1/3 (2002): 73, 74), Emperor Taizong revived the translation projects essentially for three reasons: "to promote the image of the state as a provider of literary learning and shaper of a civil society"; to fulfill diplomatic goals, "especially in enhancing Song China's image as the disseminator of high culture among neighboring steppe kingdoms"; and "from his general interest in literary learning and his recognition that the doctrine could be employed in both the internal and external affairs of the state."

18. *Seng shilue* (T 54.240b19–21).

19. Liu Changdong 劉長東, *Songdai Fojiao Zhengce lungao* 宋代佛教政策論稿 (Buddhist Policy in the Song Dynasty) (Chengdu: Sichuan chuban jiduan, 2005).

20. *Guitian lu* 1, *Sibu jiyao* (ed.), p. 1. See also *Shimen zhengtong, Xuzang jing* Vol. 130, p. 451a and *Fozu tongji* 44 (T Vol. 49, pp. 405a24–b4).

21. Albert Welter, "A Buddhist Response to the Confucian Revival: Tsan-ning and the Debate over Wen in the Early Sung" in Daniel A. Getz and Peter N. Gregory, eds., *Buddhism in the Sung* (Honolulu, HI: University of Hawaii Press, 1999), pp. 21–61.

22. *Seng shilue* (T 54.246c19–20).

Chapter 6

From Oriental Utopia to Business Ethics: Europe's Search for New Socioeconomic Paradigms in Eastern Religions and Philosophies

Gerrit De Vylder

In the eyes of European commentators, Asia represented utopias, romantic oriental empires, and spiritual wisdom. Europe reinvented Asia: sometimes from an inferior position, and sometimes from a superior position. In general, this "European Asia" had not much to do with the real Asia. Asian philosophies and religions were used to make a point in a European context. But in doing so, some traces of an authentic Asia, sometimes even forgotten in Asia itself, came to the surface.

So far, the study of the impact of Asia on European thinking has focused on the cultural or literary fields. Not much attention was paid to its impact on the socioeconomic field. To what extent did Eastern philosophies and religions influence European economic thinking? What was the image of Asia or the "East" and how did it fit into the way Europeans were reacting against their own societies and economies? Concepts like "economic equilibrium" and "sustainable development" are usually considered as concepts that originated from a growing awareness in the so-called Western world. Actually, these concepts are very old and, among others, have Eastern origins. Clearly, even if modern economic thinking was dominated by "Western" economists, its concepts and ideas may indirectly have been of Eastern origin.

SEVENTEENTH- AND EIGHTEENTH-CENTURY EUROPEAN ORIENTALISTS SEARCHING FOR AN ECONOMIC UTOPIA

The 17th century was the period in which the West-European literary world discovered, as it were, "Eastern" lands. The Oriental genre became popular. Writers like Henry Fielding and Jonathan Swift owned many such books.[1] Following the explorations undertaken by the European maritime powers, and the dispatch, by the Roman Catholic Society of Jesus, of Christian missions to the East, a series of institutes and academies were set up for the study of the languages and cultures of India, China, and Japan. In France, even the Crown encouraged the work of early Orientalists, and the discovery of the Orient was of great interest to Jean-Baptiste Colbert (1619–1683), the famous French finance minister for more than 20 years during the reign of Louis XIV. He not only encouraged travel and particularly commerce, but also granted subsidies to scholars. In the final quarter of the 18th century, Orientalism became even firmly established as a profession in the final quarter of the 18th century.[1]

It should be emphasized that, until the beginning of the 19th century, the notion of racial "superiority" did not exist as such in Western Europe. In fact, while still lacking concrete information on Eastern civilizations, many authors considered China and India as equal or even superior to Europe. By the end of the 18th century, one in three British men in India were living with Indian women; many taking on Indian ways, clothes, habits, and even religions; and crossing cultures to become, according to Dalrymple, *White Mughals*.[2] They were the living proof that the two worlds, India and Britain, or East and West, could be reconciled. A certain degree of West-European xenophobia may have existed, but "the East" was already for centuries represented as a "utopia," or even a model. Obviously, this is the link between the genre of "utopias" and "Orientalism." Just like Voltaire (1694–1778), who referred to China as the first major world civilization in his *Essai sur l'histoire générale et sur les moeurs et l'esprit des nations* (1756), Irish English novelist Jonathan Swift discovered "Eastern" empires and considered them either as an alternative or as a pretext to criticize the socioeconomic and political systems of Western Europe of his days. The difference of course is that scholars like Voltaire considered real countries like China, Japan, and India. Of all the remote regions of the globe visited by the main character of Swift's classic satirical narrative *Gulliver's Travels* (1726), Japan and Fort St. George (possibly in present-day

Chennai, in South India) are the only real places existing. Significantly, the "heathen" Japanese were portrayed in a better light than the Protestant Dutch.[3] But otherwise, Swift basically invented countries for making a point. Clearly, Swift intentionally considered only a "fantasy world," whereas Voltaire emphasized the true existence of these countries. But essentially, Voltaire's China also had little to do with the real China. This suggests that the new Orientalist genre had more to do with European yearnings than Asian or Middle Eastern reality.

However, the point is that Europeans regarded Eastern countries as superior civilizations. Even in early 18th century, France Henri de Boulainvilliers's *Life of Mohammed* presented the Prophet Mohammed in a flattering light. No other religion, he argued, was as close to reason as Islam. Increasingly, this portrait of the East had to give way to that of a sensual eroticized Orient. This tradition may have started with the publication of *Les mille et une nuit* between 1704 and 1711 by Anthoine Galland, who had been sent by Colbert to the French embassy in Istanbul. But it would take another century before the "East" had become "eroticized" and therefore inferior.[4]

There is a lot of discussion among scholars on the nature of economic thinking among the first generations of Orientalists (17th/18th century). They were especially concerned with defending physiocratic (natural balance, like the Taoist concept of "*yin*" and "*yang*") against mercantilist principles (the need for government interference in order to accumulate wealth through a positive balance of payments). In 1758, the French physiocrat, François Quesnay (1694–1774) published his famous *Tableau Economique,* advocating the economic theory that land was the source of all wealth and that the wealth of a nation could only be measured by the extent to which it returned to its natural balance. As a court physician, Quesnay compared the blood circulation of a human body to the circulation of production factors within the economy. In two books, *Laws of Nature* and *China's Autocracy,* he referred to the East as the examples of implementing the laws of nature and natural reasoning. China was a model in building its national economy on the basis of agriculture, while adhering to the reasons and principles regulated by "Lord Nature" of "Heaven," which symbolized belief in natural law and order. He lauded China's autocracy as a "rational autocratic government," which was responsible for stipulating rules within the scope of natural law. Even the monarch himself had to adhere to such rules, accepting the "rules of Heaven" as his guidelines. The physiocrats became an important branch of the Enlightenment movement. In 1756, the French king, Louis XV, took up Quesnay's advice and followed the example of the Chinese emperor to hold ceremonies on the occasion of plowing and harvesting. Quesnay was so ardent in propagating the Confucian doctrine that he became known as the "Confucius of Europe."

Similarly, another French physiocrat Jacques Turgot (1727–1781) introduced physiocratic reforms as governor of Limousin in 1761, by abolishing the levy of labor duty on farmers and replacing it with taxation. He too was keenly interested in China's developments in economics, taxation, and technology, viewing the "Oriental nation" as a practical model of natural order. While he was governor of Limousin, he came to know two Chinese students, Gao Leisi and Yang Dewang, with whom he covered subjects such as the roles of land, rental, and capital in the agricultural economy; and the technological achievements in China's paper-making, textile, and porcelain industries.[5]

Two interesting case studies that examine the relationship of the East with economic thought are the works of Jonathan Swift and Daniel Defoe, famous for his *Robinson Crusoe* (1719). Swift reported on extraordinary lands and societies—notably the minute inhabitants of "Lilliput," the giants of "Brobdingnag," and the Yahoos in "Houyhnhnmland," where talking horses are the dominant species. While Defoe described a primitive paradise,[6] Swift discovered sophisticated utopias, superior or at least equal to European civilization of his time. Being a non-Orientalist, Defoe joined a generation that believed in the noble and beautiful "savage."

One could argue that the entire history of the way East has influenced European thinking can be deduced to Jonathan Swift's message in *Gulliver's Travels.* Swift represented economics both as a utopia and as a threat. Being part of European Enlightenment, Swift viewed "Asian governance and economics" in a positive light. He genuinely considered the East as an inspiration for initiating socioeconomic reform in Britain by an open-minded monarch from above. This monarch represented a natural equilibrium, as suggested by the French physiocrats. Quesnay's admiration for Confucius as the ultimate type of leadership was never far away.

The comparison to Defoe illustrates the specificity of the role of Eastern thinking. Defoe did not look for any utopia in the East. His utopia was rather a tropical island in the West Indies. Robinson Crusoe had to be a pragmatist in order to survive all alone on his island. Defoe identified with what he considered a prospering Britain full of potential, if only it played the game the right way. This involved government intervention if required. Defoe represents 18th-century Britain (or Western Europe, in general) defending mercantilism, the kind of state capitalism that made the Industrial Revolution possible. The "East" did not have any message for Defoe.[7]

But what is remarkable was Swift's realism. Apart from idealizing the East, he simultaneously emphasized the hypocrisy and failure of man in general as a *homo economicus,* regardless of the economic system implemented, regardless of East or West. In the end, it is not the system that is wrong but man himself. Any type of leadership is bound to fail because leaders are men. One might argue that if Swift lived today, he would agree that the present rebirth of neoclassics looks very promising, reintroducing a natural equilibrium. However, "man," as a social and psychological being, is not yet ready for it. Man remains deceived by his own economic preferences, making a spiritual equilibrium impossible. Swift's refusal to detect anything positive in initiatives for promoting economic growth, and his emphasis on balance, suggests he only believed in the search for an internal balance, from within. For Swift, paradise was inside oneself.

Swift identified this wisdom with the East. Considering the spirit of the time, it was not a coincidence that all of Gulliver's travels are "Eastbound" and his descriptions of the countries concerned are a mix of admiration and critique. "Luggnaggian" society—mentioned in part 3 of the book—reflected generosity, politeness, balance, and fairness. On the last page of *Gulliver's Travels,* Swift expressed a radical view about the nature of the "East" versus the nature of the "West": Gulliver wishes "to send a sufficient number of their inhabitants for civilizing Europe" so that Europeans may also, like the "Houyhnhnms," "live under the government of reason."[8]

NINETEENTH- AND EARLY-TWENTIETH-CENTURY ORIENTALISM: PATERNALIST UTILITARIAN APPROACHES VERSUS EASTERN SPIRITUAL SOLUTIONS

Swift's Orientalism should certainly not be confused with late-19th- and early-20th-century Orientalism. The nature of Orientalism would radically change from the beginning of the 19th century. The industrialization of England was too fast and too radical and all of a sudden it seemed that "East and West would never meet again." Moreover, the economic thinking of Orientalists changed fundamentally. The Indologist William Jones, who founded the Asiatic Society in Calcutta in 1784, was already aware of economic liberal ideas, like those of David Hume (1711–1776) and Adam Smith (1723–1790), who referred to India as the ultimate example of comparative advantages in textiles throughout world history in his famous *Wealth of Nations* (1776).[9] Gradually, economists would radicalize Smith's ideas into utilitarian philosophies, like those of Jeremy Bentham (1748–1832) and David Ricardo (1772–1823). Up to the end of the 18th century, the notion of racial superiority would remain largely unknown, but the new concept of "public utility" would gradually allow paternalistic thoughts to emerge.

At first, in the first phase, Orientalist Romanticists were still looking for "divine remembrance" originating from the East. In Germany, philosopher G.W.F. Hegel (1770–1831) described India as the "richest country in the world," both in terms of physical and metaphysical richness. But it was Germany's *uomo universale* Johann Wolfgang Goethe (1749–1832) who gave Eastern religion and philosophy also socioeconomic relevance. In

1919, the *West-östlicher Diwan* (*West-Eastern Divan*), a collection of poems in Persian style, influenced by the work of Hafez, was published. Through reading Friedrich Schlegel (1772–1829), he had also become acquainted with Vedantic thinking. Goethe anticipated the imbalance caused by industrial growth. He accused scientists like Newton of dividing and splitting what he considered as "one." In his *Versuch die Metamorphose der Pflanzen zu erklären*, he took up the concept of a leaf as the fundamental organ of a plant to illustrate that everything is a variation of this one and only shape. Everything could be reduced to the elementary forms of a "genko" leaf. This simplicity made possible all diversity. For Goethe, this was an experience based on the direct observation of the subject and from this, he concluded the essential oneness of all existence. He gave this unity of nature a religious name: "*Gott-Natur.*" In his *Farbenlehre*, Goethe explained that light and darkness are involved in a never-ending struggle. They are like two opposite poles of a magnet that can influence each other but one cannot destroy the other. They are "*Ur*-phenomena" that can only be observed based on an "*Ur-Erlebnis*" or "original experience." Between these two phenomena exists "*das trübe*," a German term that is difficult to translate. It stands for an obscure, clouded, and dark existence. Human beings are caught in "*das trübe*." According to Goethe, a scientific approach to nature, including artificial instruments and mathematical considerations, is useless, as it is about rediscovering and reconfirming "what is unconsciously already known." Goethe's interpretation of nature is a philosophical and religious experience. It somehow illustrates why Vedanta did not result in science as an independent activity. It also illustrates that as "man" is trapped in an unbalanced situation, economics also is to be considered as unbalanced.[10]

Significantly, Thomas Raffles (1781–1826), the East India Company clerk who founded Singapore, investigated the Javanese temple ruins of Prambanan and Borobudur, and assumed the existence of an advanced Indian civilization in Java's history. For Raffles, civilization obviously had no skin color.[11] Likewise, Warren Hastings (1732–1818), the first governor-general of British India, spoke fluent Urdu, Bengali, and Persian. He even suggested that Persian (the language of the Mogul court and as such still the official language of India) should be included in the curriculum of Oxford University and should also be made a part of a British "gentleman's" education.

One of the last great European admirers of Indian culture was Sir William Jones (1746–1794). In 1783, he took up his position as a judge in the High Court of the British East India Company. Throughout his life, Jones's greatest passion had been the study of Oriental languages, including Arabic and Persian, and on his arrival in India, he turned to the ancient and then almost forgotten language of Sanskrit. He discovered that Sanskrit shared many characteristics with Greek, Latin, German, and other

European languages. This led him to the conclusion that all these different tongues were branches of the same Indo-European family. An interesting conclusion followed: India and Europe had common roots. But Jones's conclusions came at the wrong time, because in the next century, the psychological distance between India and Europe would only become larger.[12]

Gradually, a new Eurocentric and Victorian world was born in which most Orientalists were considered eccentric. It was the classical economist James Mill, with his famous *History of British India* (1817), who marked a turning point in the way West-Europeans considered Asia. At the end of a comprehensive attack on supposed Indian achievements particularly in mathematics and science, Mill came to the conclusion that the Indian civilization was similar to other inferior ones like the Chinese, Persian, and Arab civilizations. Unfortunately, Mill's book became a "bible for the British Indian officer," without Mill having set one foot in India during his lifetime.

Most 19th-century Orientalists were essentially supporting the classical school of economics in the utilitarian interpretation of the term. However, this manifested itself in two completely different ways. The first dominant way was to assume that all blessings came from Western Europe. These Orientalists assumed that utility in India only increased by adopting West-European concepts and technologies. They are the so-called Said types (after Edward Said, a strong opponent of Orientalism, emphasizing its collusion with imperialism).[13] It should be pointed out that many of them were socialists. Karl Marx (1818–1883) saw Hinduism, like all religion, as the reflection of social and economic realities of despotism and inertia. And Max Weber (1864–1920) saw the poor social and economic condition of India as the result of Hinduism. Both their views were based on inadequate sources and a deeply rooted Eurocentrism.

The second way was to assume that all blessings came from Asia itself and that therefore an ancient and genuine Asia had to be rediscovered. Theosophical speculation placed an emphasis on mystical experience: a deeper spiritual reality exists, and direct contact may be established with that reality through intuition, meditation, revelation, or some other state transcending normal human consciousness. Theosophists claimed that all world religions, including Christianity, contain such an inner teaching, and that the richest and most profound source of theosophical views is Hindu or Vedantic thought.

In reality, most commentators were somewhere in between. Levallois and Moussa[14] support this view by referring to the Saint Simonians (the *saint-simoniens*), followers of the French utopian economist, the Count of Saint Simon (1760–1825). Many of them were involved in the imperialist design of France for the Maghreb and Egypt. Following the footsteps of Napoleon, they sojourned in Egypt, and from the 1830s, increasingly in Algeria. Most of them genuinely tried to open up to the Muslim society and culture and to find common grounds for their utopian socialism. This attitude of "*ouverture à l'autre*" left its impact on Orientalist literature and was not completely meaningless for the French colonial policies in the Maghreb.

The "East" also received mixed comments from Victor Hugo (1802–1885) who dominated French literature during the mid-19th century. The depiction of Turks in his *Les Orientales* (1829) mixed condemnation, idealization, and crude envy. It is often cited as being representative of the "Orientalist" attitudes in much of French literature. In his essay on *Shakespeare* (1864), Hugo was more positive about the East. The Roman poet and philosopher Lucretius, one of the characters, studies Greece and its philosophers to finally, just like Shakespeare, realize the importance of India, described as "*l'infini impersonnel.*"[15] India cannot attain the level of individuality and at the same time transcend it, again indirectly referring to the problem of classical economics that its sole reference point is the individual.

Germany's and France's appreciation for *Vedanta* (Michelet, Burnouf, Lévy, Rolland, Müller, Schopenhauer, Hegel, Kant, and Von Schlegel) generally combined admiration, fascination, and paternalism. The parallel relationship between utopian and scientific socialism and the early ancient Indian-Buddhist concept of *sanghas* or democratically organized monastic communities should also be considered here.[16]

However, for the Irish theosophist Annie Besant (1847–1933), India was no longer an abstract concept but a very close reality. With her, the Said types gradually lost terrain. She was a foreigner who "genuinely" sought to restore a "genuine" India that supplied a "genuine" socioeconomic alternative to the Victorian world. Since the late-19th century, theosophy was represented by the Theosophical Society, whose headquarters moved from New York to Chennai. The leadership of the charismatic Besant gave Indians a sense of pride that they were exporting ideas of importance to the West.[17] In 1911, she proclaimed Jiddu Krishnamurti (1895–1986), an obscure South Indian youth, as the vehicle of a coming world teacher, an act that led to much controversy. Krishnamurti subsequently renounced any claims to being a world teacher, and began a career of writing and teaching. Beginning in the 1920s, he spent much time in the United States and Europe, where his books have enjoyed considerable popularity. The relevance of Krishnamurti's thought for economics and other social sciences became obvious when Europe was confronted with the absurdities of the interwar period and the Second World War. Krishnamurti argued that the ultimate trap of human sciences and of man's approach to life, in general, is the continuous intellectual effort to identify schools of thought and ideas. He considered thinking as the ultimate problem of the human kind:

> There is only one freedom—religious freedom; there is no other freedom. The freedom that the so-called welfare state brings, the economic, national, political, and various other forms of freedom that one is given surely are not freedom at all, but only lead to further chaos and further misery—which is obvious to anyone who observes.[18]

Concrete influence from Vedanta reached European socioeconomic thinking through the visits and the writings of Bengali monk and philosopher Swami Vivekananda, who became the subject of French novelist and pacifist Romain Rolland's (1866–1944) essays *La vie de Vivekananda* (1930) and *l'Evangile universel* (1930). The writings of Swami Vivekananda were essentially about overcoming duality in a genuine *Vedanta*-sense. First of all, he emphasized the need to achieve this in a spiritual way. The ensuing ethical problem of justice and injustice only existed in duality, and only by transcending individuality, this problem could be neutralized. However, there was also an economic way to overcome duality: the problem of justice and injustice manifested itself by definition in an economic way. Traditionally, there were two ways of tackling this: (1) a socialist way whereby the government redistributes and (2) the classical, utilitarian way in which the creation of opportunities and possibilities (to use a term from Amartya Sen) goes hand in hand with the rewarding principle providing incentives for focused entrepreneurship. Swami Vivekananda transcended these traditional ways.

Theoretically, Swami Vivekananda indirectly assumed a classical economic model. And, just like Adam Smith, he considered humans as economic actors behaving potentially in an economically logical and optimal way, resulting in growth and a more equal distribution. Just like Smith, he considered humans as ethically well-behaving and only temporarily disturbed by negative institutions or environment. Smith's ethically oriented actors are similar to Vedanta's principle of human beings transcending duality and attaining a perfect inner and outer equilibrium. Gradually, the free-market system combined with a growing number of people transcending duality will result in more durable development and a more equal distribution of wealth. The role of government should clearly be defined because by definition, government is controlled by ambitious and manipulating persons, supporting duality, and consequently resulting in unfair competition and artificial monopolies. On the other hand, in a free-market system, achieving inner balance or equilibrium will result in outer economic equilibrium.

But Swami Vivekananda was aware that "man" has not reached this stage yet. He considered it as a "potentiality," which can only be reached in a spiritual way, while Smith considered it as a theory, reflecting a natural reality. Accordingly, Swami Vivekananda's final conclusion was the need for Vedantic socialism. Ghosh reaches the core of Swami Vivekananda's argument:

> The Vivekananda doctrine tries to take us to a higher state of human realization where we can get rid of Maya (illusion) in order to understand that irrespective of our caste, creed, religion and nationality, we belong to the same human race.[19]

Essentially, that is what Swami Vivekananda meant when he stated: "What will save Europe (the West) is the religion of the Upanishads (i.e. Vedanta)."[20]

It does imply that the system only functions with human beings who have duality transcended to some degree. If not, one can assume that a free-market system would be disastrous for any hopes for genuine and sustainable development. Economists should acknowledge that the main issue of today's socioeconomic problems is not primarily of an economic nature, but rather of a psychological or behavioral nature (whereby, spiritual capital is the key to the solution).

Another famous Bengali, the 1913 Nobel Prize winner for literature, Rabindranath Tagore (1861–1941), also influenced Romain Rolland and introduced a spiritual, literary, and also broad-minded India to Europe and the world (cf. Rolland's "Conversations with Rabindranath Tagore"). Tagore agreed with Vivekananda that the "entire personality" of a human person has to be stimulated and not just the purely ascetic aspect or the mechanical use of fingers on a spinning wheel, the ideal activity of Gandhi's philosophy.[21] Tagore lacked any economic training. He nevertheless contributed, especially in his speeches on nationalism, to Indian thinking on politics and economics. Most of these speeches were delivered during trips to Japan and the United States in 1916 and 1917. It was as if he had to avoid war-making Europe to be able to address it. Tagore argued that all positive social relations that are not mechanical no impersonal are contradictory to the notion of a "nation." One of the major crimes of the cults surrounding a nation was the surrender by individuals of their own free will, replacing it by an abstract strictly organized national will. Tagore explained: "I am not against one nation in particular, but against the general idea of all nations. What is the nation?"[22] His concept of a nation was a complete people as an organized power. When executing this power, energy and economic means are being redrawn from the higher nature of man where he is creative and in solidarity. Nationalism, in the eyes of Tagore, is immoral, mechanical, self-destructive, and counterproductive. Already in 1908, he had written: "Patriotism cannot be our final spiritual shelter; my refuge is humanity. I will not buy glass for the price of diamonds, and I will never allow patriotism to triumph over humanity as long as I live."[23] His words would linger on during the First World War and when Fascism took over in Italy and Nazism in Germany. Not surprisingly, he became a hero to the European antiwar movement.

Interestingly, it was in Germany where Oswald Spengler's *Der Untergang des Abendlandes* (*The Decline of the West*, 1918)[24] made explicit room for heterogeneities within each culture and for the cross-cultural similarities that can be clearly observed. In fact, Spengler argued that there was nothing special about Socrates, Epicurus, or Diogenes, who all have their more ancient Indian and Chinese counterparts. Unfortunately, as Germany got trapped in economic crises and consequently the Nazi regime, both timing and location were wrong for introducing such ideas.

Other West-European scholars, like the Protestant Alsacian theologian Dr. Albert Schweitzer (1875–1965) writing his *Indian Thought and Its Development* in 1935 (English edition: 1936), were influenced by Vivekananda and Tagore. Schweitzer searched for the meaning of activity and work within Hinduism and challenged the Weberian view that religions like Hinduism and Buddhism were by nature fatalistic and counterproductive. Schweitzer made a clear distinction of early Hinduism, or Brahmanism (advocated by the Brahmins or priest caste), and later, more popular, Hinduism, which developed after 1000 BC. Brahmanism and its mysticism were specifically concerned with the uniting of the human personality to the divine personality. The divine and the human are basically one and the same. In this process, everything is subjected to world and life negation.

The new Hinduism challenged Brahmanism, but did not contradict it. It professed a belief in monotheism, probably by first worshipping Krishna, who may have originally been a deified tribal hero and later held to be an *avatar* of Vishnu. But at the same time, polytheism was preserved. "God is worshipped in the Gods," wrote Schweitzer.[25] While Christianity simply demands mankind to be obedient to God, Hinduism requires union with Him, in complete self-surrender. This "bhakti"—piety or Hindu mysticism—is concerned with the uniting of the human personality to the Divine Personality, not with the Brahmanical absorption of the individual soul into the Universal Soul: "Hinduism does not lose itself in abstract thought, but strives to remain a living piety."[26]

Schweitzer then identified a contradiction:

> So monotheistic theism, because it is the religion of the masses and at the same time under the spell of the Brahmanic world-view, finds itself faced by the task of gaining recognition for activity within world and life negation.[27]

Hindu thinking neutralized this contradiction by combining world and life negation with ethics, which basically results in world and life affirmation. Thus, Hindu thinking, instead of merely tolerating activity, prizes it as a valuable thing. It cannot do otherwise than take account of natural feeling. Only, according to Schweitzer, "Man must get rid of the illusion that his ego is the real worker."[28] Basically, the *Bhagavad Gita* comes to this conclusion. In the text of the *Bhagavad Gita,* the God Krishna will not admit the Brahmanic deduction that an enlightened person should withdraw from the play (the illusion of life) and behave as an inactive and nonparticipant spectator of it. Each person is required to play his/her part in self-devotion to God in the play God has staged. Schweitzer elaborates on this:

> Man must get to a point where he no longer accomplishes any act for the sake of expected advantage or enjoyment, or out of hatred or a spirit of revenge, like such as still live blindly in the world and seek satisfaction in it. If his heart has become free from the outward motives to action, he can perform any numbers of works; he will nevertheless remain in inactivity.[29]

Thus, Krishna suggests the outward performance of actions in combination with inward renunciation of the world. We conclude that man should be active not because of the expected results, but solely because of a pure, absolute sense of duty with no empirical foundation. The German "Enlightenment" philosopher Immanuel Kant (1724–1804) had a very similar approach. However, the *Bhagavad Gita* explicitly linked it to an ethical awareness: Krishna defines it as the totality of the obligations that naturally belong to a man's stations in life.

Of course, this interpretation comes from Schweitzer's preoccupation with affirming life. His view was that "Western" civilization was in decay because it was gradually abandoning its ethical foundations, those of affirmation of life. He looked forward to a renewed and more profound Renaissance and Enlightenment of humanity through the philosophies of the European Middle Ages and the essence of Indian Hindu thought. In this way, Schweitzer was the first West-European to derive a direct economic ethical message from ancient Hindu thinking related to West-European reality. However, his economic ethical conclusions about the essence of Hindu thinking do not contradict other interpretations. Uppal, while considering the relationship between Hinduism and economic development in South Asia, offers the following summary statement:

> According to the Gita—an individual should actively engage himself in his duty according to his particular guna [activities] but should at the same time disassociate himself from the activity itself. This is the essence of non-attachment, an important element in the Gita.[30]

On the one hand, one could argue that the gap between *Atman* and *guṇa* (qualities) can be bridged by renunciation of activities. On the other hand, transcending *guṇa* can only be reached by involving in *guṇa* itself.

This implies that salvation from work is through work itself. Uppal suggests that *Karma,* rather than being a deterrent to action, can serve as a powerful incentive to action, because it makes man himself the maker of his fortune.

During the 1920s, a Russian artist and philosopher, Nicholas Roerich (1874–1947), started expeditions to Buddhist, Hindu, and Islamic regions in Central Asia, China, and India. In his philosophic and artistic essays, Roerich created an absolutely new concept of culture based on the idea of "living ethics." Culture and ethics are based on beauty and knowledge. Economics should focus on artistic expression and beauty, as these are basic needs for a successful and harmonious humanity. His idea of an international pact for the protection of cultural treasures, signed in 1935 in the presence of U.S. President F. Roosevelt, was supported by Rolland, Tagore, and Albert Einstein. Roerich's son, Svetoslav Roerich (1904–1993), while living in India, basically continued his father's work.[31]

Finally, two traditions with roots in Islam also reached Europe. First, "perennial" Sufism was introduced to Europe through the foundation of the Sufi Order in the West in 1910 by Pir Hadrat 'Inayat Khan (1882–1927), who initially came to the Europe as a representative of classical Indian music, but soon turned to the introduction and transmission of Sufi thought and practice. His universal message of divine unity (*Tawhid*) focused on the themes of love, harmony, and beauty. He taught that blind adherence to any book rendered any religion void of spirit. Doctrinally, it held views that go against Sunni, Shi'ite, and even mainstream Sufi Islam: the nature of Allah/God is changeable, Allah/God and human beings are essentially one, and the human being is divine. It also accepted the belief in reincarnation, and promoted the idea of a feminine dimension of the sacred.[32]

Second, the Bahá'í faith was a monotheistic religion founded by Bahá'u'lláh (1817–1892) in the 19th-century Persia, emphasizing the spiritual unity of all humankind. Under the leadership of his son, 'Abdu'l-Bahá (1844–1921), the religion gained a footing in Europe and America. As Bahá'i did not consider man as innately sinful (like many of the Christian churches or conventional Islam), a free-market system is considered as a perfect way to distribute resources in a fair way. Not surprisingly, the movement reacted against the extreme forms of protectionism implemented during the interwar period. British IMF economist and member of Bahá'i, John Huddleston describes this point of view as follows:

> A spiritual society will have more rational methods of protecting its members from economic hardship than restrictions on movement of trade and peoples which cause gross inequalities and inefficiencies in the economic system.[33]

A natural evolution of mankind implies the growth of the higher, spiritual nature of man in a free-market environment. However, an emphasis on marriage and family life resulted in a certain degree of exclusiveness.

POSTWAR EUROPEAN VISIONS OF THE EAST: FROM UTOPIAN ENVIRONMENTALISM TO BUSINESS ETHICS

The Second World War had once again demonstrated how Europe was self-destructive and once again "Eastern" ideas were considered as possible alternatives. From the 1960s, specific interest was shown in Zen Buddhism, which stressed the importance of applying meditation to work and art. Mahayana (Greater Vehicle or Great Way) Buddhism, emphasizing complete Buddhahood, the perfection of wisdom and compassion, was introduced by Japanese movements in the 1960s. Together with increasing sympathy for the Tibetan cause, Tibetan communities also became very popular, attracting not only Tibetan refugees but also native French and other European nationalities. Native French *lamas* and monks "Europeanized" the movement. Later, in the 1980s and 1990s, a widespread interest developed in Vajrayana Buddhism, which involves the use of rituals to achieve both Buddhahood itself and this-worldly benefits. One of the principal agents in the advancement of "engaged Buddhism" was the Vietnamese monk Thich Nhat Hanh. Through his publications and the foundation of the *Eglise Bouddhique Unifiée,* he advocated a nonviolent engagement through Buddhism with all aspects of life, including economic activities.[34]

There were concrete influences on European economic thinking, which emerged in Western Europe of the 1960s. E. F. Schumacher's *Buddhist Economics,* first published in 1966, was widely understood as a call for an economics of peace. In the essay, Schumacher imagines a multitude of vibrant, self-sufficient villages that, from their secure sense of community and place, work together in peace and cooperation. This idea is repeated in his utopian *Small is Beautiful,* published in 1973.

In fact, Schumacher's writings and that of his colleagues derived a lot from Mahatma (Mohandas Karamchand) Gandhi (1869–1948), who was inspired by both *Vedanta* and Buddhism. While industrialist J. N. Tata and to some extent philosopher Swami Vivekananda had been industrial pragmatists, the Mahatma represented a complete economic alternative, emphasizing a "voluntary limitation of needs," leading to a better equilibrium between man and nature. He suggested setting up self-sufficient village communities in order to reach these goals. After studying the *Bhagavad Gita* and other (including Christian and Muslim) religious and philosophical sources, he had concluded that a peaceful basic needs approach should replace the modern demand-oriented economy. "True economics" coincided with "just economics." Regardless of the objective utility of their production, "Western" economies only focused on profit and return maximization. As long as industries alienate themselves from local and appropriate technologies, the economy will continue to lose touch with the objective needs of people. Man is being made subordinate to technological progress, economic policy, and the game of power this implies. He is delivered to invisible and unpredictable economic laws, which in one stroke can make thousands of people lose their jobs. A citizen living in an industrialized environment is no longer self-sufficient, becoming increasingly vulnerable, and is not satisfied with what he or she produces himself or herself.

This "ecological" point of view *avant la lettre* contradicted the "spirit of the time" in India. Gandhi and his disciples were described as moralizing old men who lacked any theoretical basis. In Europe, however, his timing couldn't have been better. He inspired generations of green and small-scale socioeconomic philosophers like Schumacher (1911–1977) and Michael Lipton (1937–). Basically, the Mahatma paved the way for the success of the green movement in Europe from the 1960s onward.

From the 1980s onward, the emphasis gradually moved from alternative "green" messages to a more practical code for businesses in an increasingly capitalist and competitive environment. A new generation of holistic thinkers explored Asian philosophical and religious traditions and applied them to modern socioeconomic leadership wisdom.[35] All these traditions refer to a basic oneness of existence, whereby the inner and outer worlds merge into one reality. The success of new religious movements (NRMs) and the New Age Movement (NAM), both frequently inspired by Asian traditions, in Europe and elsewhere reflected the need for the "unchurched but spiritual." However, the "integration of the whole person" has been interpreted either as "intensified concentration" and eventually as "greater job efficiency," or as a way for extreme alienation from society. Now, the study of the origins of concepts, principles, and rituals, and thereby uncovering their spiritual meanings, became relevant for mainstream socioeconomic ethics. Similarities with mainstream West-European Christian-inspired humanism were noted. Norwegian economist Oyvind Jaer (1998) referred to a common reference point shared by capitalism and Hinduism in the concepts of action (Karma) and structure (Dharma). He argued that the duality of action–structure is a particularly fertile "bridgehead" for cultural translation and comparison. Lindsay Falvey (2005) identified agricultural sustainability in both Christianity and Buddhism. Polish film director M. Skiba focused on the ecological awareness of the Rajasthani community of Bishnois in her documentary film *Eco Dharma* (2006). The Sant Nirankari Mission, an open-minded movement among Sikhs that had its formal beginning already in 1929, attracted attention in the United Kingdom and elsewhere because of its views against ritualism, emphasizing that God is formless and the need to maintain a balance between spiritual and material life. From an economic point of view, the mission emphasized the importance of economic activities within the context of responsibilities for family life and service to the society.[36] These are only a few examples of how a new economic ethical awareness grew from a new approach to Eastern traditions.

More specifically, the new business ethical approach also involved the Sufi concept of "self-help through remembering God" (constant remembrance and respect for origin and historical perspective), the concept of *Darshan* (seeing the divine image in everything, resulting in the sacredness of nature and its implications for ecological awareness), the concept of *Prasad* (blessed offering to the God as a reflection of the right product, salary, and price), the tradition of gurus and pilgrimages (e.g., the *Maha Kumbha Mela,* allowing both gurus and followers to cleanse themselves, reflecting the need of mutually beneficial interactions like fair play relations), the principle of *Ahimsa* (reflecting nonviolent interactions), connected to the law of *Karma* (of cause and effect, e.g., violent interactions invite more violent interactions), and the concept of *Dharma* (emphasizing the "path," i.e., the way of doing business, rather than the outcome, e.g., the profits). Simultaneously, Eurocentric views of the world received exhilarating critique by thinkers such as the development economist Andre Gunder Frank (1929–2005), who forcefully argued that Asia had played the leading role in the world economy up to the 18th century.[37]

CONCLUSION

This contribution focused on how Europe perceived Indian traditions from an economic point of view. A more conventional approach was to study the similarities between European and ancient Indian economic thinking. Both approaches are now gradually illustrating that economics as we know it today is the result of a long multicultural process. G. R. Madan already wrote in 1981:

> It is often believed that the evolution of . . . economic doctrine is exclusively of European origin. It is perhaps for this reason that a majority of the books on economic thought generally deal with western economic thought. But it is hoped that the study of ancient economic theories of India will help in dispelling such baneful illusions.[38]

From the 17th century onward, the "East" had become a "utopia"—a place to find wisdom and critique for Europe's growing mercantilist and capitalist system. Though 19th-century utilitarianism initially invited paternalistic behavior, it nonetheless paved the way for a genuine intellectual interaction between Europe and Asia. Amartya Sen[39] may be right that India was as materialistic as the "West," but was forced into spiritual thinking because this field was "still open to non-Westerners." But in doing so, India (and Asia) provided a strong critique against mainstream European economic thinking. It offered Europe again an alternative to the excesses of imperialism and capitalism. During and after the world wars, the spread of totalitarian regimes, and the economic crises of the 1920s and 1930s, some intellectuals reacted against economic chaos, violence, and fascism by referring to "Asian (especially Indian) wisdom." Later on, in the 1960s, there was yet another revival of Asia in Europe: many religious movements came over, and while yoga seemed to offer a solution to many physical problems, Buddhism and Vedanta fascinated environmentalist and utopian economists. Of late, postmodernism provided the framework for yet another renaissance of Asian thinking in Europe. This time "Asian wisdom" was introduced into business ethics. We have demonstrated that the foundations of the new role Asian thinking is playing within the framework of postmodernism go back a long time. We conclude that the psychology of the European economic and intellectual mind, with the exception of the "Said types" during the 19th century, resulted into "an East" that has criticized European economic models for centuries.

What Asian, especially Indian, traditions may ultimately teach West-European economists is not to keep looking for new economic models and theories, but to start looking for a change in human nature. India's history and today's society are certainly not models for "peaceful balance and oneness" in this respect, but Indian civilization may have delivered unintentionally the message more clearly than any other civilization.

NOTES

1. Kevin Rushby, *Paradise: A History of the Idea That Rules the World* (London: Robinson, 2007), p. 160.
2. William Dalrymple, *White Mughals: Love and Betrayal in Eighteenth-Century India* (London: Flamingo-HarperCollins Publishers, 2003).
3. Swift also wrote an unfinished essay "An Account of the Court and Empire of Japan" in 1728, which merely served as a device to satirize corruption in English politics. See Gerrit De Vylder, "The Economics of Oriental Utopia: The Case of Jonathan Swift," *Review of Business and Economics* 53, no. 1 (January–March 2008): 93–108.
4. Rushby, *Paradise*, pp. 154–60.
5. Shen Fuwei, *Cultural Flow between China and Outside World throughout History* (Beijing: Foreign Languages Press, 1997), pp. 275–77.
6. Most probably inspired by Tobago, an island in the West Indies.
7. Ha-Joon Chang, *Bad Samaritans: Rich Nations, Poor Policies & the Threat to the Developing World* (London: Random House Business Books, 2007), pp. 40–64.
8. Jonathan Swift, *Gulliver's Travels* (Ware: Wordsworth Editions, 2001 [1726]), pp. 162, 222–24.

9. Adam Smith, *The Wealth of Nations* (New York: Bantam Dell, 2003 [1776]), pp. 563–65.

10. See Richard Friedenthal, *Goethe: His Life and Times* (London: Weidenfeld, 1993).

11. See Phil Grabsky, *The Lost Temple of Java* (London: Seven Dials, 2000).

12. See John M. Hobson, *The Eastern Origins of Western Civilization* (Cambridge: Cambridge University Press, 2004).

13. A. L. Macfie, ed., *Orientalism: A Reader* (Cairo: The American University in Cairo Press, 2000), pp. 87–114.

14. See Michel Levallois and Sarga Moussa, eds., *L'orientalisme des saint-simoniens* (Paris: Maisonneuve & Larose, 2006).

15. Franck Laurent, "L'Orient de Victor Hugo: Un nom de Génie" in Levallois and Moussa, *L'orientalisme des saint-simoniens,* p. 72.

16. See the overviews by Swami Tathagatananda in *Journey of the Upanishads to the West* (New York: The Vedanta Society of New York, 2002) and *Light from the Orient: Essays on the Impact of India's Sacred Literature in the West* (Kolkata: Advaita Ashrama, 2005).

17. See C. P. Ramaswami Aiyar, *Annie Besant* (New Delhi: Ministry of Education and Broadcasting, 1992).

18. J. Krishnamurti, *What Is a Problem?* (Chennai: Krishnamurti Foundation India, 2005), pp. 2–5.

19. Sarup Prasad Ghosh, *Swami Vivekananda's Economic Thought in Modern International Perspective: India as a Case Study* (Kolkata: The Ramakrishna Mission Institute of Culture, 2006), pp. 553, 554.

20. Quoted in Santwana Dasgupta, *Social Philosophy of Swami Vivekananda* (Kolkata: The Ramakrishna Mission Institute of Culture, 2005), p. 474.

21. See Śaṅkarīprasāda Basu, *Economic and Political Ideas: Vivekananda, Gandhi, Subhas Bose* (New Delhi: Sterling Publishers, 2000).

22. Rabindranath Tagore, *Nationalism* (New Delhi: Rupa, 2002 [1917]), pp. 53–104.

23. Amartya Sen, *The Argumentative Indian: Writings on Indian History, Culture and Identity* (London: Penguin Books, 2005), p. 108.

24. Oswald Spengler, *The Decline of the West* (New York/Oxford: Oxford University Press, 1991 [1918]).

25. Albert Schweitzer, *Indian Thought and Its Development* (Mumbai: Wilco Publishing House, 2006 [1936]), p. 149.

26. Ibid.

27. Ibid., p. 152.

28. Ibid., p. 160.

29. Ibid., p. 157.

30. J. S. Uppal, "Hinduism and Economic Development in South Asia," *International Review of Economics & Ethics* 1, no. 1 (1986): 24.

31. See Svetoslav Roerich, *Art and Life* (Moscow: International Centre of the Roerichs, 2004) and *Creative Thought* (Moscow: International Centre of the Roerichs, 2004).

32. See Hazrat Inayat Khan, *The Sufi Message,* Vol. XIII (Delhi: Motilal Banarsidass Publishers, 2004).

33. John Huddleston, *The Earth Is But One Country* (New Delhi: Bahá'i Publishing Trust, 2008), pp. 140, 141.

34. Ibid., pp. 87–92.

35. See S.K. Chakraborty, *Ethics in Management: Vedantic Perspectives* (Oxford/New Delhi: Oxford University Press, 2006).

36. See C.L. Gulati, *A Mission for All* (Delhi: Sant Nirankari Mandal, 2003).

37. See Andre Gunder Frank, *Reorient: Global Economy in the Asian Age* (Berkeley, CA: University of California Press, 1998).

38. G.R. Madan, *Economic Thinking in India* (New Delhi: S. Chande, 1981), pp. 1, 2.

39. Amartya Sen, *The Argumentative Indian: Writings on Indian History, Culture and Identity* (London: Penguin Books, 2005).

Chapter 7

The South Asian Impact upon Traditional Malay Theater

Ghulam-Sarwar Yousof

INTRODUCTION

Cultural influences from various parts of South Asia started reaching Southeast Asian lands, including what was to become Malaya and eventually Malaysia, in the early decades of the Common Era, marking the beginning of the region's known history. These were followed by influences from the Chinese mainland and the Middle or Near East, in that order. Christianity was introduced into the Philippines in the mid-16th century, but did not spread any further. It remains, to this day, the dominant religion in that country. The third Southeast Asian contact with other Asian cultures, in addition to the Western, came in the 19th and 20th centuries, in the wake of European colonization. This marked the migration into Southeast Asia of vast numbers of peoples, particularly from the South Asia and the China mainland, bringing with them their own cultures and traditions. It was the first and second waves of immigration, however, that were instrumental, to a considerable degree, in shaping, reshaping, or influencing indigenous traditions of the Malays. In the case of the Malay Peninsula, which was to eventually become predominantly Islamic, the impact of Hinduism has been strong, while lesser Buddhist influences are evident in the northern states bordering Thailand.

This chapter briefly examines the highly significant South Asian influences in Malay traditional theater, influences which may be summarily categorized in terms of (1) the transplantation and development of South Asian genres into the Malay Peninsula and the development of new genres inspired by them, (2) the appropriation of literary sources for the development of dramatic content, (3) the borrowing of mythology as well as particular religious beliefs and concepts, (4) the prevalence of Hindu and Buddhist ritual practices, and (5) aesthetic principles.

THE SETTING

The tendency to take the whole of Southeast Asia as a single unit in discussions related to history and culture has, to some extent, distorted the realities on the ground. The process of Indian acculturation, for instance, was a long drawn out one and did not reach the countries in the region in any uniform manner. It was also not necessarily at all times direct. It will be seen in the case of the traditional performing arts, for instance, that most of the South Asian influences reaching traditional theater in the "Malay" region, or particular locations on the peninsula, came indirectly through the island of Java and what is today southern Thailand. Hardly anything significant in terms of performing arts reached this region directly until the late 19th century, following the establishment of a British colony on the island of Penang off the west coast of peninsular Malaysia in 1786.

This is not to deny, of course, the fact that Hindu and Buddhist settlements had long before those days been established in Bujang Valley, Kedah, as well as elsewhere as indicated by the presence of archaeological evidence in the form of temple remains as well as religious or art objects discovered at points far from the actual location of the Bujang Valley temple complex, the most significant remnants of temples discovered in the Malay Peninsula, as well as other such settlements further south in the present-day Malaysian state of Perak, close to the site of the ancient Indian settlement at Gangga Negara. Unlike the monuments in Cambodia, in particular Angkor Wat, or those in Central and East Java, the Malaysian ruins provide no indication of performing arts. Neither is there any evidence for the presence of the two major epics, *Ramayana* and *Mahabharata,* the principal sources for dramatic repertoire for much of traditional Southeast Asian theater.

It is not until almost a millennium later that the first evidence emerges for the presence in the Malay Peninsula of traditional performing arts. The mak yong dance theater is mentioned by a British observer, Frank Swettenham, in 1878. All the major traditional theater forms in the Malay Peninsula, including mak yong, menora, or lakon chatri, and the shadow play (wayang kulit), begin to get attention for the first time in the end of the 19th century following the arrival of Western observers beginning with Walter Skeat. It is, in fact, quite intriguing that no indigenous histories (*hikayat*) or literary works and no local observers, with the possible exception of the early-19th-century writer Munshi Abdullah, make any references to the traditional theater. Even when it comes to traditional dance and music apart from occasional brief references in passing to ceremonial music, there is but a single important work in this category—*Hikayat Patani* (*History of Patani*), a history of the Patani kingdom, now part of Southern Thailand, which provides a colorful picture of what was taking place in the palace in the 17th century. There is, thus, overall, a telling silence, and a situation vastly different from that encountered in Indonesia. In most Southeast Asian nations, even if there were no detailed or dedicated works devoted to the performing arts written, court records do mention those forms that received royal patronage or support. In traditional Malay theater forms, then, apart from bangsawan and boria, which reached Malaysia following the British arrival, much of what is known comes from observations in the last century or so first by colonial observers, followed by Western scholars, and finally by a handful of Malaysian researchers.

Before proceeding to the precise topic at hand, however, it should be noted in passing that with the arrival of immigrant populations—the Chinese, the Indians, the Thais, and the various communities belonging to the Indonesian diaspora from the 19th century—forms of performing arts belonging to and active within these communities came to be introduced into the Malay Peninsula. Some of these remain active to this day, virtually unchanged, in the respective communities. These include Chinese puppet theater and opera in several different dialects, the Javanese shadow play (wayang kulit purwa), lakon chatri or menora (a Thai-Buddhist dance theater form), and the southern Thai shadow play (nang talung). Malaysian versions of both the southern Thai theater genres just mentioned were developed in the northern part of peninsular Malaysia in regions south of the international border between Malaysia and Thailand, with greater or lesser adaptation. The most significant of these is wayang kulit gedek, an offshoot of nang talung.

TRANSPLANTATION AND DEVELOPMENT OF GENRES

Not taking into consideration those forms of artistic expression that arrived in the Malay Peninsula with the wave of immigrations from the 18th century to the present, forms that essentially belong to and are active within particular non-Malay communities—the Chinese, the Indians, the Thais, the Javanese, and Minangkabau communities from Indonesia, as well as the Portuguese—the most obvious example that comes to mind in connection with the current topic is the shadow play (*wayang kulit*), active in several parts of the Malay Peninsula in four traditional and several newly developed styles.

Before touching upon the major genres, it may be pertinent, for the sake of a complete picture of the situation vis-à-vis traditional Malay theater, to mention the fact that there exist three nonritualistic styles of proto-theater based upon narrative techniques, featuring solo artistes who present their performances with combinations of vocal techniques, physical movements, costumes, musical instruments, and hand properties. These are awang batil, selampit, and tarik selampit. In the past, awang batil featured an inverted clay pot (*belanga*) as an instrument, as indicated by its older name, awang belanga. The clay pot was at some point in time replaced with a brass bowl (*batil*). In selampit, the only instruments used for sound effects are the performer's body and his vocal techniques, while the tarik selampit artist accompanies himself on a three-stringed rebab. In all three genres, local legendary and romantic stories constitute the dramatic repertoire. In the style of performance, there are parallels with proto-theater genres in India, Bangladesh, and elsewhere. There are clear resemblances, for instance, between the original form of awang batil and the Indian mann bhatt that to this day uses a clay pot. Nearer to Malaysia, there are striking parallels between Malay and Indonesian forms of proto-theater, including storytelling or solo performance genres such as dalang gentrung and dalang jemplung.[1] While pointing out these parallels, the intention here is not to directly connect these Indonesian and Malay theater forms to South Asian equivalents, for theater forms involving narration, epic recitation, or storytelling, sharing many characteristics, are universally performed in many cultures. In most of these cultures, such forms are, indeed, amongst the earliest. On the other hand, given the kind of cultural relationships between South and Southeast Asia and the strong influences emanating from that region, the possibility of such connections between South Asian and Malay storytelling genres cannot be entirely ruled out.

Malay proto-theater forms include three styles of shamanism: belian, bagih, and main puteri, all active in the northeastern state of Kelantan. Additionally, belian, in various forms, shared between Malaysia and Indonesia, may be encountered throughout the northern part of the island of Borneo. All three forms involve trance or states of altered consciousness, while main puteri, the most elaborate of these, makes use of a small orchestra consisting of a three-stringed rebab, a pair of gongs, and a pairs of drums—instruments also constituting the orchestra of the mak yong dance theater. In exorcism or healing situations, depending upon the patient's malady, main puteri is at times performed in combination with other genres, particularly mak yong as well as with dances such as joget, or with silat, in complex performances lasting several nights. While belian, bagih, and main puteri come from the animistic level of Malay culture, the theater consecration (buka panggung) rituals featured in them are near identical to those performed in more sophisticated genres. These rituals, which will presently be examined, suggest more than superficial connections with similar rituals, in terms of style, content, and purpose, encountered in South Asian folk theater.

To return to the shadow play (wayang kulit) for now, there has been a strong assumption among a number of observers that this particular genre of theater originated in South Asia and thence found its way elsewhere including several Southeast Asian countries—Malaysia, Cambodia, Thailand, and Indonesia.[2] Other opinions place the origins of the shadow play on the island of Java in Indonesia, China, or Central Asia, while another view suggests several independent origins for this obviously ancient and intriguing form of theater.[3] Given that no real consensus exists on the whole issue of the origins of the shadow play, this oft-discussed problem need not concern us at this point. Enough is to say that three traditional styles of shadow play are active in the Malay Peninsula: wayang kulit Siam in Kelantan, wayang kulit gedek in Kedah and Perlis, and wayang kulit purwa in Johore. A fourth traditional style of shadow play wayang kulit Melayu recently became extinct, while several new ones, which in content and spirit have nothing whatsoever to do the traditional forms, have come into being in the past decade or so. All of these use single-character figures, rather than the large composite ones seen in the Cambodian nang sbek thom and the Thai nang yai. No matter what the immediate or even ultimate geographical origins of the Malaysian wayang kulit styles—for they certainly reached the Malay Peninsula from different directions—they betray strong South Asian influences in dramatic content, spiritual or religious notions, ritual activities featured in performances, and in other ways.

In the final quarter of the 19th century, an operatic form of theater, supported by the Parsee merchants in Bombay (now Mumbai) and, in some instances, performed by its members of that community, came into being in that city. The product of a fusion of several different strands and elements—indigenous Indian, Parsee, and Western—became a rage in Indian towns and cities from its first inception. Through association with the Parsees, who provided financial backing as well as became actively involved in it, this genre came to adopt the name Parsee theater. Both within and outside the land of its origin, it spawned several variants, which ultimately consolidated as independent forms including therukoothu in Tamil Nadu, nadagama in Sri Lanka, as well as in Southeast Asia where it found its first footfall on the island of Penang in Malaysia. Out of this style, through an intermediary form tellingly designated imitation Parsee theater (wayang Parsee tiruan), which attempted to localize the Indian form, was born bangsawan, a transitional form of Malay theater, operatic in character like its parent.

With suitable adaptations as well as the infusion of appropriate local elements—stories, music, and dance forms inter alia—bangsawan, eventually, came to be regarded as a form quite distinct from Parsee theater. In the early decades, it was very much an eclectic multicultural theater form involving members of various communities—Malays, Indians, Chinese, Eurasians, members of mixed Malay Chinese (Peranakan or Baba) communities, as well as Eurasians. It spreads rapidly within Malaya, Singapore, Brunei, and neighboring Malay-speaking territories in Indonesia.

In Malaya, following the reduction or near-elimination of non-Malay elements in the years between the Second World War and those immediately after independence in 1957, bangsawan, now associated principally with the Malay community, increasingly became an important vehicle for the assertion of "Malayness" and the articulation of Malay feudal values and aspirations, in particular through its dramatic content that gave priority to stories set in real or imaginary Malay kingdoms. Notwithstanding such a stance, it continues to be claimed by the Malaysian Baba community as their own, and in Singapore, it retains its multiethnic character, while the Indonesian bangsawan, active on Sumatra and in the Riau islands, has seen other parallel developments, including offshoots of the genre such as stambul or stamboel. The strong combination of South Asian and Western aesthetic elements in bangsawan proved vital in shaping the character of the fledgling Malay film industry, the successor of bangsawan, while the impact of Hindustani films, which, in India, succeeded the Parsee theater, continues unabated in Malaysian popular culture.

At approximately the same time as the arrival of the Parsee theater, Penang also received from South Asia another important genre. This was the religious drama form known as ta'ziyeh or ta'ziyah, traditionally performed in Shia Muslim countries during the first 10 days of Muharram, the first month of the Islamic calendar. Traced originally to various forms of storytelling, it developed to its most complete form in Iran, where it has been active for several centuries. It is also found in Shia communities in India and Pakistan. Its traditional repertoire draws upon legends connected with the family of Ali, the Prophet's son-in-law and Islam's fourth caliph, and the martyrdom of Ali's son Husain on the battlefield of Karbala in Iraq in 680 CE. Over the decades, it has undergone considerable transformation determined by religious as well as political considerations, with a consequent expansion of its repertoire. In performances staged during Muharram, the emphasis, however, still remains upon the house of Ali.

The precise development as well as character of ta'ziyah performed in Penang remains unclear due to lack of evidence. Interestingly, a recent work[4] indicates that there was a strong connection not only between trading relations, but also between Shia communities in the southern Indian kingdom of Golconda and the Thai city of Ayutthaya, which had a fairly large population of Iranian Shias. As far as the present topic is concerned, the most fascinating bit of information in this work is the reference to ta'ziyah mourning processions in Ayutthaya cited[5] from the French traveler and diplomat Guy Tachard, who stayed in the Siamese capital during the 1680s. This is possibly the first reference to ta'ziyah anywhere in Southeast Asia, and any connection that there was between the processions in Ayutthaya and elsewhere in the region remains to be investigated. The gap of almost exactly two centuries between the performance described by Tachard and the first notice of the existence of ta'ziyah in Penang, Malaysia in the late 19th century makes it unlikely that there was any kind of direct movement of this activity from Thailand to Malaysia. There are, nevertheless, other links between Islamic performances in Thailand and those in Malaysia, particularly through various forms of chanting, *zikir*. One such form, *dikir barat* that has been totally desecularized, is actively performed in Malaysia and Singapore to this day.

In both Penang and Padang Priaman on the Indonesian island of Sumatra, ta'ziyah seems to have arrived from India in the late 19th century, following the establishment of British rule in Penang. It is generally believed to have been performed by Shia members of the north Indian police (*sepoy*) regiments based in Penang, as well as by members of that community originally from northwestern India and what is now Pakistan. Available evidence, dating from several decades after its introduction into Penang, indicates that processions were an important feature of ta'ziyah, and at least some of the performers were dressed in sack cloth, a sign of mourning. Masks and face painting (mostly with charcoal) were a feature of these daytime processions, which were followed, in the evening, by dramatic presentations presumably using established ta'ziyah plots. No ta'ziyah scripts, however, have come to light.

Over time, ta'ziyah in Penang became transformed into what came to be known as boria, a name traced to the word for a gunny sack in the Urdu or Hindustani language or referring to members of the Bohri Shia community. Given the fact that the Shia Muslim community in Penang, small to start with, became numerically insignificant with the departure of the sepoy regiments and given the further fact of the changing demographic situation in Penang with the increase in numbers of Sunni Muslims as well as the Malay Indian mixed blood (*Peranakan*) community resulting from intermarriages between Malays and Indian Muslims, boria became a genre no longer associated with the Shia. With the increasing domination of this theater form by Malays, Indian Muslims and the peranakan communities became the inevitable elimination of religious themes and even the religious spirit of ta'ziyah. Choral singing, music, as well as limited dance movements, highlighted in preference to serious dramatic content, resulted in a form of boria that made use of comic skits, but nevertheless gave greater place to these other aspects of performance. Revivals of this intermediary boria style may occasionally be still seen. By and large, however, contemporary boria has been reduced to a form of choral singing with limited and simple dance steps, its performers dressed as sailors, and its purpose exclusively didactic or laudatory—in every way, a far cry from the original religious ta'ziyah.

In a discussion touching upon Middle and Near Eastern or South Asian Muslim elements in traditional Malay theater, reference must inevitably to be made, if only in passing, to several lesser theater genres, including hadrah, hamdolok, and dabus. Java clearly served as the immediate transit point for their transmission to the Malay Peninsula following suitable adaptation there. It remains a matter of speculation, however, if these genres found their way to Indonesia directly from the Middle East or through South Asia. New performance genres, based upon real or imagined events of the Middle East, were also developed. The famous Javanese hobby-horse dance (kuda kepang), active in the southern Malaysian state of Johor, is representative of this process. As in Java, local oral history strongly associates it with the early history of Islam, connecting it with legends built around military prowess of Muslim warriors. Direct links with any Middle Eastern performance genre have yet to be established. On the other hand, there is a tradition of hobby-horse dances in South India, with one particular style called poikkal kuthirai, occasionally seen in Malaysia during Tamil Hindu festivals such as Thaipusam, raising intriguing possibilities, tentatively, of inspiration from that direction.

SOURCES FOR THE DEVELOPMENT OF DRAMATIC CONTENT

As in the rest of Southeast Asia, Malay traditional theater forms make use of a wide range of sources, indigenous as well as borrowed, for dramatic content, the materials coming ultimately from sources in neighboring Southeast Asian countries as well as from South Asia, the Middle and Near East, as well as from the West. South Asian sources, amongst the earliest to come into use with the spread of Hinduism and Buddhism, are highly important in the dramatic content of traditional Malay theater. The shadow play forms, in particular, as elsewhere in the region, make use of the *Ramayana* and *Mahabharata*. The first epic is featured in wayang kulit Siam as well as in wayang kulit gedek. Wayang kulit Siam's *Ramayana* repertoire is based upon *Hikayat Maharaja Wana,* an oral version of the epic, rather than the literary *Hikayat Seri Rama.* While the central plots in both versions are more or less identical, they manifest certain important differences in detail when compared to the Valmiki, Kamban, or

Tulsidas versions of the epic. There are also significant parallels between the Malay versions and those extant further north in Thailand, Cambodia, and Myanmar, as well as in Indonesia. Similarly, many differences are to be found between *Hikayat Maharaja Wana* and Indian versions of the Ramayana, as a result of the oral transmission of the *Hikayat,* reworking of its plot through improvization, as well as attempts at making the epic acceptable within the Malay-Islamic milieu of Kelantan through a drastic reduction of Hindu elements.

One important element of wayang kulit Siam is the use of a large number of locally invented stories, designated as branch stories (*cerita ranting*) of the epic. They are, in fact, imaginative extensions of the *Ramayana,* if that description may be loosely used, with no real basis in that epic. The events contained in these stories are indicated as taking place after the completion of the parent epic with the return of Seri Rama and Sita Dewi to Ayodhya. Several central characters of the *Ramayana,* in particular Seri Rama and his family, have been retained in these extension stories with the hero given new adventures, some of which have been based upon episodes from the Javanese Panji romance. The emphasis, however, shifts away in stages from the hero himself to Laksmana, to Seri Rama's sons, Lava and Kusha (in Kelantan renamed Kusi and Serawi), and, following that, to locally developed characters not found in the *Ramayana.* The pair of clowns Pak Dogol and Wak Long, not seen in any version of the epic and regarded by puppeteers as local manifestations of Semar and his fellow clowns of the Javanese theater, are highly important in wayang kulit Siam. Attempts to see the derivation of Semar and his kin from the Vidushaka of the Sanskrit theater and Indian folk traditions have not been entirely convincing.[6] The clown characters have found an important place, too, in the *ranting* stories in company with a whole range of other totally invented characters, which, in most instances, appear as antagonists to the firmly established central characters or as additional comic figures. In the development of the plot and some of the principal themes of the ranting stories, the puppeteers have clearly made use of the highly popular Javanese Panji romance, whose themes and motifs betray many similarities to the *Ramayana* and to other romance cycles, as well as their fertile imagination.[7]

The *Ramayana,* this time based on the Thai *Ramakien,* also forms the core story of wayang kulit gedek. Additional sources for its repertoire include both Thai and Malay popular literature. Recent developments have seen the gradual diminishing of the *Ramayana* story in this genre in favor of totally invented materials. The *Mahabharata,* locally designated *Hikayat Pandawa Lima,* has a significantly lesser place in traditional Malay theater. It is principally encountered, with certain innovations, in wayang kulit purwa, which spread from Indonesia and has been active for several decades in the southern part of peninsular Malaysia. One important element in wayang kulit purwa, the fusion of Hindu and Islamic elements as seen in mystical interpretations of the *Mahabharata,* is totally absent in Malaysia.

In traditional Malay theater, as a whole, there are hardly any examples of other Hindu-oriented stories apart from those derived from the pair of epics. The medieval Panji cycle of stories may be mentioned in passing, for the record, as an important source of repertoire in the rarely seen wayang kulit Melayu, developed from the Javanese wayang kulit gedok, whose entire repertoire was based on this romance. Elements from the *Mahabharata* get combined with those from the Panji romance in stories featured in this form of shadow play.

Wayang kulit Siam's extremely rare ritual (*berjamu*) performances are staged for initiation of new puppeteers, paying homage to teachers (*sembah guru*) or strengthening the spirit (*semangat*) of retired ones. Such performances, lasting over three nights, include episodes from the Ramayana as well as certain other stories never done in entertainment-oriented performances. The most important of these is a story dealing with the birth of the demon Kala, who is depicted as a son of Vishnu and Bentara Omar disguised as a woman, rather than a form of Vishnu as in the *Vishnu Purana,* a possible ultimate source of the story. Growing up instantly into a giant moments after his birth, Kala is ready to consume his yet tiny elder brother. This is prevented by Vishnu, who instead gives permission to Kala to eat other living beings. Kala chases a woman, whose blood he has smelt as she accidentally cuts her finger. She manages to elude the demon's assault by hiding in a shadow play theater where a show is in progress. The puppeteer is in fact Wak Long, the second clown figure in wayang kulit Siam. Distracted by the performance, Kala forgets his victim, who thus escapes. Known in Kelantan as *Hikayat Putrakala,* the same episode, in different versions, is also incorporated into ritual performances of the Javanese wayang kulit purwa and the Balinese wayang kulit parwa for similar purposes of redeeming the life of someone who becomes a potential victim of Kala due to unfortunate circumstances. In all likelihood, the three versions of this story as performed in the wayang kulit come from a single source in Java.

Due to the fact that mak yong and lakon chatri are performed in the same geographical areas, that is southern Thailand and northern Malaysia, there has been much cross-borrowing between the two genres, and even the development of a form in Kelantan that combines the two genres. Mak yong's extended repertoire thus includes a number of Thai stories, some of them with a Buddhist coloring, with possible links with Buddhist literature in countries on the fringe of Thailand. An important category of such stories is that classified as Jataka stories that deal with the Buddha's previous lives, before his birth as Prince Siddharta or Sakyamuni. In addition to the official Jataka, 50 such stories, known as the *Pinnasa Jataka,* of extra-canonical Buddha-life stories were collected in northern Thailand. They appear to have come from various sources including from Hinayana Buddhist literature. A number of these stories have found a place in traditional theater and dance in the Buddhist countries of mainland Southeast Asia. The best known, in terms of their connections with theater, are the story of Prince Sudhana (locally Phra Suthon or Paksuton), the swan-maiden Manohara (locally Nang Nora or Nora), and the tale of the Prince of the Golden Shell (known in Thailand as *Sang Thong*). The former is the principal story in the lakon chatri dance theater in both Thailand and Malaysia, while *Sang Thong* is featured in lakon nok. Renamed *Anak Raja Gondang* in Malaysia, it's one of the core plays in the dramatic repertoire of the mak yong dance theater.

A third category of South Asian tales, featured in bangsawan, was originally borrowed from the extensive and varied repertoire of the Parsee theater. Both Parsee theater and bangsawan eschewed epic-based material, and even religious themes are rare in its repertoire, although the genre, like the Parsee theater, made extensive use of Middle Eastern and Persian romances. Bangsawan's so-called "Indian" or Hindustani tales—which, in some instances, have their origins outside the Indian subcontinent—include legendary or historical romances, fairy tales, and purely invented stories of fantasy, all of which reached the genre through the agency of the Parsee theater. Its most important legendary or historical tales include the well-known story of Raja Harishchandra as well as Padmavati, which have Hindu settings. South Asian Muslim fairy tales or romances include *Sabz Pari wa Gulfam* (better known as *Indra Sabha*), *Gul-i-Bakawali, Hawai-i-Majlis,* and *Laila Baba.* Also transmitted through the Parsee theater in Urdu/Hindustani versions, rather than in the original Arabic Persian, were several Middle and Near Eastern stories including the mystical romance *Laila Majnun* and stories from the *One Thousand and One Nights,* particularly Ali Baba and the Forty Thieves. More recent stories from literary sources as well as from Hindustani film include *Gulzar-i-Neki* and *Anarkali.* In bangsawan, unlike in the Parsee theater, no attempt was made to use original scripts of these tales. Instead, a great deal of improvization took place on the basic scenarios.

This trend of using legendary or historical stories, fairy tales, and romances from South Asia and the Middle or Near East (through South Asia), first introduced by the Parsee theater into bangsawan, continued into Malay films when the new medium of the cinema began to replace bangsawan in the mid-1930s. With the involvement of directors from Bombay or Madras and ideas for stories as well as production styles borrowed from subcontinental films, the South Asian influence continued into the mid-20th century. Beyond that era, although the practice of directly borrowing particular plots from erstwhile popular South Asian and Middle

Eastern sources diminished considerably, South Asian influences have remained ubiquitous and continue to be pervasive—their new sources being not Parsee theater or bangsawan, but the highly popular Hindustani films.

MYTHOLOGY

Unlike in Java and Bali, apart from the *Ramayana,* no religious texts or other writings connected with Hinduism or Buddhism have been discovered in the Malay Peninsula. This includes the mythology. Archaeological finds in the form of statues or deity images currently placed in museums such as the Archaeological Museum in the Bujang Valley complex, by no means substantial, add to our knowledge of the gods and goddesses who may have been introduced into the peninsula during the long period of Hindu and Buddhist influences until the arrival of Islam in the 14th century. The oral tradition of the Malays, and in particular the lore of the bomoh with roots in animism, indicates some awareness of the higher mythology of Hinduism, and clearly, there is a substantial corpus of myths and legends derived from the epics as previously mentioned. It is noteworthy, however, that outside the epic itself, the principal characters of the *Ramayana* have a separate mythic existence in the ritual context. Hanuman serves as the special guardian spirit or helper of certain bomoh or puppeteers. Seri Rama, Sita Dewi, Rawana, and Hanuman are associated with different locations of the environment and with the upper regions or heavens. In ritual wayang kulit Siam, together as host of animistic beings, they are invited through a trance medium to partake in the final feast offered upon the completion of performances intended for the initiation of puppeteers or the salutation of teachers.

If these characters represent a Vaishnava strand in the Malay belief system, a look at sources independent of the Ramayana makes it clear that Shiva as Bhattara Guru or as Nataraja and Ganesha, in particular, appear in invocations consecrating the theater, indicating some parallels and possible connections with rituals in Indian folk theater, in which these two gods also have highly significant roles. A goddess simply known as Dewi, apparently some kind of eponymous mother figure, also figures in certain bomoh rituals, once again echoing Hindu, and in particular Tantric, elements. It may be that this belief has colored the main puteri shamanic dance for puteri, meaning princess, is strongly suggestive of the possibility that the original performers of this shaman ritual were in fact females. Although now male-dominated, there still are female main puteri performers as well as signs that male shamans may have made a later appearance in the genre. Apart from these major deities, there is a strong presence of ogres, goblins (*raksasa,* cf. Sanskrit *rakshasha*), or bota (cf. Sanskrit *bhuta*) as well as numerous benevolent and violent spirits in rituals used in theater performances involving purification and healing as already demonstrated. The bomoh, when necessary, exorcise those connected with particular problems in his patient performers or call upon them occasionally to assist him personally, such as enhancing his charisma, making him irresistible to his audiences, or as a means of ensuring the success of performances in other ways. Actors and actresses involved in the major traditional dance-theater genres similarly seek the assistance of spirits, also termed *jin,* with similar intentions. Some of the more interesting ones—not belonging to traditional mythology or even to myths imported from Hindu and Buddhist sources, but invented by the storytellers or dramaturges—appear as supplementary characters in wayang kulit episodes, while in mak yong, which does not derive its repertoire from Indian sources, a number of these ogres and ogresses assume greater roles as characters within the stories. One of the most outstanding examples is the Ogre Princess (*Puteri Bota*) in the play entitled *Raja Tangkai Hati.* Later, through the influences from Islam as well as Middle Eastern literature featured in bangsawan, the word *jin* became familiar to Malay theater practitioners and audiences. The animistic and Hindu spirits were redesignated *jin.* Like the fairies (*peri*), they then became part of Islamic rather than Hindu mythology.

RITUAL PRACTICES

Due to the nature of their origins, Malay traditional theater genres are deeply rooted in a variety of beliefs, derived from animism, Hinduism, Buddhism, and Islam. The ritual proto-theater forms, in particular, betray the fundamental beliefs prevalent in the country prior to the arrival of the most significant external influences through the major religions. The genres, in particular, that are performed in situations requiring the involvement of a bomoh in the processes of healing—such as the three examples, belian, bagih, and main puteri, mentioned earlier—as well as ritual performances of the more elaborate shadow play and dance theater forms have to do with beliefs connected with the presence of spirits—malicious and benevolent—in the natural environment, as well as to beliefs related to the nature of the soul, to the spirit or the vital substance (*semangat*), to illnesses, and the manner of their treatment.

The arrival of Hinduism contributed another layer to this basic first level of belief by introducing Hindu concepts of spirits and deities, disease, and healing. The bomoh, now having to deal with these, thus became a master not just of the traditional spirits of his own culture, but also those that he now borrowed from the Hindu tradition. Possible elements of Tantrism have been noticed in the rituals of the Malay shaman: "Hinduism in Tantric form fortified the Malay shaman by corroborating the efficacy of fasting and seclusion and confirming the notion that trances bring supernatural power."[8] Given the strong Hindu influence, it is not surprising that some of the bomoh's invocations (*mantera,* from Sanskrit *mantra,* mystical formulae from the Veda) indicate his assumption of a superior role as possessor of spiritual power (*sakti,* cf. Sanskrit *shakti*) bestowed upon him by the Hindu gods, or as a *siddhi,* possibly a confusion in terms with *siddha.*[9] Acccording to Garrett, Siddhas are beings of an intermediate order between men and gods, while siddhis refer to eight faculties. These details are not generally spelt out by the Malay bomoh. Apart from being a part of healing rituals per se, these new concepts found their way into theater consecration rituals and even more so into rituals varieties of performances, thus turning the healer or shaman into a central figure in these special varieties of performances.

On the simplest level, ritual elements are seen in virtually every performance of traditional Malay theater. The principal objectives are to obtain the permission and goodwill of environmental spirits, teachers, and at times higher deities. This is usually done through extensive invocations. The goodwill of the invisible beings ensures that no mishap—such as illness of performers, who actually impersonate spirits and gods in their plays—takes place, and that audiences too are not affected in any negative manner. The activities involved in the opening of the theater (*buka panggung*) ritual ensure all this by propitiating the invisible entities and giving them offerings. The panggung building is cleansed with incense smoke and turmeric rice, and the performance can then take place. Invocation texts used vary between different genres, different bomoh, and even different localities due to local influences. Lakon chatri rituals, for instance, even if done in Malay communities, have invocations in the southern Thai dialect, some of them addressed to Mesi Mala, the female shaman who is said to have founded the genre; wayang kulit gedek invocations too feature strong Thai ritual elements. In the Malay genres, a sprinkling of texts in the Arabic language, verses from the Holy Quran, and names of Sufi saints and angels are included. Then, in virtually all genres, there are invocations to animistic environmental spirits as well as to figures from the pantheon of Hindu gods and spirits, as well as characters from the *Ramayana.* Needless to say, the overall picture is a highly complex one given the multiple layers of spiritual influences that have colored these genres of traditional theater since ancient times.

Rituals connected with the opening of the theater, and following them, such as the introductory section of the wayang kulit Siam performance (*dalang muda* or young puppeteer's section) and the opening dance and song sequence (*mengadap rebab*) in mak yong, continue to reiterate this connection of the traditional performing arts with the divine, at times disguising the whole process through highly interesting symbolism. In *mengadap rebab,* for instance, the mystery of the guru lies subsumed, in essence, in the three-stringed rebab, mak yong's lead instrument.

Performances, on the other hand, become or turn totally into rituals on particular occasions. Such rituals performances may be seen in terms of three categories: (1) annual or periodic performances to pay homage to ancestors and teachers (guru); (2) similar performances for the purpose of restoring an artist's *semangat* when necessary; and (3) occasional performances for purposes of exorcism and healing done at the request of a patient or his family, involving angin (literally wind), but in fact referring to illnesses caused by emotional or psychological upheavals or suppressed urges or desires, including the desire to perform mak yong, particular kinds of dances, etc., due to obsessive identification with particular characters from the traditional repertoire of stories.

One of the key concepts that came with Hinduism, possibly modified in Java to some extent, is the idea of the guru in Hindu tradition, representative and vehicle of divine owner, and therefore entitled to receive the most implicit obedience from his disciples. As in Indian traditional arts, an apprentice performer is not entitled to do independent performances unless he has paid homage to the teacher through a special ritual performance. Tradition links this teacher, and all teachers, to the first, original or ultimate guru (*guru yang asal guru yang mula*); the *adiguru* often remains unnamed. From him or her, as seen in the case of Mesi Mala, the bomoh or artist claims to have inherited his art, be it the art of the theater or that of the healer. The most important traditional performing arts forms are traced to divine or semidivine beings, eponymous ancestors, and human teachers who form such a link in a chain reaching back to the ultimate teacher, sometimes with the Prophet Adam (Nabi Adam), as the first performer, himself occupying the penultimate position. As in Indonesia and in Malaysia, this original or ultimate guru sometimes gets identified with Semar, the principal comic figure in Javanese traditional theater, who in reality is believed to be a god in clown appearance. Javanese attempts to "trace" the origins of Semar have led to interesting theories linking him with the gods in the sky country (*Kayangan*) and with Shiva or Betara Guru (cf. Sanskrit *Bhattara Guru*), who is regarded as his brother. Without any doubt, the mud-covered Semar is seen as a god in base earthly disguise; his amorphous shape and his dark or jet black color suggesting in dual symbolism of his connections with heaven as well as earth, as also does his character as an androgynous being.

In Islamic Malaysia, the name of this ultimate guru is never mentioned in performances even though homage is paid to him. One suspects, however, in spite of the significance of the Javanese variant of this picture—connecting the ultimate teacher with Semar—the ultimate teacher with the unmentioned or unutterable name is none other than Shiva. To fend off accusation of wrong doing, or possibly out of genuine ignorance of the reality that, in fact, it is Shiva who is present in their rituals, performers express the view, albeit rarely and with considerable hesitation, that this ultimate guru is in fact God (Tuhan). This device—the use of the name Tuhan instead of Allah, the proper Islamic name for God—clearly allows them to skirt the central issue, for the mention of Allah in this context would be blasphemous from the Islamic point of view.

Following his encounter with Islam, the Malay bomoh was to appropriate certain beliefs and practices from the new religion, further enriching his rituals. Apart from certain Sufi beliefs, the influence of Islam is reflected, once again, in invocation texts in the form of the Basmala and selected verses from the Holy Quran. The bomoh now claims that any attempt on the part of unfriendly entities to bring failure to his role as healer or ritual specialist would, in fact, be frowned upon or even punished by Allah, for the perpetrator of such a crime would, in fact, be disobedient or disloyal (*derhaka*) to Allah, and thus merit divine punishment. Allah is thus perceived as protector of the bomoh. To use a phrase borrowed from Winstedt, the Malay bomoh was now no longer just shaman and Saiva, but also Sufi. Despite this apparent shift from one belief system to another, the Hindu elements stand vastly apparent, even dominant, in the theater rituals alongside Islamic elements.

AESTHETIC CONCEPTS

Traditional Malay theater genres can be described as presentational rather than representational. This is particularly obvious in bangsawan, but, typically, the term "presentational" also characterizes the styles of various dance theater forms and even the shadow play. The manner of staging—including acting techniques, set designs where used, makeup, etc.—make this conclusion inevitable. The very notion of realistic representation is, of course, as in many non-Western societies, a fairly modern importation from the West and something not necessarily in keeping with local cultures and worldviews.

As already seen, the plays of traditional Malay theater are by and large fantasies or romances with value as entertainment or as vehicles for the teaching of social, moral, or religious values. Tragedy and comedy—not in themselves counters for classification of dramatic texts, for as in Indian theater, no true tragedy is to be found in the Malay repertoire—are certainly present in an admixture in most plays. The plays, in some sense, adhere to the Indian concept of heroic drama (*nataka*), with love and heroism as central themes. Plots are characteristically extensive, discursive, and episodic in character, allowing for the presentation of selected episodes rather than full plays. This is particularly true where a story, dance, vocal and instrumental music, as well as stylized acting are indispensable elements, to the extent that even the shadow play that makes no use of human actors does have a semblance of dance in the movements of the figures—movements that, in a sense, are choreographed.

Characters, with few exceptions, in keeping with the repertoire, are derived from mythology and fantasy, and, even when scripts are based upon historical events as in some of the bangsawan plays, no attempt is made at realism in the delineation of characters. They are, instead, presented in a stereotyped manner, as in much Asian theater, with the concepts of the hero and heroine based almost entirely upon Indian models or, depending upon the story, upon a combination of Indian and Middle Eastern models, particularly when the influence of Sufism makes itself felt. Gods and goddesses, fairies, ogres, and animals often rub shoulders with human characters, thus precluding any realism in their presentation. The hero is a divine or semidivine being, or alternatively a legendary figure. He has his close confidante, and the idealized heroine, whether semidivine or human, has her companions as do the heroines of Indian folk and classical plays. When noncontemporary stories are selected, the Indian cinema, itself an inheritor of ideas and techniques from the Parsee theater, serves as a model.

Here and there, in writings on Southeast Asian performing arts, occur allusions, mostly in passing, at the possible influences of South Asian aesthetic concepts and ideas upon the region's dance, in particular, and traditional theater. *Natyasastra,* the ancient work on Indian dramaturgy, attributed to Bharata Muni, thus becomes the point of departure for the analysis of the region's performing arts. While, given the undeniable intensity of South Asian influences upon the region's traditional performing arts, this may seem a valid approach, it, nonetheless, needs to be questioned for in it lie couched the assumptions that, by and large, Southeast Asian traditional performing arts are, firstly, devoid of originality and, secondly, homogenous. This is not to deny the South Asian impact in several important areas of traditional theater, as this chapter has demonstrated. Additionally, such influences are apparent in dance, in music, in costumes, in concepts related to stage designs, as well as in the carved figures of the shadow play, occurring, by and large, in clear combination with features from other cultures—Middle and Near Eastern, Thai, Javanese, as well as in the more recently developed bangsawan theater, Western—all placed upon an indigenous base. Some of the traditional Malay genres cited in this chapter have already given a picture of their multicultural character.

As far as aesthetics is concerned, two items, specifically, have been given considerable importance in this "Indian" approach to Southeast Asian performing arts: *abhinaya* and the *rasa* theory. While to some extent Southeast Asian dances have been described, albeit not adequately enough, from the perspective of *abhinaya,* the available picture is far from complete. It is even less so in the traditional theater. This is also the case with the use of the *rasa* theory. The suitability or otherwise of this theory, highly important in Indian aesthetics, for an examination of Malay, and even in Indonesian arts forms, has yet to be adequately determined. The use of the word "rasa" for emotions, feelings, and sentiments certainly belongs to the broader fund of borrowed words in the vocabulary of Malay Indonesian languages and dialects, words that come from a wide spectrum of languages. It is thus tempting to assume that the aesthetic concept of rasa is also to be found in Malay Indonesian art forms. While there is no denying that this may ultimately prove to be true, at this point in time, such a connection must remain but tentative.

An important alternative entry into an examination of almost any of the traditional performing arts forms, as well as to their particular components, and beyond that, broadly, of all art forms, is the concept of *halus-kasar,* refined and coarse. An understanding of this concept and its manifestations is as vital to an appreciation of Malay Indonesian arts as is that of rasa to approaching South Asian arts. In the Kelantan shadow play, the Seri Rama puppet is the example of a *halus* figure par excellence. In this context, the term *halus* applies not just to the physical form of the figure, but also to the hero's character, his nobility, his conduct as a person, his manner of movement, his language, and so on. The opposite, essentially negative, concept of *kasar* would apply to the figure of Ravana, generally considered the epitome of evil. It is evident that, while in the designs of puppet figures or the physical preparation of actors and actresses representing these characters in the human theater (in Javanese or Balinese wayang wong, for instance), one may see reflected elements of iconography seen in Indian counterparts of these characters, their development in the Malay Indonesian region certainly reflects a fusion of indigenous, South Asian, and other foreign elements. The Malay traditional theater forms have certainly evolved through such syncretism.

CONCLUSION

There is much, therefore, that may be discerned as common between Indian and Malay traditional theater forms, particularly through the spread of religious ideas and rituals, literatures, as well as art forms. The possibility has, nevertheless, to be constantly borne in mind that certain elements of traditional Malay theater may, in fact, be indigenous rather than Indian, as shown through commonalities and parallels with other forms within the Southeast Asian region. This may also be the case with aesthetics. For instance, the vital concept of rasa, a fundamental aspect of Indian aesthetics, may not altogether reflect Malay apperceptions of art and beauty. It would, consequently, not make much sense to impose the rasa concept upon the Malay traditional theater, with the danger that something not actually present in it may, in fact, be seen to exist through an overfertile imagination or an inordinate desire to search for connections. Given the universality of feelings and emotions and the fact that emotions find overt, even uninhibited, expression in many Asian cultures, something inevitably manifested in the art of the theater, it may well be necessary, given our present concern with traditional Malay theater genres, to seek new ways to examine the manner in which Malay performers as well as their immediate neighbors themselves view emotions and their expression in the arts. This would also be the case in virtually every aspect of Malay traditional theater. Thus, while there is demonstrable evidence of a high degree of borrowing, of strong cultural and artistic influences from South Asia, it appears, all the same, that for a complete picture vis-á-vis traditional Malay theater, one has to remain open to other possibilities.

NOTES

1. For details regarding the various kinds of theater performances mentioned in this chapter, refer to Ghulam-Sarwar Yousof, *Dictionary of Traditional South-East Asian Theatre* (Singapore: Oxford University Press, 1994).
2. Jacques Brunet, "Attempt at a Historical Outline of the Shadow Theatres" in Mohd Taib Osman, ed., *Traditional Drama and Music of Southeast Asia* (Kuala Lumpur: Dewan Bahasa dan Pustaka, 1974), pp. 127–29.
3. James R. Brandon, *Theatre in Southeast Asia* (Cambridge, MA: Harvard University Press, 1967), pp. 42, 43.
4. Muhammad Ismail Marcinkowski, *From Isfahan to Ayutthaya: Contacts between Iran & Siam in the 17th Century* (Singapore: Pustaka National Pte Ltd, 2005).
5. Ibid., pp. 56, 57.
6. Jayadeva Tilakasiri, *The Asian Shadow Play* (Ratmalana: Vishva Lekha, 1999), pp. 19–26.
7. The Panji stories dealing with the adventures of Raden Inu Kertapati and Galuh Chandra Kirana came into being in the 15th century in East Java. From there, they spread into the Malay peninsula as well as into Thailand and Cambodia in slightly different versions as a result of localization. The romances are used in several traditional theater forms in Java, Bali, Cambodia, and Thailand.
8. Richard Winstedt, *The Malay Magician, Being Shaman, Saiva and Sufi* (London: Routledge and Kegan Paul, 1951), p. 28.
9. John Garrett, *A Classical Dictionary of India* (New Delhi: Rupa & Co., 2000), p. 514.

Chapter 8

Javanese Narrations of Rāmāyaṇa and Mahābhārata: Products of a Peaceful Process of Integration

Malini Saran

Peace has never been more urgent than in today's multipolar, multicivilizational world where the politics of religion, race, and economic development escalate international conflicts. In the Preface to his influential 1996 book *The Clash of Civilisations and the Remaking of World Order,*[1] Samuel Huntington qualifies his thesis by saying that he has been exposed to "all the major civilizations except Hinduism." It might be useful, then, to pause and reflect on non-Western civilizational encounters in world history, specifically between India and Indonesia, in the period before the evolution of modern nation-states.

From the beginning of the Common Era, the language of Sanskrit and Indian literatures traveled to Afghanistan, Tibet, and China, and to East and Southeast Asia. Over time, it became the cultural property of Buddhist countries such as Burma, Cambodia, Thailand, and Vietnam—and, most relevant to this chapter, the property of the Indonesian archipelago, especially the island of Java.

Globalization, as we know, is the 20th-century version of something that started 2,000 years ago, when overland and maritime trading routes from Rome to China were active, with a steady stream of people carrying not only precious goods such as silk, spices, ivory, and gold, but equally precious handwritten manuscripts in a script never before seen in Southeast Asia. These manuscripts, written in the sacred language of Sanskrit, contained new systems of political and religious thought, Hindu and Buddhist ritual and cultural practices, art and architecture, and a poetry and literature so vast and beautiful that it gripped the imagination of the poets and raconteurs of Southeast Asia.

In Java, the epic literatures of Rāmāyaṇa and Mahābhārata were absorbed as a legitimate cultural motif within the frameworks of different religious practices—Shaivite, Vaishnavite, syncretic Shiva Buddhistic adaptations, and explorations of Tantra. Less well known is the story of its peaceful transition from a Hindu Buddhist social milieu into an Islamic framework, and of how the stories of Rama, and the great war of the Bharatas, became the staple diet of a largely Muslim population on the island of Java.

This chapter discusses how the Hindu icons of Rama and Krishna were skillfully and peacefully transformed into cultural heroes in Indonesia, and how they acquired an iconic but secular status in the largely Muslim society of a different land. The little island of Bali is intentionally left out of this discussion because its Hindu identity remained intact even when Javanese courts adopted Islam in the 16th century.

The scope of this chapter allows only a brief overview of the huge body of works that represent Rāmāyaṇa and Mahābhārata in their diverse manifestations, to emphasize their unbroken longevity in Java. The classical Old Javanese language scholar Supomo observes that, in the poetic literature discussed in Zoetmulder's survey of *belles lettres*, more than half have heroes and heroines from Mahābhārata as their main characters.[2] This chapter selects a few narrations from literature and sculpture to illustrate the increasing integration with the Hindu Buddhist Javanese ethos between the 10th and 15th centuries, and discusses literary references and *wayang* (shadow puppet) theater plays to demonstrate how the stories of the Rāmāyaṇa and Mahābhārata were equally assimilated into the Islamic mould over the next half-century.

Both Rāmāyaṇa and Mahābhārata were borne to Indonesia not by conquering armies or fervent missionaries, but by the tide of a powerful intellectual and religious movement that by 400 CE was sweeping over Southeast Asia. This peaceful, dynamic movement bore a vast body of knowledge that included religious art and architecture, political philosophy, and literature in the highly developed language of Sanskrit, written in a script unknown in Southeast Asia. The first Sanskrit inscription on a stele appeared in Vietnam, recording a temple dedicated to Valmiki where daily recitation of Rāmāyaṇa and Mahābhārata occurred.

But it was in Java that the deepest fascination for this body of knowledge was suddenly on display in the middle of the ninth century, when an efflorescence of Hindu temples appeared on the plains of Central Java. In the largest of them known as Prambanan, we witness the sculptural depiction of a complete Rama story in the Shiva and Brahma temples and a Krishna story in the Vishnu temple—in a way that combined a mature understanding of Indian tradition with a rare genius for its uniquely Javanese interpretation. The same qualities are evident in a superb work of Old Javanese poetic literature that appeared coevally, known as the Rāmāyaṇa *kakawin* or the Old Javanese Rāmāyaṇa. It is the first full-length literary classic created in Java. Both works were sponsored by the king of the Sanjay dynasty and were clearly rooted in the Hinduized culture of the Central Javanese court. However close these works were to their Indian source at this stage, Javanese sensibility left a discernible stamp on the final product. This was the first and last time that a complete Rāmāyaṇa would be illustrated in temple sculpture in Java. The nature of Javanese tradition dictated that hereafter only selected episodes would be depicted.

Kakawin, the Javanese equivalent of Sanskrit *kavya,* was a poetic work written in Old Javanese, a language that drew heavily on Sanskrit to enrich its vocabulary, syntax, and prosody. Rāmāyaṇa *kakawin* was modeled on the Sanskrit *Ravanavadha* by Bhatti, hence known as *Bhattikavya,* and written in Gujarat *circa* seventh century, which was not only a narration of the Rama story along Valmikian lines, but also a vehicle to illustrate some of the more complicated rules of Sanskrit grammar. In the hands of the Old Javanese poet, it became not a translation but an extraordinary transcreation, a literary *tour de force,* and one that exerted a major influence on literature, political, and moral philosophy and the performing and plastic arts in the islands of Java and Bali.[3]

The Prambanan reliefs stand as the most comprehensive illustration of the Rama story from the Balakanda to the Uttarakanda, in that period anywhere in the world. Both *kakawin* and the sculptural telling were sponsored by the king in a court and are clearly Shaivite in their orientation. While they were born in the same cultural ethos, and could be even contemporaneous, one does not seem to have been based on the other. They are often dissimilar in their treatment of the story; the most obvious being the *kakawin* ends with the coronation of Rama and Sita, whereas the temple sculpture goes on to depict the final canto of the epic, the Uttarakanda.

In their choice and portrayal of episodes too, there are marked differences, but what unifies them is the fact that both works are intrinsically Javanese. While the *kakawin* is heavily influenced by the Sanskrit poetics and prosody in the work of its Indian counterpart *Bhattikavya,* and the temple forms and sculptural style are of Indian inspiration, the crafting of both is in essence Javanese. With their changed emphasis and characterization, these works could only have been produced in Java. The enhanced dramatic elements evident in both creations are reminiscent of the performance arts. The depictions of flora and fauna, the clothes, jewelry, the posture of sitting bear, and a Javanese flavor—e.g., Sita's abduction taking place in a Javanese household and Rama shooting at a row of seven coconut trees, commonly found in Java rather than the *sala* trees of Valmiki—are all situated in Java. Indian rules have been applied in the portrayal of Javanese ideals of beauty of the human form or in nature. In the *kakawin,* it is through the cultivation of beauty or *kalangwon* that the poet builds his temple of words.[4]

Certain emphases are shared that remain key features of the Rāmāyaṇa narrative in Java for the next 1,000 years. What makes both works unique is their portrayal of the main characters and their role in the episodes chosen. The characters of Rama and Sita are shown in royal attire, not in the forester's garb, as described in the *kakawin*. Rama is seen as the heroic valiant king who embodies valor and justice, fighting against evil with outstanding valor. Sita in the *kakawin* is the loyal but outspoken wife with a mind of her own, and when wronged by her husband, he is defended by an equally spirited companion Trijata, the daughter of Wibhisana. In the reliefs, Hanuman (the loyal monkey) and the giant *rakshasa* Kumbharkarna, battling unto death for his brother Ravana, receive much attention; the latter appearing in 3 of a total of 30 reliefs, more frequently than Ravana, the king of Lanka. These traits become increasingly significant with the passage of the centuries, so that in the *wayang* plays by the 19th century, the giant Kumbhakarna becomes a major character synonymous with fraternal loyalty—"my brother right or wrong," and the personification of physical might and valor.

Certain exchanges between characters go on to become central to Javanese political culture. One such in the *kakawin* is the extensive discourse on *nitishastra*[5] delivered by Rama to Wibhisana, paralyzed with grief for his dead brother, Ravana, whom he had earlier abandoned because of his wickedness. Rama praises the fallen brother, but urges Wibhisana to put his grief behind him, perform the last rites for his dead brother, and then assume the throne of Lanka and his duties as a king. Under the title *Asthta-brata* (the eightfold meritorious act), the discourse goes on for 40 verses, elaborating on the merits of 8 divinities that are embodied in the king and should be his role models. For example, these are the eight gods to be followed: Indra, Yama, Surya, Chandra, Anila, Kubera, Baruna, and Agni—Indra for his generosity in giving rain to his people, Yama for punishing evildoers, Surya for taxing people in a gentle way as the sun absorbs water, Chandra for kindness and tenderness, Anila for investigating the conduct and character of people, Kubera for enjoying the pleasures of life without excess, Baruna for sternness to the wicked, and Agni who can burn and destroy the enemy.[6] Rama then calls upon Wibhisana to pay close attention to the rules set out by Manu. The *Ashta-brata* became the best-known text on kingship in the courts of Java for centuries and retains that status until today, and the Old Javanese Rāmāyaṇa went on to become the single most influential literary work created in Java.

This idea of redemption in reading the Rāmāyaṇa aloud was firmly rooted in Javanese culture and its echoes are heard down the centuries beginning with the Old Javanese Rāmāyaṇa:

> May the story of Rama which contains excellent words [of guidance], be like fragrance that penetrates the hearts [of men]. The great yogins will become proficient [in the Vedas], the good people will obtain a pure mind after reading it. If it is read to the unfortunate people, be they high or low in rank, they will understand it beyond doubt, which will lead them to heavenly Bliss.[7]

The custom of the patron king identifying with the deity invoked in the work persisted through the centuries. Among the benefits of recitation, the empowerment of the king in a political and spiritual sense was a major reward. Religious state ceremonies and rituals were closely connected with performances based on the epics of recitation, theater, and dance.

The Vishnu temple in the complex illustrates the story of Krishna, although no literary work on the Mahābhārata is known for this period. Neither was there a literary equivalent of the Uttarkanda, although episodes from it were illustrated on the walls of the Brahma temple. Both burst onto the scene a hundred years late in a distinct genre known as the *parwa* literature.

At the end of the 10th century, King Dharmawangsa Teguh Anantawikramottunggadewa of East Java presided over an historic enterprise in his court—the creation of the *parwa* literature. These were prose adaptations into Old Javanese of the original Sankrit *parwas* of the Mahābhārata. The Uttarakanda, the seventh and final *kanda* of Valmiki's Rāmāyaṇa, was included in this exercise.

By this inspired act, a new and influential genre of literature was born. Only 9 of the 18 *parwas* of Mahābhārata have come down to us,[8] and we may never know whether the others were lost or never completed. The final *parwa,* the Uttarakanda, is an unusual categorization, as we know it to be the seventh and final *kanda* of Valmiki Rāmāyaṇa. The *parwa* literature played a pivotal role in the dissemination and understanding of Mahābhārata and Rāmāyaṇa to the Javanese people.

Only four parwas (*Uttarakanda parwa, Adiparwa, Wirataparwa,* and *Bhishmaparwa*) have an introduction that eulogizes the name of the king, Sri Dharmawangsa Teguh Anantawikramottunggadewa, under whose patronage they were written. They are ascribed to different authors. In fact, this king is identified in the beginning of the Adiparwa with Shiva himself, to whom homage is paid. The god is credited with regenerating the world after its destruction, which begins through the mystical union with his consort on the summit of Mount Kailash.

Like the *kakawin* literature in Java, the *parwas* too were considered sacred, as the commencement of the recital of *Wirataparwa* and its end was recorded in a conversation between the king and a Brahmin, which leads us to the precise date of October 14–November 12 in 996 CE. In the *Wirataparwa*, the introduction is first addressed to Krishna Dwaipayana, who is the same as Vyasa, the mythical author of the Mahābhārata, asking that "he may be a source of blessing to him who is going to render the Wirata story into the vernacular."[9] The Bhismaparwa also opens with an act of homage to Vyasa and then to the king of the island of Yawa, who is eminently worthy of bearing the name of Hari. "He can be called Hari because he Wisnu being a bearer of Śri; because he is a protector of the world; because he is a lion."[10] In the Uttarakanda, Valmiki, the author of Rāmāyaṇa, is first praised and then homage is paid to King Dharmawangsa, who, because of his heroic nature and power, dominates the world and churns it, so that the elixir of life issues forth and inundates his realm in abundance like an ever flowing fountain. The fact that Dharmawangsa Teguh is identified in the manggala of these *parwa* with the power of both Vishu and Shiva suggests a relaxed inclusivity of religious belief that allows both gods to be enlisted in the cause of furthering the prestige and power of the king. It also reiterates the belief that literature is like a temple in words. It is interesting to recall that in the Prambanan temples, the Rama story is depicted on the Shiva and Brahma temples, but the Krishna tale is illustrated in the Vishu temple.

The *parwas* in Java are simple, direct, and lucid translations into Old Javanese prose of the original Sanskrit books (called *parvas* in Sanskrit) and adapted to be comprehensible to ordinary people. They were often shortened in length and "whole fragments probably considered less relevant to the main purport of the story have been left out."[11] Snatches of Sanskrit *ślokas* are embedded throughout to enhance its magical and sacred character, to heighten its sanctity, and add to its prestige and authenticity. Although its stories were already well known in Central Java as seen by their illustrations on the stone balustrades of the Brahma temple in Prambanan, it was perhaps felt necessary to give the stories a literary form. It is interesting that the distinction between the two epics has blurred, as the Uttarakanda *parwa* is part of the body of the Mahābhārata *parwas*. The Uttarakanda *parwa* has kept largely to the Sanskrit original. This particular reservoir of stories ignited the creativity of poets, sculptors, and performance artists for generations to come. These *parwas* were a reservoir of stories for the *wayang kulit* or shadow puppet theater and known as *wayang purwa*. When the genealogies were being reconstituted to include the kings of Java for the *wayang* repertoire, its focus perhaps was on genealogies that explain this classification of Uttarakanda as a *parwa*. It presages the development in the Javanese *wayang* literature during the Islamic period that would historically link the Rāmāyaṇa with the Mahābhārata in the framework of lineage. In a later period, the Javanese *suluks* would replace the Sanskrit singing of *ślokas*.

A remarkable feature of Rāmāyaṇa and Mahābhārata from their very first mention in an inscription dated 907 CE is their popularity. Written in Old Javanese, this inscription issued by King Balitung confirms the granting of freehold land to the monastery of Dalinan.[12] A variety of performances marked the celebration of this event that may have been the most important for the whole region. The performances include singing (*mamidu*), play acting (*mamirus*), clowning (*mabanol*), a spectacle with songs in which a certain Nalu recited the story of Bhimakumara and danced as Kicaka (*macaritaken Bhimakumara manigel Kicaka*), a recitation of Rāmāyaṇa by Jaluk (*macarita Rāmāyaṇa*), and a *wayang* performance by Galigi with the story of Bhimakumara (*mawayari buat hyan macarita Bhima ya kumara*).

The use of the word "*macarita*" is revealing. Its meaning, Supomo the reputed scholar of Old Javanese explains, is to tell a story and is often used in the sense of "to recite a prose work at a performance."[13] He suggests that the narrator of the Bhimakumara episode recited a Sanskrit text and then explained it in Javanese to the audience. He compares it to the Indian institution of *harikatha* or public reading of the epics and the Puranas by trained masters of the art, in which a priest reads and explains a religious story in the common language to his audience. This seemed to have been a popular pastime, as it took a couple of weeks to complete the story and the audience met for a few hours every evening in a temple. It was possibly the method by which ordinary people who could not access classical literature in Sanskrit became familiar with the Rama story. Such was the method also employed in Java, and in Bali even today, when people gather at *mbasan* to listen to the recital of a poem in Old Javanese and its interpretation by an expert in the local dialect of Balinese.

The precise episode is from Rāmāyaṇa; whether it is Valmiki or the Old Javanese is not mentioned, but that it is Rāmāyaṇa is not disputed. In the case of Bhimakumara, Indian scholar H. B. Sarkar suggests he might be "the son of Bhima," i.e., Gatotkaca, but others disagree and think it could be "the young Bhima" or Bhima as lover.[14] Whatever the precise reference, it seems logical to infer from this royal inscription that in the first decade of the 10th century at the latest, stories based on episodes from the epics were an important part of the shadow puppet theater and other performing arts. To this day, Bima (as Bhima is now known) and his son Gatotkaca are continuing favorites of the Javanese people. In the 12th-century Kediri court, a complete *kakawin*, known as *Gatotkacasraya*, was dedicated to the exploits of this hero. In this story, Gatotkaca is abetting Arjuna's son, Abhimanyu, in the pursuit of his beloved Siti Sundari, Krishna's daughter, in opposition to Baladewa, Krishna's brother, who is against the marriage.

A remarkable feature of the *Gatotkacasraya* is the first appearance of *panakawans,* the clownish but astute old servants in a Javanese literary work. Said to have their origins in Javanese folklore, they are the mainstay of a *wayang* performance with their humor, playful roguishness, and childish pranks, which they combine with utterances of divine wisdom. They are mentors of the hero, and their appearance is the hallmark of Javanese authorship.

With the death of Dharmawangsa and his nobles in 1016 CE in an attack on the *kraton,* a period of chaos ensued. This ended when one of East Java's most famous kings rose to power, Airlangga. This king patronized Shaivites, Mahāyāna Buddhists, and rishis or ascetics. But he, like other kings of this era, identified himself predominantly with avatars of Vishnu, the god whose duty was to protect the world and to free it from evil powers. Airlangga was known for his practice of penance to enhance his power and increase the prestige of the court, which inspired the creation of a classic work of Old Javanese literature, *Arjunawiwaha.* The asceticism of Arjuna in the *kakawin* is a reference to its real-life counterpart in Airlangga. Once again an episode from one of the *parwas*—the Vanaparwa—is taken as the barest outline, and an elaborate and original story is woven around complete with fresh plots and new characters.

This famous and deeply cherished *kakawin,* known as *Arjunawiwahawa* (Arjuna's nuptials), was composed probably to honor the marriage of the king. Its subject matter is Arjuna's penance on Mount Indrakila for obtaining the magic weapon *Pashupati.* Indra dressed as a hunter visits Arjuna to test his motives for doing penance and, in the conversation that follows, instructs him on the true meaning of power and pleasure. On a hunt in the forest, Arjuna clashes with Shiva in the form of a hunter, when they claim the same boar. A dispute follows, and then a struggle in which Arjuna proves himself worthy, Shiva grants him the invaluable Pashupati weapon that will be his most powerful one in the war against the Kurawas. Arjuna vanquishes the demon Niwata Kawaka whose secret weapon lies at the tip of his tongue. (His name is borrowed from the Niwatakaca group of demons well known in Indian mythology and mentioned in the *Wanaparwa*). Finally, Arjuna's sojourn in the heavenly abode sporting with the heavenly maidens as a reward for overcoming the demon is described.

Very different from the Rāmāyaṇa *kakawin* that was written a century earlier, this *kakawin* heralds a new trend in Javanese literature. The Javanese poets take the barest outline from Indian sources and embroider them with fresh plots and new characters. As no definitive known source can be ascribed to this highly inventive *kakawin,* scholars have pointed to a possible infusion from *wayang lakon* tradition of stories. In a typical *wayang* performance, the subject matter is often altered to suit the patron's circumstances, which may have inspired the parallels in the *kakawin* of

Arjuna's asceticism with the practice of penance of the royal patron King Airlangga to enhance his power and prestige.

Two centuries later, this story would be etched into stone reliefs in the temple of Surawana in East Java; and in the 18th century, during the Islamic period, this *kakawin* would inspire poets to create the mystical character of Minta Raga who became the counterpart of Bima Suci, known for his search for the water of life and quest for esoteric wisdom.

In the interest of a peaceful succession, King Airlangga divided his kingdom into two before his death in the middle of the 11th century. The court of Kediri became the more powerful where many *kakawins* were composed, earning this period the reputation of "the golden age" of *kakawin* literature. Only one *kakawin, Sumanasantaka* written at this time, chose a story distantly related to Rāmāyaṇa for its subject—that of Aja, the grandfather of Rama, and his beloved queen Indumati. The theme of several *kakawins* in this period revolves around Krishna, e.g., *Hariwangsa, Krishnayana,* and *Bhomatanka.*

It was not until the middle of the 12th century that a *kawi rajya* or court poet under the patronage of King Jayabhaya undertook the task of composing a *kakawin* based on the Mahābhārata. Known as the *Bharatayuddha* or the war among the Bharatas, it was in the words of the poet "the war between the Pandawas and the king of the Korawas," beginning from the Krishna's mission to Hastina to the complete victory of the Pandawas. The writing was started by one poet Mpu Sedah, but completed by another Mpu Panuluh.

The Old Javanese *Bharatayuddha* is a greatly pruned version of the Sanskrit Mahābhārata. The 20,000 stanzas that comprise 6 *parwas* have been reduced to 711, and only the barest outline of the most significant events of the war are retained, while all nonessential episodes and digressions are omitted. Supomo tells us, in his detailed study of the text, that the first parts of the *Bharatayuddha* are more dependent on the *parwas* than the original Sanskrit Mahābhārata. An astonishing omission in this telling is the absence of the *Bhagavad Gita,* despite the fact that Krishna's admonitions to Arjuna at Kurukshetra constitute a considerable part of the Old Javanese Bhismaparwa. Yet, the poet Sedah spends no more than 2 lines in Canto 10 on this teaching.

> As for the Pandavas they ranged themselves in the battle array of the sharp pointed thunderbolt. Arjuna, Bhima and Shikhandi were ensconsed in front, Sweta Stayai and Dhrshtadhumya were at the rear, Yuddhisthira and all the kings were in the centre. (11)
>
> As Arjuna looked about him he was visibly overwhelmed by emotions and sadness, for his enemies were all relatives, not a single stranger among them. There were cousins from both sides of his parents, as well as uncles, foremost among them being Krpa, Salya, Bhishma and his teacher Drona. (12)

> This was why he spoke to Krishna imploring him to prevent the war, for he was filled with compassion at the sight of the Korawas. But Krishna earnestly urged him to fight with all his might for it was forbidden for a ksatriya to withdraw from the battlefield. (13)[15]

Another noteworthy difference from the Indian Mahābhārata tradition, Supomo points out, is when Krishna arrives in Hastinapur, which gives the poet the opportunity to describe the *nagara* and how the people, especially the womenfolk, flock to the observation stands to welcome him. The lengthy conversation on *dharma, artha,* and *kama,* which occurs in Mbh 5.90–91 between Krishna and Vidura, is dispensed within two lines. Instead, the poet spends 25 stanzas on descriptions of nature and amorous sport. A great deal of attention is paid to the presence of women in the battlefield—Draupadi takes part in the march of the two armies into the battlefield. Apart from Draupadi, seven other women are mentioned by name—Kunti, Subhadra, Hidimbi, and Uttari are known, but three others are unknown figures: Ksitisundari, who is Abhimanyu's second wife (14.5c); Sitisundari (15.7a, 12a), Salya' s wife (38.1b); and Sugandhika, the maidservant of Satyawati (44.5b; 45. b). When the heroes die on the battlefield, there are scenes in which women take the center stage.

Another Javanese invention is seen in the account of the killing of Salya by Yuddhisthira with a magical book:

> Thereupon Kṛṣṇa enjoined the son of Dharma to discharge his book, and the latter, not aware of what he had to do, was glad to comply with the request. He swiftly grasped his weapon, the book Kalimahosadha, and successfully transformed it into a blazing lance. (42.5)
>
> Then he was struck down by the excellent weapon in the form of a book which was gleaming and luminous for it was a staff of jewels and gold. It pierced through his breast and like a rainbow it drank his blood that gushed forth. Such was its power. Salyas's soul then returned to the abode of the gods. (42.8)[16]

Centuries later, in the Islamic context, this magical weapon will be integrated into an Islamic story.[17]

In the court of the Majapahit era king, Hyam Wuruk, in the second half of the 14th century, two *kakawins* related to Uttarakanda were composed by the poet Tantular, although Rama does not figure in either. One was the noteworthy *Arjunwijaya* (the victory of Arjuna) and the other *Harisraya,* less well known. *Arjunawijaya* concerns itself not with the Arjuna of Mahābhārata but with the 1,000-armed Arjunasasrabahu, who vanquishes Ravana prior to his misadventures with Rama. The *kakawin* starts with the genealogy of Ravana, the descendent of the god Brahma via his father the sage Wisrawa, and his doings before he meets Rama. It then turns to King

Arjunasasrabahu, from which point onward only the skeleton of the story comes from Uttarakanda. Most of the rest is poetic invention. The encounter with Ravana occurs at the point when Arjunasasrabahu, true to his name, assumes his 1,000-armed *trivikrama* form across the river Narbada, to form a lake for the pleasure of his wife and her companions, in which they can swim and amuse themselves. This causes a flood upstream where Ravana is at his prayers. Enraged at being disturbed, Ravana wages war on Arjuna. In the violent battle that follows, Suwandha, Arjuna's prime minister, determined not to disturb his royal master disporting in the river with his wife, lays down his life. His fearlessness, loyalty, and ultimate sacrifice has earned him lasting fame among the Javanese people, endowing him with the status of the ideal serviteur for a king. Ravana is overpowered, bound in chains, and put in a cage. In the meantime, Queen Chitrawati commits suicide having heard false reports that her husband is dead. But she is restored to life by the goddess Narbada, and Ravana's grandfather, the great sage Pulastya, arrives to successfully plead for the life of his vanquished and disgraced grandson, which is graciously granted. Arjuna urges Ravana to abandon arrogance and conceit in his powers "for these qualities are not proper for a king."[18] The *kakawin* ends happily with the great sage's magical power reviving the fallen soldiers. While the story largely follows that in the Uttarakanda, the characters of both Suwandha and Chitrawati are Javanese inventions, and later become icons respectively of bravery and loyalty and wifely devotion in the Javanese *wayang* theater.

In the 14th century, a major temple complex known as Panataran was home to the last major series of reliefs on Rāmāyaṇa and Mahābhārata seen in East Java. The king was a regular visitor, and both Shaivites and Buddhist devotees worshipped the lord of the mountains at this shrine. The temple itself was like a terraced shrine, laid out in three courtyards, against the backdrop of the mountain. Chosen episodes from the Rama and Krishna stories were pictorialized on the terraced walls of one shrine of the largest temple complex in East Java. Hanuman is the hero of the Rama series. His adventures, in great detail, form the subject matter in this sculptural telling. Of great interest is the fact that it closely follows the Old Javanese Rāmāyaṇa. Of even greater interest is the style of the *wayang* puppets in which it is executed. Here we see the world of *wayang* theater meet with the literary and sculptural arts, mingling in a harmonious illustration of the organic melding of Rāmāyaṇa with the sacral and artistic traditions of Java.

Of the episodes from Krishna's life, his conquest of Rukmini appears to be one of the most popular in Java. These are illustrated in a series of reliefs in the same temple, on one level above that of Hanuman in Lanka. In contrast, this sculptural telling is not depicted in the *wayang* style. Krishna and Rukmini forms the subject of a *kakawin* by Mpu Trguna known as *Krishnayana.*

By the 16th century, the courts of Java in the northern coastal belt had adopted Islam and the majority of people followed suit. Javanese mythology credits the spreading of the religion of Islam to the *walis sembilan* or the nine saints of Java, principally Sunan Kalijaga, to whom is also ascribed the authorship of a large number of books, including the Rāmāyaṇa. In the way Valmiki was thought in India to have been a reformed robber, so too Sunan Kalijaga is reputed to have been a highway bandit converted to Islam by another of its saints, Sunan Bonang. In another Javanese story, King Darmakusuma (Javanese for Yuddhishthira) of the Pandawas tells the story of his ancestors, which is the Mahābhārata, to the same Sunan Kalijaga, who uses the *kris* or dagger he had received from Nabi Kilir to write it down on palm leaves. "Thus, to Javanese Muslims, Mahābhārata is the work of a Javanese Muslim saint and can be regarded as Muslim literature although not a single letter is changed."[19]

As a final example, in the following story of Kalimasada told by Soewito Santoso, we see how *Bharatayuddha* was adapted to the Islamic worldview. King Darmakusuma could not die because he is unable to read the scripture in his possession known as Kalimasada (originating from the word "*Kalimahoshadha,*" the book that turns into a lance in *Bharatayudda*). God tells him that if he succeeds in reading the book with the help of a certain saint, Sunan Kalijaga, he might return to Heaven. So the king wanders in the forests around Demak and finds Sunan Kalijaga, who explains to him that Kalimasada was in fact *kalima sjahadah,* the creed of Islam, and that by pronouncing and studying it, one became a Muslim. King Darmakusuma agreed to convert to Islam and soon died.[20]

In all likelihood, Sunan Kalijaga also saw the opportunity to exploit the popular shadow puppet theater as an effective channel of mass communication to spread his faith. He is reported to have said:

> The wayang show is indeed a [mirror] image of the One, one can call it the image of the Law. The wayang then stands for all mankind [and] the dalang is to be compared with Allah, the creator of the Universe.[21]

With the adoption of Islam by the rulers of Java from the 16th century onward, the Indonesian Rāmāyaṇa and Mahābhārata tradition experiences profound change in dramatic new manifestations. It seemed understood that if a people's mythology could not be erased from the collective memory, any effort at conversion would be better served by building on the familiar and loved. With this practical approach in a congenial environment, the Rama and Bhārata tales became even more firmly established as they acquired secular traits acceptable to Islam without conflicting with its tenets. The gods remained but in the form of prophets, and through *wayang* were linked to the age-old mystical tradition of Java. They also retained their most significant characteristics of being the touchstone of ethics, morality, and political wisdom. One likely reasons why Malay society readily embraced Rāmāyaṇa and Mahābhārata was that its characters and ideals synchronized with those upheld in Java and provided a language for ethical discourse. With the removal of previous religious connotations, and a careful consonance with the tenets of the new religion that forbade the worship of any god but Allah, the stories are easily transformed into secular tales of love and war and valor, advocating loyalty both to the king the country.

The subtle transformations that slowly occurred in Rāmāyaṇa and Mahābhārata during the Hindu Buddhist period see obvious changes in the Islamic period. The major innovations in episodes and the relationship of its characters that modern scholars once thought were designed in Java to discredit Rāmāyaṇa can actually be traced to the alternate oral and folk traditions of India, circulating among the traders and merchants for centuries that were also familiar to the *wayang* theater. We will hear echoes from Prambanan in many of them.

The *Hikayat Seri Rama,* the first known Islamic Rāmāyaṇa, was composed in Malay, the spoken language of the traders but written in an Arabic script. In Malay literature, the *hikayat* came to stand for a prose tale, whose subject was generally concerned with myths or legendary history as well as with historical chronicles. Like the *kakawin,* it was probably meant to be read aloud at gatherings. It seems probable that popular literature of an earlier period was inserted into the genre of the *hikayat* to legitimize its links with Malay society's pre-Islamic past, as well as to ensure its continuity in the Javanese present. In its mode of narration and arrangement of material, *Hikayat Seri Rama* differs from all Indian Rāmāyaṇas and is a distinct contribution to Rāmāyaṇa literature. The rich assortment of episodes from the orally told reservoir of Rama stories, which traveled to Southeast Asia over the centuries, was eclectically incorporated into the *Hikayat* tradition.

A few examples will suffice to illustrate the above point. Shiva fathers Hanuman, a motif that is already seen in the Shiva Puranas; in some recensions, Rama is the father; but in both cases, it is the Wind God who carries his semen to Anjana (or Anjani), echoing the Valmikian episode in which Vayu is the father of Hanuman. Hanuman is born with earrings, and a divine voice tells Anjana that these earrings will, sometime in the future, enable the child's father to recognize him. This episode has a close parallel in the Telugu *Ranganatha* Rāmāyaṇa. Ravana deceives Dasarata into surrendering his wife Mandudari, but she cleverly kneads the waste from her skin and turns it into a frog, which she converts into a clone of herself called Mandudaki, which the unsuspecting Ravana takes home. Mandudari's ingenious device echoes the well-known Indian story of how Parvati creates Ganesha. Dasarata has a daughter Kikewi Dewi, who maliciously engineers Sita's banishment by Rama by drawing a portrait of Ravana to sow suspicion in Rama's mind about his wife's chastity. Such a daughter with a similar sounding name of Kakua is also found in Chandrawati's Bengali Rāmāyaṇa.[22]

The phenomenon of Sita's birth has ignited the imagination of storytellers since the earliest recorded Rāmāyaṇas in India. In several Rāmāyaṇas of Southeast Asia, she is seen as the daughter of Ravana, or as the daughter of Dasarata in the Buddhist stories. In the *Hikayat Seri Rama,* we see a conflation of both the stories and Sita is respectively the daughter of Dasarata and Ravana, or could be the daughter of either. The unusual birth stories of Sugriva and Valin find parallel in the Rāmāyaṇas of Orissa and Tamil, both regions with historic trade connections with Indonesia.[23]

The *Hikayat* of the 16th century has an intriguing link with the temples of Prambanan built 500 years earlier. Many intriguing episodes depicted on the balustrades of the Shiva and Brahma temples that are not part of Valmiki Rāmāyaṇa are found in this Malay text. For example, at the scene of Sita's abduction by Ravana, Jatayu flies to her rescue and she drops her ring in his beak, which is later shown as being brought to Rama by a large parrot-like bird. Another interesting episode is the one of a tearful Sugriva sitting on a tree, while an unsuspecting Lakshman below, unaware of his presence, collects these tears in a container. In the depiction of the duel of the monkey brothers, we see Sugriva wearing a root around his body rather than a garland around his neck to distinguish him from his brother.

In the *Hikayat Seri Rama,* Nabi Adam intercedes on Ravana's behalf with Allah. As punishment for his misbehavior, Ravana is sent off to Bukit Serendip or Lanka, where he practices asceticism for 12 years by hanging upside down over a fire. He is visited by Nabi Adam and pleads with him to intercede with Allah to grant him four kingdoms: the Earth, Keindraan (the heavens), the Sea, and the Netherworld, which Adam agrees to do on condition that Ravana rule according to law and justice. It is interesting that no mention is made of the incarnation of gods and nowhere is Rama claimed to be an incarnation of Vishnu.

Another example of the contemporization of ancient literature was the *Hikayat Pandawa Jaya* that takes the war between the Kurawas and the Pandawas as its theme, and symbolizes the conflict between the evil and the good.

Over time, the old language of Java was replaced by modern Javanese, the new language of cosmopolitan Java. In the 16th century, a fresh Rāmāyaṇa telling known as Serat Kanda was created in the Pasisir, the northern coastal region, in this new language. This telling was rooted in the new structure of Pasisir universal histories that united all known myths, legends, and histories in a single frame and came to be known as Serat Kanda or Book of Tales. They retained a symbiotic link with the *wayang* theater, which created the concept of *Serat Kanda ning ringit purwa,* or the *Book of Tales of the Wayang Purwa.* In the Serat Kanda, the Rāmāyaṇa and Mahābhārata legends are treated as historical figures through a mixture of Islamic (Old Testament) and Hindu mythical figures. Hindu gods merge into an Islamic genealogy, e.g., Shiva (guru) becomes the great-great-grandson of Nabi Adam. The birth of Vishnu and Vasuki after the Great Flood provides a bridge to the genealogy of the mythical Javanese rulers, until we come to the ancestors of Rama and Rahwana (Javanese for Ravana). Then follows the Rama story, which runs broadly along the lines of the *Hikayat Seri Rama* albeit with many differences. The concept of a harmonious continuity of rulers from one dynasty to another was of great importance to Javanese tradition. To underline this continuity in *wayang* without offending the requirements of Islam, the status of the gods was transformed into that of historical heroes who were seen as ancestors of the Javanese king.

Serat Kanda played a significant role in the transmission of the epic stories, as this body of literature, composed in verse using the indigenous *macapat* metrical system, incorporated countless legends that has been sung for generations. These also fed into the multivolume work entitled *Pustaka Raja,* a book that contains 300 stories in 3 cycles of epic tales, all told in simple verse.[24] Even today, this provides the source of many *wayang* plots.

Despite these new trends, the rich legacy of the Old Javanese *kakawins* continued. In the 17th century, a new kingdom known as Mataram came to power in Central Java, and its greatest ruler Sultan Agung, harking back to the glory of the Majaphit kingdom, extolled the virtues of *kawi,* as Old Javanese came to be known, that all descendants of the Mataram should have a thorough knowledge of *kawi* because the *kawi* texts were the repository of all knowledge. Fortunately, these old texts had been preserved by laborious copying not only on the island of Bali where manuscripts were meticulously preserved, but in Java also where the tradition continued in limited circles, albeit riddled with errors. Nonetheless, these very manuscripts became the source of an extraordinary reinterpretation into modern Javanese of the Old Javanese classics (in two forms known as *macapat* and *jarwa*) in the 18th-century court of Surakarat by the court poets, father and son Jasadipura 1 and 11. A series of historical upheavals had led to the division of the kingdom in 1755, and the ruling elite, tired of war, abandoned it as an instrument of policy. Hence, the need of the hour called for stability and balance, and a resurgence of old values. Despite the corrupted manuscripts, these old classics were given a new lease of life in the form of *Serat Rama* based on Rāmāyaṇa *kakawin, Bratayuda* on *Bharatayuddha, Minta Raga* on *Arjunwiwaha,* and *Serat Lokapal Kawi* on *Arjunawijaya.* The *Ashta-brata* from Rāmāyaṇa *kakawin* was refurbished and given a contemporary look.

Bima Suci is a uniquely adapted story of Bhima. Popularly known in Java as Bima and Werkadura, he must be the most loved of the five Pandawa brothers in the Bharatayuddha, as Javanese call their own telling of this story. In the puppet form of the *wayang kulit,* his character is a painted leather puppet that is physically large, equal in size to that of the rakshasas, the evil characters who are ranged on the right side of the Tree of Life, which divides the screen on which the shadows play. On the left side, amongst whom Bima takes his place, are the halus or refined or good characters: their forms tiny in size, their eyes like the kernel of rice, their noses sharp and elongated in postures of refinement, with feet together. Bima has characteristics of both sides. His nature might be *halus* or refined, but his physical manifestation is *kasar* or coarse, embodied in his big round eyes, a large bulbous nose, and a stance that only the rough use—legs wide apart and a loud raucous voice. A prominent feature is his large curved nail with which he tears apart his opponents. Multiple stories are associated with this impulsive rowdy character, but because he is flawed and therefore human, in contrast to refined perfection of the halus characters on the good side, he is best loved.

This character plays to the gallery with his extraordinary physical power annihilating enemies with uprooted tree trunks performing acrobatic feats of physical prowess like a modern day Superman, yet it is around this very character that some foundational ideas of Javanese mysticism are enacted. It is the *wayang lakon* called Dewa Ruci. Javanese people describe in it the struggle of the soul that results in the conquest of passion, a pilgrimage to the self that is often seen as a mystical experience of the Kabah in Mecca.

In this *lakon,* we hear that his beloved teacher Durna (or Drona in India) instructs Bima to search for the water of life, hidden in a place that will require great effort to discover. His brothers, the other Pandawas, attempt to dissuade him fearing that Durna, being the teacher of their enemy the Kurawa brothers, might try and kill him, but Bima, placing absolute faith in his teacher, sets out on the quest. On the way, he encounters two ogres on Mount Candramuka who attempt to kill him. Bima destroys them, but fails to find the water of life. He plunges into the ocean where he encounters a giant naga. A mighty struggle ensues that ends by Bima killing it with his long thumbnail. Then in the very center of the ocean, he meets a tiny replica of himself, Dewa Ruci, who tells him to have faith and to enter his tiny body. The enormous Bima is astonished but complies with the request. Entering the miniature Bima through his ear, he finds that it contains the entire world. Dewa Ruci then reveals the secret of union with Allah and orders Bima to return to the world. Bima wishes to remain in this state of union and refuses to return, but Dewa Ruci explains that such a stay is possible only after death.

Santoso tell us that the *wayang lakon,* in its very structure, articulates the introspective formulation of the path to Allah in the course of life. It is divided into three segments that represent the symbolic representation of the three stages of life: youth, maturity, and old age. The term "*lakon*" is derived from the Javanese word "*laku*," which means to walk, and the life cycle is referred to as *anglakoni urip,* which in Javanese is to walk through life.

The traditions of innovation and renovation in Rāmāyaṇa and Mahābhārata continue today in Java, and role of its mediators cannot be overemphasized. Dynasties changed, as did centers of power from Central Java to East Java, and then to the north coast and then back to Central Java. Languages changed, old religions outgrew their usefulness, and new religions were adopted. But through it all, Rāmāyaṇa and Mahābhārata endured, not through coercion or the dictate of a ruler, but through their relevance to the lives of people who had made these stories their own. "Even today the great war between the Pandawas and their cousins the Korawas is still the best known story among the Javanese people," Supomo tells us.[25] Born in a small village in Yogyakarta that was the center of Javanese culture, he became well acquainted with Abhimanyu, Gatotkaca, Arjuna, Karna, and other heroes of the *wayang* world. Being familiar with their appearances before he started his primary education, he could easily recognize the timbre of their voices even when he lay half-awake throughout the night of the *wayang* performance.[26] Together yet separate, the epic stories played a significant role in that same cultural space, whether sacred or secular. They were patronized by kings who identified themselves sometimes with the power of Shiva, at others with Vishnu. But the association of *sekti* or power with texts gave them a special place. They came to be regarded as *pusakas,* or the sacred heirlooms of Javanese heritage, that empowered the kings and sultans of Java.

Although introduced to Java in the Hindu Buddhist ethos of the courts, Rama and Krishna were never worshipped as gods. Rama was the ideal king and enlightened ruler, and the *Ashta-brata* his guiding principal. The *Bhagavad Gita* did not make the same impact on Javanese consciousness as it has done in India, yet the characters and situation of Mahābhārata provided the language of ethical discourse in Java.

It is interesting that no major *kakawin* on the subject of Rama and Sita was written in Java between the 10th and 14th centuries. Perhaps, the Old Javanese Rāmāyaṇa and the Uttarakand *parwa,* combined with an impressive knowledge of Rama lore in the oral tradition, were sufficient for their continued vocalization in recitation, visualization, and performance, as the inscriptional records attest. They have redemptive qualities and provide methods of teaching that combines entertainment with instruction. In the hands of the 18th-century court poets, they were refurbished or renewed, yet retained their familiarity to the Javanese. The familiar characters of Seri Rama, Devi Sinta, Arjuno, and Kresna joined the lineage of their ancestors. They are the guardians of their country and protectors of their souls. Beloved equally by the king and by the common man, they became Javanese cultural property.

They were seen and heard in a collective context rather than silently read as an individual experience. Furthermore, it penetrated the consciousness of people through explanation and contextualization. Episodes of stories from the larger story of Rāmāyaṇa or Mahābhārata stories are popularly enacted in a multitude of performance arts and focus on relationship between the central and minor characters often in ways unknown or unheard of in India. Bhima encounters Hanuman. Rama battles with Arjuna. Finally, they merge into a single historical framework in a linear progression of two cycles. Rama incarnates into Kresna, Lesmana into Arjuna, and Dewi Sinta into Sumbhadra, the sister of Kresna.

Such incidents demonstrate to us the capacity of the Javanese to receive a variety of diverse sources from a different civilization and amalgamate them with their own narrative framework. This results in an eclectic mix of stories from the Sanskritic tradition with the folk and oral ones blended with preexisting origin myths, not to mention those of the local storytellers who shape and enlarge, adjust, or invent the plot and characters to situate the narrative in his time and render it suitable to the circumstances of patron. The origins are of no relevance. They belong simply to the Javanese tradition.

Admittedly, this slow acculturation occurred over a period of 15 centuries, but the process was a peaceful one, without war or violent imposition and so merits our attention. The present tendency to view Islam as a monolithic religion within a rigid framework of belief and practice, and to define the whole complex range of beliefs by the fundamentalist minority is to ignore the history of countries such as Indonesia in which the Islamic majority of people follow various shades of Islam—from the Sufi brand of mysticism to normative piety demanded by the Shariat—into which their ancient Hindu heritage has been so successfully integrated that its origins for the average man on the street are totally obscured.

NOTES

1. Samuel P. Huntington, *The Clash of Civilizations and the Remaking of World Order* (New York: Simon and Schuster, 1996).

2. S. Supomo, *Bharatayuddha: An Old Javanese Poem and Its Indian Source*, Sata-Pitika Series Indo-Asian Literatures, v. 373 (New Delhi: International Academy of Indian Culture and Aditya Prakashan, 1993), p. 1.

3. Malini Saran and Vinod C. Khanna, *The Rāmāyaṇa in Indonesia* (Delhi: Ravi Dayal Publisher, 2004), p. 89.

4. Petrus Joseph Zoetmulder, *Kalangwan: A Survey of Old Javanese Literature*, KITLV Translation Series 16 (The Hague: Martinus Nijhoff, 1974), p. 36.

5. A close comparison reveals that the Old Javanese poet had turned to chapters V and IX of the *Manusmṇti* for the specific idea of eight divinities who are embodied in the king. Vinod C. Khanna and Malini Saran, "The Ramayana *Kakawin:*

A Product of Sanskrit Scholarship and Independent Literary Genius Khanna," *Journal of the Royal Institute of Linguistics and Anthropology* 149, no. 3 (1993): 240, 241.

6. Soewito Santoso, *Rāmāyaṇa Kakawin* (Singapore: Institute of Southeast Asian Studies/New Delhi: International Academy of Indian Culture, 1980), Canto XXIV, verses 81–86.

7. Ibid., Canto XXVI, verse 50.

8. They are *Adiparwa, Wirataparwa, Udyogparwa, Bhishmaparwa, Asramaparwa, Mosalaparwa, Prashthanikaparwa, Swargarohanaparwa,* and *Sabhaparwa.*

9. Zoetmulder, *Kalangwan,* p. 100.

10. Ibid.

11. Ibid., p. 87.

12. Himansu Bhusan Sarkar, *Corpus of the Inscriptions of Java up to 928 A.D. (Corpus inscriptionum Javanicarum),* v. 11 (Calcutta: Firma K.L. Mukhopadhyaya, 1972), pp. 85–89.

13. Supomo, *Bharatayuddha,* p. 3.

14. Zoetmulder, *Kalangwan,* p. 209.

15. Supomo, *Bharatayuddha,* p. 179, Canto X, verses 11–13.

16. Ibid., pp. 237, 238, Canto XLII, verses 5–8.

17. Mark R. Woodward, "Islam in Java Normative Piety and Mysticism in the Sultanate of Yogyakarta," *The Association for Asia Studies Monograph No. XLV* (Tucson, AZ: The University of Arizona Press, 1989).

18. S. Supomo, *Arjunawijaya: A Kakawin of Mpu Tantular,* Vol. 2 (The Hague: Martinus Nijhoff, 1977), Canto LXX, verse 2.

19. Santoso, *Rāmāyaṇa Kakawin,* p. 21.

20. Ibid.

21. Laurie J. Sears, *Shadows of Empires: Colonial Discourse and Javanese Tales* (Durham, NC: Duke University Press, 1996), p. 54.

22. Saran and Khanna, *The Rāmāyaṇa in Indonesia,* pp. 136, 137.

23. Several more such episodes are listed in ibid., p. 137.

24. Sears, *Shadows of Empires,* p. 54.

25. Supomo, *Bharatayuddha,* Preface, vii.

26. Ibid., p. 1.

Chapter 9

Multilingual Scholarship in the Study of Religion

Joseph T. O'Connell

BASIC APPEAL FOR "MULTILINGUAL FLUENCY" IN SCHOLARSHIP ON RELIGION

It should be obvious that scholars of religion at any time, but with much greater urgency after September 11, 2001, must strive to understand as best they can the religious dimensions of the mentalities and ways of acting of persons and populations globally.[1] For scholars whose cultural formation is basically Western, as is mine, this includes striving to understand better those men and women whose mentalities are shaped in terms of non-Western languages and cultures.[2] So far as professional academic study of religion is concerned, most of the practitioners at present are Westerners or Western in professional training and orientation even if born and raised in the embrace of non-Western languages and cultures. It may also seem obvious that drawing competent scholars raised and initially trained in terms of non-Western cultures into the academic study of religion would enhance understanding of the religious aspects of those cultures within the profession as a whole and among the wider public that scholars of religion are expected to inform. The Institute of Islamic Studies in McGill University over half a century ago under its first director, Wilfred Cantwell

Smith, sought to institutionalize such broadening of religio-cultural understanding in its own operations by aiming to have as many Muslims as non-Muslims among its faculty and likewise among its students.[3] At much the same time, the Center for the Study of World Religions at Harvard University under its first director, Robert H. L. Slater, began to enroll and domicile in its residential-*cum*-academic building graduate students and senior scholars from diverse countries, languages, cultures, and religious traditions around the world. Half a century later, we find in universities throughout the West quite a few scholars of religion, especially those concentrating on non-Western religious traditions, who grew up in countries where the basic culture is non-Western. In my own University of Toronto, since my retirement in 1998, the majority of new appointees across the whole gamut of South Asian studies are South Asian by cultural background (and the majority of these are women, a stunning reversal of the dominance of European and North American male scholars of South Asia in my generation and earlier). This phenomenon clearly constitutes a major step toward global cultural (and gender) inclusiveness in the academic study of religion.

Despite such openness to non-Western cultural backgrounds among newly appointed professors, however, I would still contend that a yet more vigorous commitment to multicultural capability, to what I call "multilingual fluency," in religious scholarship remains a desideratum within the profession. So far as I can tell, even among the recently appointed scholars whose initial cultural orientation was non-Western, their professional training, their modes of research, their academic publications, and, I would guess (though in individual cases I may be guessing wrongly), their scholarly thinking are predominantly done in English. Accordingly, in this chapter, I propose that yet more intensified "multilingual fluency" would further enable scholars of religion worldwide, still overwhelmingly Western or professionally Westernized, to understand and interpret the influence of the religious aspects of the lives, public and private, of fellow humans globally. After the tragic events of September 11, 2001, and their yet more tragic repercussions, such enhanced understanding—on a globally plural scale—of how other peoples think and feel, and hence act, takes on all the more urgency. This much should be obvious. How best to gain such enhanced understanding may not be so obvious.

One broad proposal for enhancing such understanding is for scholars to develop greater multilingual capability, especially scholars of religion. Multilingual capability becomes all the more urgent in the wake of the September 11 violence and the traumatic reverberations from it because of the need to understand as intimately and accurately as possible the mentalities of persons whose culture, ideology, religion, and language differ markedly from one's own. One essential key to understanding another person or group is to know his, her, or their language, to know it well, to listen patiently so as to grasp what the other really means, and then, where feasible, to respond in ways that will in turn be understood.

Let me first call into question what seems to me to be a tacit assumption (a certain complacency, perhaps, one in which I have indulged) too widely shared in our profession as scholars of religion. We tend to be satisfied with a pattern of scholarship that on the one hand aspires to understand humanity at large in its religious aspects while carrying on our work primarily in one dominant language, English, supplemented by certain other European languages, with but minimal recourse to languages from non-Western civilizations (except for specialists in one of the latter and for the as yet too few academic scholars of religion trained in non-Western countries). In the West, of course, "world religions" scholars and specialists in non-Western religion may be expected to learn at least one non-Western language (classical and/or modern vernacular) for research purposes. But generally, we are content to read and some of us to speak a bit in the non-Western language(s) we study, but are rarely expected to think and feel or even write, teach, or publish through the medium of that/those language(s). We may strive to think and feel imaginatively or empathetically like those whom we are studying, but typically we "imagine" or "empathize" in English. As languages go, English is probably quite a good one for scholarship. But operating exclusively in English and within a Western cultural context, inevitably places limitations, unnecessary limitations I would contend, on how sensitively and perceptively we may be attuned to the ideas and feelings of fellow humans whose languages and cultures are significantly different, and on how able we are to comprehend novel conceptual categories and gestalts of emotions and images.

Moreover, it seems reasonable to expect that if within the profession of academic study of religion there were more leading voices effectively employing languages other than English (and its more influential Western European cousins) in the effort to understand human religiousness, more progress could be made toward the objective set out by the late Canadian historian of religion, Wilfred Cantwell Smith:

> The fact is that we do not have available to us, and must work towards forging, concepts that will serve us generically (for accurate interpretation, let alone self-interpretation). Even when concepts are attained, the words though which to communicate them in this language or in that may prove inadequate, less for some persons or groups than for others.[4]

There has been for quite some time now sustained criticism of the Orientalist West for cultural and political-economic imperialism, for its hegemonic impact on colonial and postcolonial ways of life of both the dominating and the dominated peoples. But there remains the irony or paradox that much (most perhaps) of the eloquent and influential postmodern and postcolonial critique is carried out in English, French, or other European hegemonic (post)colonial language. This seems to be the case even when done by intellectuals whose primary cultural roots are non-Western. Such privileging of Anglo-European languages, I suggest, continues even at the highest levels of critical theoretical discourse to entrench, though disguising, the continuing hegemonic influence of English and European languages and the cultural and political-economic interests they articulate. It does so at the cost of marginalizing and inhibiting non-Western, in particular South Asian, languages and the cultural and political-economic interests they articulate. Also, if it is only in terms of one dominant language (or family of languages) that scholarly conceptualizing of religion is to be sought, then we gratuitously restrict—and to that extent distort—the capacity of scholars and of humankind as a whole to recognize and comprehend the full range of human religious sensibility.

Many articulate and talented academics, writers, and other cultural figures with non-Western linguistic-cultural roots are drawn away intellectually from those roots in order to operate professionally within Anglo-European linguistic-*cum*-cultural discourses, notwithstanding the hegemonic implications of doing so. Not a few, especially among the most talented, move physically to the West, where they are yet more persistently drawn away from their primary linguistic-cultural roots and into a predominantly Western cosmopolitan mentality. Given the economic-political structure of global power relationships, this may be to a large extent an unavoidable dilemma facing intellectuals hailing from relatively less wealthy and powerful countries, classes, cultures, and languages. It may be the price to be paid if his or her critical voice is to be heard at all in the centers of global power and influence as well as in peripheral zones other than one's own. Be that as it may in general terms, we as professionals in the academic study of religion have some modest scope within our own professional field to reduce, rather than tolerate or augment, the impact of linguistic hegemony and its attendant marginalization of alternative cultures and languages resulting in a Euro-American-centric narrowing of capacity for understanding the innate diversity of human religious mentality, feelings, and actions.

I am, of course, aware that there are practical and historical reasons why Anglo-European linguistic hegemony prevails within the academic study of religion. Thus far in its relatively short history, this field of scholarship is still largely a European American enterprise and English currently is the most convenient language for global communication, not least thanks to the ubiquitous Internet. Dynamics somewhat parallel to the hegemonic influence of English language in South Asia are, no doubt, operative to some extent in other regions where there remains from colonial times some residual dominance by French or other European colonial language-*cum*-culture. Russian presumably had similar influence in the erstwhile Soviet Union and still has in relation to other languages in use in the Russian sphere of influence today. There is also the far older and more deeply entrenched hegemony of Arabic among Muslim populations in many countries throughout the world, one that in fact resists the inroads of English among them. In many of those countries, though not (or not yet) in South Asia, Arabic has effectively uprooted indigenous languages and become the standard vernacular. Chinese may come to have a dominant linguistic influence in East Asia in the foreseeable future. Thus far, however, none of these alternative hegemonic languages has had nearly the impact on academic study of religion worldwide as has English. We academics hardly have the leverage to change massively the course of human linguistic history. But we may at the very least take stock of what we may be losing in our zone of responsibility by perpetuating the overwhelming dominance of a single language, English, as the medium of global scholarly conceptualization and communication, in particular, in relation to South Asian languages and cultures. For other parts of Asia and the Middle East, some such dominance may be exercised by Chinese, French, or Arabic. The points being made here regarding English would likely apply to those languages in those areas as well. Because the focus of my remaining remarks is on South Asia, in particular India and Bangladesh, when speaking hereafter of "multilingual" scholarship, I am for the most part referring English in relation to South Asian languages.

At this point, something may be said about the virtual absence of academic study of religion within South Asia itself, though only briefly here. This problem, which currently is gaining considerable attention, has been discussed in detail elsewhere.[5] Strange as it may seem to those unfamiliar with the history of modern education in India, Bangladesh, and other countries in South Asia, religion as an explicit subject for study and research is largely taboo. The reasons vary from country to country. In India, which much of the world sees as a country richly endowed (or plagued) by a luxuriance of modes of religious life, several factors combine to account for the extreme paucity of university departments, centers, or chairs for the study of religion. Among these, governmental and administrative fear of stirring up religio-political "communal" discord, the ideologically left-leaning secular orientation of a generation or more of modern Indian intellectuals, lack of interest in or suspicion of critical academic scholarship by traditional leaders of religious institutions, and the absence of religion from the disciplinary structure of the University of London are said to have been the model for Indian universities begun during British colonial rule. There may be only two Indian universities having departments dedicated to the academic study of religion.[6] In Bangladesh, where the population is almost 90 percent Muslim, there is a marked cleavage between those for whom affirmation of Islam leaves little scope for appreciative study of other religious traditions and those of secular political-intellectual orientation who (even though personally Muslim) tend to be extremely suspicious of organized religion a weapon of fanatic movements and repressive regimes. Hence, the launching a decade ago of the country's first Department of World Religions in the University of Dhaka is noteworthy.[7] In Pakistan, political turmoil and assertiveness of certain Muslim groups combined with the absence of all but miniscule non-Muslim populations have inhibited academic study of religion in that country. In Sri Lanka, Buddhist scholarship has been significant, but intense religio-ethnic conflict has limited academic study of religion as such, even though the presence of considerable Buddhist, Hindu, Muslim, and Christian populations might have, in other circumstances, facilitated study of religion on a pluralist basis.

To enrich the linguistic capability of religious studies as a profession, I would urge Western scholars, especially comparative religion scholars and specialists in non-Western religion and culture, to strive to become more effectively multilingual in their own (our own) thinking, writing, and speaking, modest though such success may prove to be, especially among us North Americans, who are less accustomed to linguistic plurality in daily life than are many of our European colleagues. Where more dramatic progress might be hoped for is with those scholars of religion and culture—still relatively few now, but who we may expect to be much more numerous in the near future—hailing from non-Western countries and raised amid non-Western religio-cultural traditions and languages. These latter I would urge to persevere in thinking, writing, and speaking academically at a rigorous professional level (as well as in public civil society discourse) in their respective first languages even as they continue to master English (or French, Arabic, Chinese, Russian, or whatever) for international professional communication.

PRACTICAL MULTILINGUAL STEPS TO SUPPORT STUDY OF RELIGION IN SOUTH ASIA

What follows is a "wish list" of what might be done to foster the sort of "multilingual fluency" in religious studies in South Asia that seems to me to be needed if religious studies are to develop in the region and are to contribute optimally to understanding human religiousness globally. First listed are measures to enhance the capability of the scholars themselves to function in a multilingual way. Then follows a list of types of academic publications and pedagogic materials—primarily in the languages used in the region, which are needed but still largely nonexistent—for teaching and research on religion in South Asian colleges and universities. Most of these suggestions would likely be applicable in regions beyond South Asia as well.

Measures to Enhance Scholars' Own Multilingual Fluency

1. In both South Asia and the West, making "multilingual fluency" basic to the professional training and "job description" of the next generation of comparative religion/world religion scholars and, of course, those specializing in a particular region or area of South Asia.[8]
2. Special funding and customized programs (including periods abroad) for research training of multilingual junior scholars based in South Asia.
3. In-service training (including periods abroad) in academic study of religion for more senior multilingual South Asian scholars already trained in disciplines other than religion but interested in religious phenomena.
4. Periodic appointments of Western scholars (and non-Westerners whose primary appointments are in the West) for teaching in South Asian institutions in the language used in the region, if in that language they have some competence, even if underutilized.
5. Encouraging and enabling multilingual students and senior scholars in South Asia to do research and reflection on religious subjects appropriate to their own regions.[9]
6. Encouraging multilingual scholars to prepare parallel versions of some of their publications, and at least summaries of others, in both English and a South Asian language.
7. Translating, individually or jointly, important scholarly works and primary source texts from English to a South Asian language and vice versa.
8. Bilingual (i.e., using a regional South Asian language and English) teaching at introductory levels, where students may still be weak in English, and to some extent at more advanced levels, where using the South Asian language to express more subtle and technical matters, would challenge teachers and advanced students to think rigorously in the South Asian linguistic and cultural terms as well as in English about basic categories and issues.

Multilingual Resources Needed to Facilitate Religious Studies Education

Teachers and students in regions where South Asian languages are currently used in colleges and universities may be consulted for identifying the educational materials most needed. Scholars should be acknowledged professionally and duly rewarded for producing educational materials of good quality, not just for research publications. Governments, foundations, and commercial publishers may be solicited for support of larger projects, while smaller ones may be part of the standard practice of individual scholars or departments. Some such written texts, audiovisual presentations, and digital materials should be produced in South Asian languages and some in English in formats and at levels appropriate for the intended students. Such materials may include the following:

1. Introductions to the history of academic study of religion and its methods and theories, but modified as appropriate for regions within South Asia[10]
2. Introductions to each of major discipline-specific ways of studying religion
3. Introductions to major religious traditions or subtraditions, especially those current in the particular regions of South Asia
4. Lectures and essays on significant topics and issues in study of religion, recorded or transcribed and disseminated in print, CD, DVD, or Internet media
5. Textbooks for basic courses geared to students' abilities[11]
6. Selected annotated bibliographies of South Asian and English language publications to support study and research, especially those dealing with religious topics pertinent to the respective regions within South Asia
7. South Asian language translations of religious "scriptures" or "classics" (or selections from them) chosen from priority lists prepared by competent scholars
8. South Asian language translations and/or digests or paraphrases of major scholarly books and articles on religion in English and other languages similarly chosen
9. Academic journals in South Asian languages (or in South Asian languages and English) geared to needs and interests of readers in the respective regions of South Asia

CONCLUDING REMARKS

There are, as indicated above, basically two contexts in which I am urging that efforts be made to develop more fluent and effective multilingual scholarship on religion with a regional focus on South Asia. The first context involves motivating and training scholars—both those whose first language is English and those whose first language is a South Asian one—to become as effectively fluent as they can in both languages (and more than two for those capable of doing so). The potential to contribute most substantially to multilingual religious studies would seem to lie with a new generation of scholars whose first language is South Asian, provided they are also very competent in English. But to be optimally effective as multilingual scholars, they should remain committed to drawing substantially upon the South Asian (vernacular and/or classical) languages (and religio-cultural resources) available to them and to thinking and writing professionally in South Asian languages as well as in English (or other non–South Asian language) about the issues they encounter in their study and research. It will likely be harder for most Western scholars to attain comparable levels of fluency in thinking, speaking, and writing in South Asian languages, but they may contribute substantially by translating and by speaking and writing to the extent they can. Their evident commitment to being effectively multilingual should in any event reinforce the importance and contribute to the success of the overall multilingual project.

The second context calls for producing and upgrading teaching-*cum*-research resources appropriate for use in South Asian educational institutions. Most, especially at introductory levels, may be in South Asian languages, but some appropriately designed introductory English materials would be helpful too, especially for more advanced students (and for teachers). If academic study of religion is to flourish in the various linguistic regions of South Asia, and not be exclusively the preserve of those in elite universities (and not be a less than optimal exercise even for them), it would seem to me advisable that a broad spectrum of South Asian language resources for teaching and studying about religion be produced and brought into play, sooner rather than later.

Underlying both of the above sets of proposals is the basic claim that optimal understanding of human religious life globally is more likely to be attained if a plurality of religio-cultural mentalities, articulated through a plurality of languages, become integral to scholarly thinking and communicating about human life in its religious aspects. If only one dominant language, currently English, is virtually the sole linguistic medium of global professional academic thought and communication, then insight into human thinking, feeling, and motivation for action at subtler and deeper levels is likely to be arbitrarily restricted to what that language and its inherent cultural patterns can readily accommodate.

If this claim and its attendant recommendations seem sound, then those of us who are scholars in the study of religion should make concerted efforts through our universities, professional associations, and elsewhere to elevate the priority of multilingual fluency in professional training and career expectations for scholars in our field. Likewise, we may advocate among colleagues, university administrations, professional associations, foundations, governments, and international bodies for the production of publications and related educational materials in South Asian languages (and some in English) pedagogically beneficial for the study of religion in South Asian colleges and universities. Needless to say, much of what is sketched above in relation to South Asia should apply, with necessary regional and local variations, to much of Southeast Asia, the Middle East, and elsewhere beyond the West.

Meanwhile, on the ground in India, Bangladesh, and elsewhere in South Asia, and among our colleagues wherever our home universities may be, we may initiate a variety of measures and small projects to foster multilingual teaching and learning incrementally. Out of such modest initiatives pilot projects may emerge that could eventually have much wider application and impact. If certain departments or universities would commit themselves to adopt and implement particular multilingual projects and if those that do would coordinate their efforts in the interests of maximum effectiveness, then momentum could be developed and substantial progress could be made. The Swedish South Asian Studies Network in collaboration with several Indian universities and relevant scholars is taking several major initiatives in this direction.[12]

NOTES

1. This chapter is a revised version of a draft prepared for a roundtable on "Academic Study of Religion" in the *Global Congress on World Religions after 9/11*, held at Jamia Millia Islamia, New Delhi, January 17–20, 2009. I wish to acknowledge Denise Couture (Université de Montréal) for recommending that the focus on "bilingual fluency" in that earlier draft be readjusted to "multilingual fluency" and Madhu Khanna (Jamia Millia Islamia) for several editorial suggestions.

2. The categories "Western" and "non-Western" are used in this chapter in the very broad sense of those cultures (and the countries in which they are dominant) that derive from European civilization and those that do not, respectively, and with awareness that there are great variations within each category. It should also be acknowledged that there has been for a long time sophisticated development of academic research on religion, especially, but not exclusively, on the Buddhist tradition in Japan. I must leave it for Japanese scholars and others expert in Japanese matters to comment on how Japanese linguistic and cultural patterns may influence academically rigorous scholarship in Japan and to what extent Japanese scholarship has been able to influence thinking about religion on a global scale. Something of the same may be said of recent Chinese and Middle Eastern contributions to scholarship on religion, but their respective contributions are not yet well known in the West.

3. Wilfred Cantwell Smith, "Comparative Religion: Whither—and Why?" in Mircea Eliade and Joseph M. Kitagawa, eds., *History of Religions: Essays in Methodology* (Chicago, IL: University of Chicago Press, 1959), pp. 31–58.

4. Smith goes on to say:

> The processes of intellectual history are in part those of old words' attaining new meanings for small or large sectors of various communities. What persons perceive in their environment, external or internal, is largely but need not be wholly a function of the words and phrases in terms of which

> they or their group think; and it is their responsibility, certainly if intellectuals, to see to it that their meanings for those words correspond as closely as may be to what they are in a position to see and to know. The history of religion (other people's and our own) has made us aware of things for which it is now our task to construct adequate conceptual categories and terms.

Towards a World Theology: Faith and the Comparative History of Religion (London: The Macmillan Press Ltd., 1981), p. 181. See also his *Faith and Belief* (Princeton, NJ: Princeton University Press, 1979) in which he devotes entire chapters to exploring Buddhist, Islamic, and Hindu conceptualizations of what to some extent corresponds to what in English may be called "faith." This is done in the quest of more globally inclusive ways of thinking about human religious experience.

5. A special panel in the January 2008 conference in New Delhi, *Rethinking Religion in India I,* dealt with "Approaches to the Academic Study of Religion from within Contemporary India." This was followed by a three-day workshop on Academic Study of Religion in India at Visva-Bharati in February 2008. "A Conversation with Vasu Narayanan Concerning Religious Studies in South Asia" appears in *Religious Studies News,* October 2008. Joseph T. O'Connell's paper "Academic Study of Religion in Bangladesh: Challenges and Opportunities" is forthcoming in *Nibandhamala,* Bulletin of the Centre for Advanced Research in the Humanities, University of Dhaka. The 2009 Annual Meeting of the American Academy of Religion (Montreal, November 7–10, 2009) included a plenary panel on "Global Perspectives on Religious Studies." See also *Religious Studies in South Asia: The Dhaka Initiative,* special issue of *Bangladesh e-journal of Sociology* 8, no. 1 (January 2011).

6. Visva-Bharati (Santiniketan, West Bengal) has the Department of Philosophy and Religion, and Punjabi University (Patiala, Panjab) has the Guru Gobind Singh Department of Religious Studies, each with a very small contingent of academic staff. Jamia Millia Islamia (New Delhi) has the Centre for the Study of Comparative Religions and Civilizations. The University of Madras (Chennai) has several chairs dedicated to particular religious traditions. Many Indian universities, most notably Banaras Hindu University (Varanasi), have departments of philosophy where Indian religio-philosophical studies take place, and many have departments of Sanskrit or Sanskrit and Pali where Brahmanic, Buddhist, and Jain texts are studied. Departments of history and of social sciences in major Indian universities may support rigorous research from their respective disciplinary orientations on subjects that include religious aspects, the wider ramifications of which may or may not be duly acknowledged. Christian, Muslim, and Jain colleges and universities, like explicitly Hindu institutions, may treat in detail their own religious traditions, usually from a confessional perspective, and some may address other religious traditions to some extent.

7. In the University of Dhaka, the Department of Comparative Religion, quickly renamed World Religions, was authorized in 1999, thanks to the unremitting efforts of Professor Kazi Nurul Islam. It now offers a four-year undergraduate honors program plus M.A. and M.Phil. programs. It is authorized to prepare students for the Ph.D., but so far has produced only one Ph.D. (jointly with another fledgling Department of Peace and Conflict Studies). Recently, Centre for

Interfaith and Intercultural Dialogue, also the result of Professor Kazi Nurul Islam's strenuous efforts within and beyond the university, has been linked to the Department of World Religions. There are at least three Islamic universities in Bangladesh whose concern for the study of religion is largely confined to confessional Islamic study. Some small private universities offer a course or two but as yet no full program in religion, so far as I know. Professor Muinuddin Ahmed Khan has been trying for some time to launch a program in comparative religion with a theological emphasis in a private university in Chittagong.

8. Institutions responsible for training such scholars should be prepared to allow additional time and additional funds to enable scholars to learn thoroughly the appropriate languages. In many cases, the best arrangement will entail an extended period of study in an area where a language is spoken and embedded in an ambient culture. At the University of Toronto, by contrast, where I taught until retirement, there is a rather rigid policy of four years of financial support for all doctoral students in the study of religion, regardless of whether the candidate's research is on religion in English-speaking Canada or in a foreign area in which language and culture are dramatically different and would require much more time to be assimilated. Such rigidity should be overcome.

9. Modest steps in this direction by the new Department of World Religions in the University of Dhaka include a series of multidisciplinary seminars on religion in Bengal, a special issue of the *Bangladesh e-journal of Sociology* based on presentations from those seminars, a textbook in preparation (initially in English but with the possibility of Bangla translation or paraphrase) on the history of religion in the Bengal region, and preparation of a teaching-*cum*-research bibliography (of Bangla and English/European publications) on religion in Bengal.

10. The Oxford Centre for Hindu Studies is committed to preparing such an introductory textbook and curriculum for religious studies suitable for India and elsewhere in South Asia. See also Joseph T. O'Connell, "Indian Conceptual and Symbolic Resources for Method and Theory in the Study of Religion," paper presented at conference on *Rethinking Religion in India I*, New Delhi, January 21–24, 2008.

11. An introductory text for sociology of religion suitable for India is being prepared by a group of Swedish scholars in conjunction with the Department of Sociology, Jadavpur University.

12. For details, see http://www.sasnet.lu.se/relhistgbg.html.

Chapter 10

Politicization of Religion and Its Possible Impact on the Academic Study of Religion in India

Madhu Khanna

I

Even after 60 years of independence from British rule, there is no institutional forum in India that considers academic study of world religions to be relevant. By denying an academic forum on the study of religions in our universities, India is unwittingly giving into colonization of knowledge. Today, our understanding of religion is based on Western and Orientalist assumptions so much so that an indigenous view of Hinduism or Islam in a nonprejudicial manner seems inconceivable.

The 20th century has witnessed the collapse of our most cherished "isms"—Marxism, Socialism, and Capitalism. There is no single ideology that commands universal respect. There is neither a prophet nor a political leader who can offer us a panacea to modern ills. Humanities and science have both failed to give us a blueprint for a future ethos. As there is no firm conviction or compulsion to follow a punitive ideology, there is no "real" history of nations. The prophets have warned us that when the boundaries of our self-definition get blurred, we live as "missing" persons. It is an established fact that societies grow and decline in proportion to their vitality and authenticity of their value system and their creative potential.

The social situation in which we live in India is one of conflicting values, a mood of cataclysmic turbulence unmatched in history. We, in India, are poised between two conflicting worlds. We cannot erase the imprints of our tradition, into which we are born, nor can we fully comprehend the "atomized" modern world. Our inner dislocations lead us ultimately to legitimize hypocrisy that veils our true authenticity. Ours is, therefore, no mere social crisis, but a massive spiritual chaos. The human predicament today is a moral one: the forces that are meant to foster the dignity of man tend to destroy it.

II

We seem to have lost our civilizational axis in the coreless enlightenment project of modernity, which comes burdened with a host of secular ideologies. The idea of secularism was the bedrock on which the colonial educational project was adopted by India—an oppressed society that needed to be redeemed albeit, civilized through modern Western values. Secularism has become an overused, unsubstantiated idea, verging on rhetoric. This rhetoric is not interested in the religious or civilization roots of our polycentric diversity that has sustained India's composite culture and its quest for *Satya* (truth).

The proponents of secularism in India sharply criticized and rejected the very idea of including religious studies as a part of our education policy. Thus, religious studies as a critical academic discipline was not given its due place of importance. In India, the secular constitution made it mandatory that religious traditions should be indirectly approached through the study of ancient history or as a handmaiden of philosophy. This reinforced a total alienation of universities from an unbiased, objective, wisdom-oriented speculation of religions in India. Religious studies per se as an autonomous *sui generis* discipline has remained an underprivileged and underresearched area in Indian academia. After 60 years of freedom, the alienation of study of religion from mainstream education has deepened. Over the years, the problem of secularism has been addressed in the public sphere, with arguments being spun both for and against it. The crucial question of the idea of secularism in a traditional society with its deep roots in religion has never been fully addressed. As one critic puts it aptly, "the constitution has never been able to define or redefine the term properly for India (secularism = the state's equi-distant from, indifference to, or equal love for all religions?)."[1] Unfortunately, the study of religion as an independent discipline has taken a beating. In the event, even after 60 years of freedom, India once again has to wait for the "secular" modernity of the West to redefine and reinterpret its home-grown religions.

A more notorious impact of this omission is that the educational agenda of the secular state has not helped us at all to understand better religions and cultural traditions, nor bring us closer to our roots. In direct conflict with the age-old traditional structure of governance, the modern state views religion and its belief structures as a threat to its growth. The conflict manifests itself on different planes: political (between religious elites and government officials), institutional, and cultural (over authority and definition of worldviews) resources. In fact, the tussle for legitimate cultural authority provides an enduring site for conflict and controversy. Modern states reassert their claims by quoting rules from constitutional provisions, statutory laws, and overbearing formal procedures, while the religious specialists quote rules from religious texts and genealogically established procedures, written or oral, handed down from generation to generation through master–pupil lineages (*guru-śiṢya paramparā*). Nor is there an attempt to understand the values of "secularity" of Indic religions. The roots of modern secularism can be sought in the dominance of the church in Western society. Unlike the Western monolithic model, Indic/Hindu society has remained multireligious and multifaceted and has preserved the autonomy of secularism in the religious sphere. Up to a great extent, our society provides a unique example of coexistence of heterogeneous racial, linguistic, and religious groups.

The visceral indifference to the study of religions in India has resulted in strong opinions with miniscule scriptural knowledge, self-taught views/antischolarship views, reading of scriptural texts out of their contexts, and with a mixed bag of analysis—a critical discernment "deficit." When a civilization has no conscious self-understanding of its cultures supported by authoritative scholarship, it subconsciously gives into misinformed judgments about one's religion and culture. We must not forget that it is not secularism but religion that has taught us that life of mind, self-reflection (*svādhyāya*), self-understanding, and self-correction should be pursued constantly. Problematizing the conceptual distinction between "the religious" and "the secular" and its pseudocharacter in the context of India, Inden has observed, "after independence governments implemented secularism mostly by refusing to recognize the religious pasts of Indian nationalism, whether Hindu or Muslim, and at the same time (inconsistently) by retaining Muslim 'personal law.' "[2]

III

The rising tide of the current political ideology of Hindutva produced by the modern patriarchs of the BJP–RSS–VHP combine pose serious threat to the unbiased, dispassionate, and objective study of religion. The irony is that those who claim to protect Hindu religion are ruthless supporters of Hindutva ideology. In recent years, their misreadings and distortions of the Hindu religious texts have precipitated rage, hatred, and religious violence between Hindus and non-Hindu communities. The gut-wrenching genocide that took place in Godhra, Gujarat, is but one example of this human tragedy.[3] The misrepresentation of Hindu tenets has allowed a reinvention of a new genre of politically based normative Hindu ideology, unknown to classical Hindu theologians. This has had far-flung ramifications in all stratums and spheres of civil society. Hindutva is involved in a discursive struggle for "ideological dominance" on several fronts, simultaneously: a struggle to rewrite a racist history, to redefine concepts of secularism and equality, to resurrect gender models and gender roles in increasingly subordinate terms, and to reinvent a legal discourse through a falsification of scriptural injunction and their exegesis, and above all, the political legitimization of sacred Hindu scriptures. I shall attempt to outline the hidden patterns of pseudotheorizing, which has become a *sine qua non* of fundamentalists. What had begun as a by-product of the British rule has now become a permanent feature of communal politics in India. The divide is precipitated by the communal distortions of religious history.

To take one example, the Sangh Parivar is actively engaged in communal interpretations of Hindu scriptures, where they misquote and misinterpret scriptural passages to promote their nationalistic agendas. Arguing for secularism in a legal document, they have quoted the *Yajur Veda* (38.18) that beckons one to look upon all humans as a friend and the *Atharva Veda* (XII.1.45) that speaks of the greatness of the mighty earth that accommodates people of diverse languages and cultures. Many other scriptural passages are freely quoted as a support for their argument to justify the normative ideals of harmony and justice between people. A lavish sprinkling of quotations from the Hindu scriptures mean little if the multicultural ethos of India is subsumed under a monolithic and communal definition of nationhood/Hinduism. As quoted in one of their legal documents:

> The word Hindutva, is used and understood as a synonym of "Indianisation," i.e., development of uniform culture by obliterating the differences between all cultures co-existing in the country.[4]

This ideology filters through their political slogans that proclaim non-Hindus must adopt the dress, mannerisms, language, clothes, and food habits of the Hindus. By misquoting the passages from the scriptures, the Sangh Parivar has broken away from the fundamental truth about the all-inclusive nature of our composite culture extolled by our scriptures. When, for example, the *Atharva Veda* (Bhūmi Sūkta XII.1.45) speaks of the ideals of tolerance, coexistence, and harmony between people, the text presupposes and revalidates a multiethnic cultural identity that celebrates the existing cultural diversity of India. The scriptures idealize the unity between people while they retain all the cultural differences of their respective communities. In this respect, the traditional Hindu view and the Sangh Parivar's view are fundamentally in opposition. The Hindu view accommodates cultural differences, yet opts for unity and harmony between diverse communities. The Sangh Parivar, on the other hand, outrightly rejects cultural differences between Hindu and non-Hindu communities, and opts for a homogenous life style dictated by the Hindus. The Sangh Parivar misreads the passages from the religious text by claiming that the differences between Hindus and non-Hindus should be obliterated.

Furthermore, the sublime and lofty quotes from the scriptures that the Sangh Parivar often use to justify their claims lose their luster on the evidence of reports about vandalism inflicted upon non-Hindu scholars. A recent report reveals how a vast treasure of Sanskrit scriptures owned by a non-Hindu scholar was smashed, looted, and burnt to ashes by a reckless mob of vandals. Such instances are steadily on the rise and run counter to the traditional Hindu reverence for religious texts. The encounters between traditional theology and Sangh Parivar interpolations have meant a descent into a savage stage of human history. The Hinduism preached by the Sangh Parivar has nothing to do with the scriptures, but reflects the pathology of a religion-centered nationalism. It is a task left to the theologians and scholars of religion to critique such pseudotheorizing. But who? How? And where? Is there an institutional base where scholars of religion can voice their views?

We may take another example. The category of Dharma (rule, conduct, and law) has also undergone serious misreading. The notion of Dharma is explained through randomly selected passages from authoritative texts such as the *Ṛg Veda, Taittirīya Upaniṣad, Manusmṛti,* and *Bṛhadāraṇyka Upaniṣad,* suggesting its commonality and universal nature:

> It is such deep-rooted unshakable, everlasting principles and values evolved in this land from times immemorial that are collectively called "Dharma": In common parlance called "Hindu Dharma," Hindutva, Hinduism or Hindu Sanskrit as also "Bhartiya Sanskriti."[5]

Further:

> Any person who follows his own religion would be acting within the rules of Dharma or Hindu Dharma. The appellant and his party sincerely and honestly believe that for the country which is facing widespread decline of moral values, exploitation of caste, religion and language in politics, disunity, crises of character, and many other ills, resurrection of Dharma or Hindutva alone is the remedy.[6]

In the Hindu context, the notion of Dharma is neither immutable nor absolute. Dharma represents a relative notion that has varied with time and changes with usage, convention, and custom, with the result that from the time of the Vedas down to the Tantras, several dissenting traditions and protest movements questioned the notion of Dharma. There is a varying scale of Dharma defined by caste, location, gender, family, and geography—for example, *loka-dharma, deśa-dharma, rāja-dharma, jāti-dharma, kula-dharma, strī-dharma,* etc. In other words, Dharma refers to a personal law with variability and flexibility attached to it. In contrast to this view, what Hindutva preaches is a territorial law with total disregard to the diversity of social and ethnic groups, or origins.

The other aspect of significance is that, unlike the Western juridical system that is grounded on the concept of legality, the traditional Hindu system is based on authority, dictated by "good custom" (*sadācāra*). The transition from the way good custom is accepted as law was instituted by an authoritative assembly (*pariṣad* or the traditional Supreme Court). The assembly consists of several experts: three Vedic experts, one logician, one mīmāṁsaka (an exegete), one scholar of etymology (*nirukta*), one expert on Dharma Shastra, and three others (a celibate, a householder, and an ascetic). The most important element here was the quality of virtue. The assembly adopted precise techniques of interpreting scripture. Controversial issues were resolved by adhering to precise techniques of interpretation following the *mīmāṁsā* method of exegesis.

In contrast to this traditional exegesis, the Hindutva ideologues give an oversimplified, haphazard, schoolbook interpretation. Verses from scriptures are arbitrarily selected and glued together in a cut-copy-paste to promote their political agenda. Randomly selected texts make for distorted, out of context, and stereotyped explanations of scripture. What is more disturbing is that such pseudotheorizing is legitimized in legal documents. Semantic manipulations of this nature denigrate the original validity of scriptural authority that had, thus far, endured through time.

Forms of the Political Mobilization of Religion

The BJP has long recognized the mobilizing potential of diverse religious symbols. All the political projects of VHP–BJP combine are geared to the formation of a Hindu identity, with an emotionally charged sense of Hindu nationalism. Communal mobilization is rooted in the perception that there are identities based on personal faiths and religious beliefs. Such identities can be exploited to gain political power and mobilize religious sentiments of the populace. The forms of political mobilization vary considerably.

The BJP activists have set themselves the task to rewrite a "Hindu history of India" with the sole aim of correcting "distortions" by professional historians. The aim of this project of power is to give a contracted albeit distorted view of history that could be the basis for revivalism of Hindu cultural heritage, excluding other cultures that make up the composite matrix of Indian society. This project legitimizes their agenda to spread communal disharmony between diverse communities, as it privileges one community (namely, Hindus) over others. Dovetailed with this is their educational program. Under this, they have set up a wide network of RSS-affiliated primary schools, numbering not less than 10,000 all over India, called Sarasvati Shishu Mandirs, centrally coordinated by Vidya Bharati. Under the guise of following the curriculum and textbooks prescribed by the government, these schools have introduced several pro-Hindutva elements. A variety of cocurricular activities, like physical education, cultural activities, daily prayers, and talks, are used for promoting a distinctly Hindu identity. Two sets of books, *Sanskar Saurabh* and *Naitika Siksha,* are in circulation. The cover of the book has an image of Bharat Mata, goddess India, holding a flag superimposed on a map of Greater India. The back cover shows a popular muscular image of Sri Ram with bow and arrow propped on the proposed temple at Ayodhya. Lessons in the book are highlighted to promote Hindu religions consciousness and communal ideology. In the *Sanskar Saurab* No. 3, one lesson narrates the martyrdom of two youths in the cause of the temple at Ayodhya, and eulogizes them as modern heroes.[7]

Since 1960, the VHP–BJP combine has juggled with many cultural symbols, drawn from Hindu religious tradition. Among the many strategies of mass manipulation was the sacrifice for a unity processions, based on the format of religious processions organized by temples. Held in 1983, these processions crossed the entire country. Instead of the conventional chariot, they used a truck carrying an image of the goddess Bharat Mata, along with a large sacred vessel filled with Ganges water and smaller pots containing holy water. The statue of Bharat Mata embodies the land and all the goddesses in India rolled into one. Similarly, the Ganges water and smaller pots embodied the sacred waters of India to mirror the unity of India.

In all these instances, religious symbols have been brought into the public sphere, and have become a battleground where their communal project of knowledge is manipulated to seek hegemony and dominion over the populace. One of the most potent of all symbols exploited by them is the universal symbol of "mother goddess" as the image of the nation. The mother archetype is played upon in several different contexts. The first overt proclamation of this equation is found in the Bharat Mata temple in Benaras, which was built around the early period of the 20th century. The spacious temple houses a massive relief map of India, instead of the statue of the goddess. Here the mother goddess is a nation, a "fixed bounded space," imminent and tangible to the eye.

Their urge to map the secular nation as a divine goddess is expressed once again in the newly constructed Bharat Mata temple in the pilgrim site at Haridwar. The temple has been looked upon by its critics as a means to popularize Hindu communal ideology and to raise funds to further the process of Hinduization. The temple consists of many floors, is fully dedicated to the "defenders of the Hindu nation," and is led by Veer Savarkar. The selection of heroes is made by the founder of the temple and includes a number of freedom fighters: Madan Mohan Malviya (the founder of Banaras Hindu University), Veer Savarkar, Subhash Chandra Bose, Chatrapati Shivaji, Guru Gobind Singh, Chandra Shekhar Azad, Rani of Jhansi, etc. Pandit Jawaharlal Nehru is conspicuous by his absence. The statues receive some sort of rituals, and the priest marks the forehead of visitors with a vermilion mark and urges them to donate money. The place is more like a "museum of Hindu nationalism," rather than a customary temple for religious worship.[8]

In the pre-independence era, religion was used as an ideology to unite the people of India. The image of India as a sacred land, personified as goddess—Bharat Mata, was used by the nationalists to unite the nation. Mahatma Gandhi adopted the *sarvadharma* ideology to bring people of all faiths together. After independence, the role of religion has changed drastically. The ideology of Hindutva purports to move away from the pre-independence ethos.

In this scenario, there exists a large agenda to be addressed, to overcome and counter the invisibility and marginalization of the study of religion in India. The major problem is not religion per se, but how it is interpreted. This issue centers around the crisis of religious authority. Who settles religious disputes? Who has the authority to reinterpret Shastra? What rules do they follow? Who empowers them? Today, in Hindu India, there are few authoritative voices who command undisputed respect. Unfortunately, at the same time, any illiterate, politically based individual feels free to cite the Vedas in his support. There are no trusted theologians to challenge their interpretation. There are, of course, a large number of journalists having a secular stance who are supported by rival political parties, and whose agenda is to outstrip Hindutva ideology. But this is not the same as understanding the essence of religion per se.

The only legitimate discourse that will change attitudes toward religion, whether it is Islam, Hindu, or Buddhist, is a constructive and critical internal discourse. Scholars should aim to reinterpret and highlight the positive role that religion has played and is still playing in our lives. Presently, religion in our societies is seen as a force that obstructs democratic values. The scholar's mission should be to separate the study of religion from modern statecraft. Religion and political discourse cannot flourish unless there is a clear-cut separation of religion and state. In this context, the scholars attempt should be to start an internal debate and discussion on the major world religions in order to create (1) an Asian voice, (2) a social space for such discourse, and (3) a political space where our collective voices can be heard. Right now, all our energy goes into maintaining credibility in our respective disciplines. This is a narrow and self-centered position.

As scholars, we are trapped between two extreme views, and modern critiques of religion fall into two camps. The fundamentalists distort and misrepresent religion and use it for political ends. Their critics, who are frequently staunch adherents of Marxism, give a materialistic and often oversimplistic interpretation of religion. For them, religion is an instrument of despotism and theocracy that gives the privileged class a free hand to exercise unlimited authority over all other classes. In both instances, religion comes across as a negative force even though it is one of the most powerful resources of an ancient civilization. There is no Hinduism, Islam, Christianity, Jainism, etc., in an abstract sense. Religion is lived by people. Its contours are adapted and defined by its believers and thinkers. When we speak of resurgence or a degeneration of religion, it is not Hinduism but people to whom we refer. Religion is what people make of it, and thus, it is the responsibility of the scholars, practitioners, and the believers to protect it. Religion can be used for peace or for war, as a force to facilitate human rights, and to promote social justice and conserve democratic values of a nation. How religion is used depends upon the kind of interpretation we give to a particular religious text and the creed it embodies, and responsibility for interpretation lies solely with the scholars of religion.

IV

Quite contrary to India, universities in America and Europe have preserved the "new old" wisdom of faith that goes deep in the study of scripture and traditions of interpretation. There are over a hundred departments of religious studies all over the world. These departments pursue academic study of Semitic and Eastern religions, and have facilitated our understanding of classical heritage and its direction in the modern world. Friedrich Max Müller initiated the comparative study of religion during the middle of the 19th century. Inspired by Goethe who had said, "He who knows one, knows none," Müller's approach to the study of religion was rooted in comparative studies in linguistics, mythology, and the science of religion. His efforts culminated into his grand program of translating the *Sacred Books of the East* (1870ff), in which some of the seminal texts of oriental religion were translated into English. Müller's philological approach was supported by the view that language was the key element of understanding the evolution of human thought.

At the advent of the 20th century, novel approaches to the religion emerged from the scholarly works of sociologists such as Max Weber,

Emile Durkheim, and Franz Boas; psychologists such as Sigmund Freud and Carl Gustav Jung; and the founders of the phenomenology of religion such as Rudolf Otto and Gerardus van der Leeuw, who contributed to the comparative science of religion. Today, the central theoretical questions raised concerning religion such as its definition, origin, scope, structure and meaning, form, and function are explored by a variety of interdisciplinary, cross-cultural approaches including "new humanism" and "creative hermeneutics."[9] Our secular critics, who do not support the view that religion should be taught in the academia in India, are perhaps unaware that today, scholarly enterprise in the field of religion brings together both orthodox and liberal views. Today, theology is no longer the "queen of sciences" dictating each aspect of our endeavor. The scope of religious studies has widened and horizons have expanded. Today, religious studies has emerged as a composite and hybrid field of study. The explorations are based on methodological pluralism, influenced by specializations, local traditions, and cultural traditions. At the same time, on account of diversity of approaches to the study of religion, the subject revels in a web of epistemological tensions. These approaches range from the historical, philological, anthropological, and sociological to the phenomenological approaches in the extreme.

Many of the criticisms that were applicable to the restricted study of theology are no longer valid. In most cases, the traditional study of theology is integrated into religious studies. This integration was considered to be necessary, as it now draws upon work of other disciplines such as anthropology, sociology, history, etc. engaging both critically and constructively with their methods and theories. The result of this fusion is that the study of religions may not be in competition with traditional theology. It seems to be an egalitarian enterprise of learning, which does not replace or exclude age-old patterns. In contrast, the university system in India appears to have branded and cut off their links with traditional scholars and religious specialists. The latter are marginalized and are a dying breed today; at worst, they are considered suspect.

By consigning the academic study of religions to the dustheap of history, India will once again loose out on its grand ideal of retaining autonomy of knowledge of its historical past. As we move up the 21st century, the challenge before India is to put the historical knowledge base of its civilization back on track. This requires critical reflection, self-reflexivity, and a self-conscious research, using critical tools of scholarship. At the same time, a generation of Indian scholars will need to critique the misinterpretation and distortions that constantly appear in current scholarship. A recent book *Invading the Sacred—An Analysis of Hinduism Studies in America*[10] gives several instances of American scholarship on India that distorts and undermines Indian cultural icons. The scholars of the counterforce declared Ganesha's trunk a "limp phallus," classified Devi as the "mother with a penis" and Shiva as "a notorious womanizer" who incites violence in India, and pronounced Sri Rama Krishna a pedophile. These hasty, undigested, insensitive, and myopic readings break down our certitudes about unbiased scholarship.

Traditionally, the right to interpret reality/truth belonged to the philosophers of the diverse religions, who were the honorable custodians. One may ask why only one section of the academia (namely, the social scientists) should enjoy this right. Why is there monopoly over Satya? This is a pertinent question after 60 years of India's independence.

We have given a broad overview of strategies of mass manipulation by Hindu fundamentalists. The ironic fallout of the essentialization of Hinduism has trapped the modern scholar in an abyss of ignorance. It is, as Ashish Nandy states, "culturally hollow, it is nothing more than a post-seventeenth century, European concept of nationality and nation-state projected back into the Indian past developed by the Orientalists as a convenient label to meet the demand of political representation."[11] We need to restore the "dialogic notion of identity and plurality of models for religious articulation." This is only possible if we treat religion as a separate category of academic discourse, institutionalized through the modern-day university system.

The pioneer efforts of Jamia Millia Islamia to establish the Centre for the Study of Comparative Religion and Civilizations, with the sole aim to promote an objective and interdisciplinary study of world religions, is a small step to redress the imbalance in the current educational system. It may well become the third eye of the nation.

NOTES

1. Ananya Vajpeyi, "Teaching against Communalism: Role of Social Sciences Pedagogy," *Economic and Political Weekly* 37, no. 51 (December 21–27, 2002): 5093–96.

2. Ronald B. Inden, *Imagining India* (Bloomington, IN: Indiana University Press, 2001), p. xii.

3. Siddharth Varadarajan, ed., *Gujarat: The Making of a Tragedy* (New Delhi: Penguin Books, 2002). Varadarajan gives a thorough account of the Godhra tragedy in his opening essay "Chronicles of a Tragedy Foretold" (pp. 3–41). The anthology is a permanent archive of the tragic event that took place in Godhra. For some excellent reappraisal and analyses, see Shail Mayaram, "Genocide of the Idea of Gujarat," pp. 404–7 and Achyut Yagnik, "The Pathology of Gujarat," pp. 408–15 in Siddharth Varadarajan, *Gujarat*. See also Praful Bidwai, "From Pokhran to Gujarat," *The Hindustan Times*, May 16, 2002, and Virendra Prakash, *"Hindutva" Demystified* (New Delhi: Virago Publications, 2002).

4. M. Rama Jois, *Supreme Court Judgement on "Hindutva": An Important Landmark* (New Delhi: Suruchi Prakashan, 1996), p. 50.

5. Ibid., p. 16.

6. Ibid., pp. 17, 18.

7. K.N. Pannikar, *Communal Threat Secular Challenge* (Chennai: Earthworm Publications, 2007), Chap. 4, pp. 73–88, 97.

8. Lisa McKean, "Bharat Mata" in John Stratton Hawley and Donna Marie Wulff, eds., *Devi Goddesses of India* (Berkeley, CA: University of California, 1996), pp. 251–280.

9. Armin W. Geertz and Russel T. Mc Cutcheon, *Perspectives on Method and Theory in Study of Religion* (Leiden: Brill, 2000), pp. 3–36.

10. Krishnan Ramaswamy, Antonio de Nicolas, and Aditi Banerjee, *Invading the Sacred—An Analysis of Hinduism Studies in America* (Delhi: Rupa & Co., 2007).

11. Ashis Nandy, Shail Mayaram, and Achyut Yagnik, *Creating a Nationality: The Ramjanmabhumi Movement and Fear of the Self* (New Delhi: Oxford University Press, 1995), pp. 63 ff.

Chapter 11

Human Rights in Cross-Cultural Perspective

Joseph Prabhu

The concept of human rights—i.e., the rights that attach to a human being, *qua* human being, quite apart from their place in a social order and apart from considerations of citizenship, ethnicity, class, religion, or gender—is a relatively recent one. It has its origin in the natural rights tradition of Hobbes and Locke in the 17th century and was given perhaps its most rigorous formulation by Kant in the 18th century. I shall in this chapter not be concerned with these classic formulations of this idea but with its modern incarnation in the Universal Declaration of Human Rights (hereafter UDHR) adopted by the General Assembly of the United Nations on December 10, 1948. What interests me is the history of this document both at its inception and during its subsequent *Rezeptionsgeschichte* over the past 60-odd years. Studying this history might help to shed light on the prospects of cross-cultural dialogue on this question.

The declaration marked a new chapter in a history that began with the great charters of humanity's first rights movements in the 17th and 18th centuries. The British Bill of Rights of 1689, the U.S. Declaration of Independence of 1776, and the French Declaration of the Rights of Man and Citizen of 1789 were all born out of struggles to overthrow autocratic and despotic rule and to establish governments based on the consent of the governed. They proclaimed that all men were born free and equal, and that the purpose of government was to protect man's natural liberties. They gave rise to the modern language of rights, but what was unique about UDHR was that unlike these nationally generated bills of rights, UDHR was universal in origin and scope and the language it spoke and the norms it articulated were meant to apply to all the different societies and cultures of the world.

From the outset, that language of rights divided into two dialects. One, influenced by continental European thinkers, especially Rousseau, provided more room for equality and fraternity and tempered rights with duties and limits. It cast the state in a positive light as guarantor of rights and protector of the needy. Charters in this tradition—the French constitutions of the 1790s and the Prussian General Code of 1794—combined political and civil rights with public obligations to provide relief for the poor. In the late 19th and early 20 centuries, these paternalistic principles evolved into social and economic rights, overseen by a social welfare state.

The Anglo-American dialect of rights language emphasized individual liberty and initiative more than equality or social solidarity and was in general infused with a greater mistrust of government. Especially in the American context, ever since the founding of the nation, this emphasis and the ambiguity of the notion of "liberty" have led to heated and profound debates as to the implications of such liberty. Is it the freedom to be left alone and to get government in particular off the backs of citizens or is it the freedom to participate in government and share in the creation of policy?

In 1948, the framers of the UDHR attempted to achieve a distinctive synthesis of previous thinking about rights and duties. They made a deliberate attempt to be global in their approach. After canvassing sources from all parts of the world, they believed they had found a core of principles so basic that no nation would wish openly to disavow them. They wove these principles into a unified document that quickly displaced all antecedents as the principal model for the rights instruments in force in the contemporary world. It is that document that I wish to analyze, and I will try to do so in four sections.

In the first, I review something about the declaration itself, its background, its content, and its purposes. In the second, I examine some challenges both theoretical and practical that have arisen to the consensus achieved in the declaration. In the third, I suggest a way of understanding this fraying of consensus and attempt to spell out its implications. Finally, in the fourth and concluding section, I attempt to sketch a way forward that tries to preserve what is most valuable about the notion of human rights, while still being sensitive to the valid points raised by the challenges.

UDHR: ITS BACKGROUND AND CONTENT

If we look back from our contemporary perspective at the drafting of UDHR in 1948, it seems extraordinary that such a document could ever have been written and almost unanimously agreed on. It seems fair to say that it would simply not be possible today with all the cultural, ethnic, social, and religious differences that are a prominent part of our present-day world. Indeed, the period between the U.N. Charter of 1945 and the UDHR on December 10, 1948 was a very special time in recent history. In February 1947, the Cold War between the two superpowers, the United States and the former USSR, and the subsequent division of the world into two ideological camps had begun but was not yet so advanced and bedeviled with ideological paranoia as to make all headway impossible. While problematic figures like Andrei Vyshinsky, Stalin's prosecutor in the Red Terror, participated in the deliberations and made sure that the entire Soviet bloc abstained in the final vote on the declaration, they did not sabotage it altogether. The Chinese delegate to the drafting committee was a scholarly and liberal Confucian named Peng Chun Chang, who had studied with John Dewey at Columbia University, earning a Ph.D. in philosophy in 1921. The Arab League spokesman Charles Malik, a student of both Whitehead of Harvard and of Heidegger at Freiburg, was another gifted and cosmopolitan philosopher, whose philosophical stance was deeply influenced by Thomism. In spite of heated debates between Chang and Malik and the other members of the drafting committee, they were still able to rise above their differences and work out a consensus.

Likewise, decolonization was underway in Asia, but the newly independent nations did not as yet feel impelled to challenge the hegemony of Western rights discourse and insist upon the distinctiveness of their own moral traditions. This had partly to do with the fact that many of the leaders of these nations had received a Western education and with the fact that the countries themselves had not had the time to assert their own cultural particularity in global form. Whatever the reasons, the great philosophical and cultural conflict between "the West and the Rest," to adopt Samuel Huntington's notorious phrase, still lay in the future. The challenge of radical Islam, the so-called Asian values debates, the conflict between socialist and capitalist human rights philosophies, and the challenges from women's groups that UDHR did not adequately address the concerns of women, all these were still ahead.

But no doubt the greatest factor making for universal agreement about a bill of human rights was the memory of the recent world war and the Holocaust in particular. Men and women throughout a shattered world were yearning not only for peace but also for a freer and better existence in the future. Thus, the preamble of the U.N. Charter of 1945 says, "We, the peoples of the UN, are determined to save succeeding generations from the scourge of war, which twice in our lifetime has brought untold sorrow to mankind . . . to promote social progress and better standards of life in larger freedom." In such a climate, it was easy to link the reduction of the likelihood of war with the prevention of large-scale violations of people's rights. The emphasis on liberty in the declaration is inseparable from its call to social responsibility and respect for fundamental human dignity. The opening words of UDHR read, "Recognition of the inherent dignity and of the equal and inalienable rights of all members of the human family is the foundation of freedom, justice, and peace in the world." Human rights, in theory at least, would provide individuals—and later, groups—some moral protection against the oppression of governments and majority groups in a society.

The Holocaust made the declaration possible, but its influence was also paradoxical. The declaration envisioned a world where, if human beings found their civil and political rights as citizens taken away, they could still appeal for protection on the basis of their rights as human beings. In theory, therefore, beneath the civil and political rights stood the fundamental and natural rights. But the Holocaust showed that once civil and political rights were taken away, human beings in practice were often defenseless. As Hannah Arendt wrote in a haunting sentence in her *Origins of Totalitarianism* published in 1951: "It seems that a man who is nothing but a man has lost the very qualities which make it possible for other people to treat him as a fellow human being." It was this nakedness that the provisions of the UDHR attempted to dignify and bolster—at the very moment when the world had seen it spurned. As Michael Ignatieff has expressed it, "The Holocaust laid bare what the world looked like when natural law was abrogated, when pure tyranny could accomplish its unbridled will. Without the Holocaust, then, no Declaration. Because of the Holocaust, no unconditional faith in the Declaration either." Like all moral documents, the UDHR attempts to mold and sensitize human consciousness; it does not provide guarantees.

Having dealt with the background and context of the declaration, let me come to its content and purposes. It might be easier to analyze its content in terms of the heuristic device provided by Rene Cassin, who was the chief legal counsel for De Gaulle in his government-in-exile and one of the key participants in the framing of the declaration. He compared the declaration to the portico of a temple, a word carefully chosen to point to his faith that the declaration could never be more than an entryway to a better world. In Cassin's image, the preamble with its seven stately clauses represents the courtyard steps of the portico. The general principles of dignity, liberty, equality, and brotherhood (contained in Articles 1 and 2) are the portico's four foundation blocks. The main body of the declaration consists of rights arranged in four columns. The first pertaining to individual as such (Articles 3–11) includes such fundamental rights as the right to life, basic liberties, and security; the rights of *habeas corpus;* and due process in legal proceedings and equal protection before the law. The second pertains to the rights of the individual in relation to others and to various groups in civil society (Articles 12–17) and includes such rights as the rights of freedom of movement, asylum, privacy, marriage, personal integrity; and the right to property.

The third concerns spiritual, public, and political liberties (Articles 18–21) and covers freedoms of thought, conscience, and religion; freedom of opinion and expression; and freedom of democratic participation. The fourth deals with economic, social, and cultural rights (Articles 22–27) and includes the rights to work, social security, a just wage, education, health, and basic material necessities. The declaration is crowned by a pediment (Articles 28–30) linking the individual and society and placing the enumerated rights in the context of limits, duties, and the social and political order in which they are to be realized.

When read as it was meant to be, namely as a whole and as an integrated document, the declaration can be seen to rest on the concept of the dignity of the human person, not just as an individual but also as a person within the human family. In substance as well as in form, it is a declaration of interdependence—interdependence of people, nations, and rights grounded in the link between individual freedom and social solidarity. What the scope and limits of this interdependence are is debatable—whether, for example, it provides sanctions for military campaigns like those in Bosnia and Kosovo. But it is certain that the modern doctrine of human rights weakens the presumption in favor of state sovereignty and strengthens the presumption in favor of international intervention when massacre and deportation become state policy. It definitely points to a post-Westphalian international order.

Having articulated the content of the declaration, let me now spell out some of its salient characteristics and implications. First, human rights are indeed *rights,* i.e., entitlements carrying claims against other parties. Should these parties fail to discharge their obligations, they are violating the rights of the rights holders, who can then impose sanctions. This is what is implied by the notion of "exercising" rights. Beyond benefiting their holders, rights actually empower them. To claim that there are human rights is to claim that all human beings, simply by virtue of being human, have rights in this sense.

Second, these rights are held to be universal and universally applicable. This implies that characteristics such as race, sex, religion, ethnicity, social position, and nationality are irrelevant to whether one has human rights.

Third, human rights are held to exist independently of recognition or implementation in the customs or legal systems of particular countries. These rights may not be *effective* rights unless legally implemented, but they nonetheless exist as standards of argument and criticism, independently of legal implementation.

Fourth, these rights imply duties for both individuals and governments. These duties, like the rights with which they are linked, are alleged to exist independently of acceptance, recognition, or implementation. Governments and people everywhere are obligated not to violate a person's rights.

Finally, these rights establish minimal standards of decent social and governmental practice. The nearly two dozen specific rights contained in the declaration are alleged to be the minimal provisions consistent with the dignity and worth of human beings and the requirements of domestic and international peace and security. In describing the declaration as a "common standard of achievement," the framers were setting up moral standards rather than legal rights. Leaving them as universal moral norms reflected the framers' desire for a document of broad application that would endure through changing times and differing interpretations and forms of implementation.

How well has the declaration in fact held up in the intervening 60-odd years?

CHALLENGES TO THE PRESUMED MORAL UNIVERSALITY OF THE DECLARATION

Fired by both the horror of the war and the Holocaust that they had just witnessed and by the window of opportunity that they discerned in the period from the war's end in 1945–1948, the drafters of the declaration seized the moment and were able to achieve consensus about a bill of rights. But they harbored no illusions about how deep the agreement they had reached went. As Jacques Maritain, one of the thinkers consulted, put it cryptically, "Yes, we agree about the rights, but on condition that no one asks us why."[1] Maritain and his colleagues did not regard this lack of consensus on conceptual foundations as fatal. When Eleanor Roosevelt, widow of the late American president, first convened a drafting committee meeting in February 1947, the Chinese Confucian Chang and the Lebanese Thomist Malik, both of them good friends, got into such an argument about the philosophical and theological bases of rights that Mrs. Roosevelt, ever the pragmatist, quickly concluded that having such discussions was not the best path to follow in this context. The only feasible goal was to achieve agreement not on the basis of common speculative ideas, but on common practical ones, and not on the affirmation of one and the same conception of the world, of man, and of knowledge—which was impossible—but upon the affirmation of a single body of beliefs for guidance in action. If there are some things so terrible in practice that virtually no one will publicly approve them and some things so good in practice that virtually no one will oppose them, a common project can move forward without agreement on the underlying reasons for these proposals.

An international Declaration of Rights would provide a framework within which divergent philosophies, religious worldviews, and economic, social, and political theories might fruitfully be discussed. The challenge was to make the framework sufficiently definite to have real focus and significance, both as an inspiration and as a guide to practice, and also sufficiently general and flexible to apply to all men and women. Furthermore, it had to be capable of modification to suit people at different stages of social and political development.

Only five years later, the entire scene had changed. The Soviet Union had tested a hydrogen bomb, China had fallen to the Communists, the Korean War between the Communist North and the pro-Western South had broken out, and the superpowers increasingly regarded human rights as a tedious obstacle to the pursuit of great power politics. From 1948 until the Helsinki Final Act in 1975, there were in fact two distinct human rights cultures sharply opposed to each other—socialist and capitalist. The former gave primacy to social and economic rights, the latter to civil and political rights. Polemics and hostilities between these two camps made a genuinely universal human rights culture impossible. With this initial fraying of consensus came other challenges over the years that further whittled away at the agreement reached in the declaration. There was first the obvious and glaring lacuna in the declaration about enforcement and accountability. Agreement on high principles was made easier by leaving the matter of their enforcement unresolved. Nothing in the declaration mandated the right of member states to intervene in another country's affairs to stop human rights abuses, which made intervention in Kosovo, for example, so problematic. In the absence of clarity about questions concerning enforcement, accountability, and sanctions, human rights treaties, agencies, and instruments multiply and yet the volume and scale of human rights abuses increase steadily. In part, this is not only a problem of success—abuses are now more visible and more documented—but also a sign of failure. The discrepancy between what states agree to in treaties and what they actually do in practice is so large that talk of human rights can easily evoke cynicism and ridicule. Cambodia, Sudan, Bosnia, Chechnya, Rwanda, East Timor, Columbia, and now Kosovo, just to choose a few examples, show that the diffusion of a global human rights consciousness has done little to halt senseless and widespread killing and what some moralists call "a culture of death."[2]

It is not just this bad faith and unwillingness to keep promises, implicit or explicit, that have of late caused demoralization about human rights discourse, but there is also a philosophical crisis, a sense that the pragmatic silences that paper over vast differences lying just below the surface need to be confronted. In a changed world, where the special circumstances surrounding the drafting of the declaration no longer prevail, these differences impinge not only on the diversity of worldviews but also on the practical beliefs guiding action. The gap between theoretical and practical reasons that Maritain and others hoped to exploit in order to arrive at some common principles of basic rights is not always easy to bridge. This is especially true in a postmodern world, where the language of universality is not easily accepted and where, on the contrary, claims of difference and of particularity tend to get emphasized.

In this section, I briefly discuss two sets of challenges—there are obviously many more—to the moral universality implied in the UDHR, and then in the following section, I draw out and elaborate on some of their implications. There is first of all the calling into question of the predominantly secular character of the declaration. A cloak of silence was thrown over the question of religion, not only because of reasons of universal appeal, but also because of the vast diversity of religious sentiment and the complications of having to deal with it. As the preamble to the declaration indicates, "human dignity" was chosen as the foundational concept on which the notion of human rights was based, without further inquiries into where that dignity came from and why that dignity ought to be protected with rights. By what right do human beings have rights in the first place? In recent times, these questions have been asked not just by Islamic traditionalists, who are very skeptical of Western notions of human autonomy and of the secularism that goes along with it, but also by religious thinkers in the West. To the extent to which the declaration makes man the measure of all things, and nature and God are completely ignored, they see disturbing evidence of idolatry.

That this is not just a theological nicety, but one that also has serious practical consequences may be seen by revisiting the Salman Rushdie affair. This played out in the West by and large as a straightforward instance of a clash of secular freedom versus religious authoritarianism, a case of fundamental freedom of expression being thwarted by theocratic rule. But this is a simplistic and quite unsatisfactory account of the issues involved. For one thing, it puts religious sensitivities unqualifiedly in the camp of theocracy and authoritarianism, ignoring the fact that many religious Muslims who found *The Satanic Verses* deeply offensive, nonetheless, decried the harshness of Ayatollah Khomeini's *fatwa* or death warrant. For another, it absolutized the notion of artistic freedom of expression and allowed it in all cases to trump religious sentiment relating to the sacredness of texts and figures. From a human rights standpoint, it may be asked, "Why the freedom of expression of one individual ought to be given priority over the spiritual sensibilities and feelings of an entire religious group numbering close to one billion people?"

To raise these questions is by no means to agree with or condone the *fatwa*. The important question in our context is that within the prevailing secularism and the individualistic cast of the declaration, there is no adequate space for such questions to be satisfactorily discussed. The Western Enlightenment conceptions of virtue and the human good are not prescriptive for non-Western peoples, although they play a big part in the underlying justification of human rights in the declaration. To think that they are prescriptive is to be guilty not only of a form of cultural imperialism but also of a form of secular fundamentalism, which can in its own way be as damaging to human dignity as any other form of fundamentalism.

If the secular nature of the declaration is one area of criticism and protest, the Western origin and cast of both the legal forms of right and the underlying individualism that is seen to ground them have also been strenuously objected to. Perhaps, the clearest form of this challenge is the so-called Asian values debate. In the interest of summarizing a very wide-ranging and multifaceted discussion, I cite a famous set of remarks by Lee Kwan Yew, the former prime minister of Singapore, as a way of highlighting both the tone and substance of the criticism: "I find parts of [the American system] totally unacceptable: guns, drugs, violent crime, vagrancy, unbecoming behavior in public—in sum the breakdown of civil society. The expansion of the right of the individual to behave or misbehave as he pleases has come at the expense of orderly society. In the East the main object is to have a well-ordered society so that everybody can have maximum enjoyment of his freedoms. This freedom can only exist in an ordered state and not in a natural state of contention."[3]

The basic notion here is that Western rights practice is seen as deficient and as unsuitable for other societies, in particular East Asian ones. It supposes that individuals are the possessors of rights and encourages them to go out and aggressively make good their rights claims. But this has a number of bad consequences. First of all, it makes people focus on their rights, what they can claim from society and others, rather than on their responsibilities and duties, what they owe to the whole community or to its members. Thus, it encourages people to be self-regarding, self-centered, and acquisitive, and leads to an atrophied sense of belonging and community. This in turn leads to a higher degree of social conflict, tending ultimately to a Hobbesian war of all against all. Social solidarity weakens and the threat of violence increases.

It may be worth mentioning in passing that this rhetoric of Lee Kwan Yew is the mirror image of the imperialist rhetoric that the British used to justify their policy of colonization, a language that Yew had no doubt often heard as a colonial subject. In both instances, authoritarianism is justified on moral grounds to curb a purported decadence: in one case, the moral laxity of people in South- and Southeast-Asian colonies of the British; in the other, the laxity in the West that must not be allowed to infect upright and decent Asians. Whatever the deeper, and I might add highly dubious, reasons behind Lee Kwan Yew's rhetoric, in terms of the validity of its critique, it certainly articulates a discomfort that many have with at least one form of human rights discourse, the highly individualist, acquisitive version, which the Canadian political theorist C. B. MacPherson once called "possessive individualism."[4] Thus, a communitarian like Charles Taylor can say of Yew's criticism: "It seems to have elements of truth . . . in fact, there is a long tradition in the West warning against pure rights talk outside a context in which the political community has a strong positive value. This 'communitarian' theorizing has taken on a new urgency today because of the experience of conflict and alienation and the fraying of solidarity in many Western democracies."[5]

Both the criticisms I have mentioned, the first against the secular tone of the declaration and the second against its supposedly Western character, highlight philosophical difficulties. I have suggested that the special historical circumstances prevailing at the time of the drafting of the declaration were able to smooth over and contain these rough edges. Today, when universalisms of various kinds are being questioned and particular identities being affirmed in a so-called politics of difference, that containment is no longer possible. What then does the present debate around the issue and the future prospects of human rights discourse look like?

MORAL UNIVERSALITY UNDER SIEGE

It was not as if the dialectic of moral universality and cultural particularity was completely ignored by the drafters of the declaration. In 1947, they received a long memorandum from the American Anthropological Association, which expressed worries about ethnocentrism—the tendency to pass off the particular values of one's own culture as normative for other cultures: "How can the proposed Declaration be applicable to all human beings and not be a statement of rights conceived only in terms of values prevalent in the countries of Western Europe and America?" In particular, the anthropologists highlighted three propositions for the Human Rights Commission to consider: (1) the individual realizes his personality through his culture, hence respect for individual differences entails respect for cultural differences; (2) respect for differences between cultures is further validated by the scientific fact that no technique of qualitatively evaluating different cultures has been discovered; and (3) standards and values are relative to the culture from which they derive, so that any attempt to formulate postulates that grow out of the beliefs or moral codes of one culture must to that extent detract from the applicability of any declaration of human rights to mankind as a whole. What is held to be a human right in one society may be regarded as antisocial by another or by the same people at a different period of their history.

That there is a whole set of culturally biased assumptions in the declaration cannot be denied. This is simply unavoidable. Thus, the very notion of human rights rests on the basis of a supposedly universal human nature common to all peoples. Furthermore, this common human nature is believed to be inherent in man and a part of common knowledge. Otherwise, human rights could not be declared universal by a group that made no claims to privileged knowledge. This is made plain by the use of the word "declaration," which stresses the fact that it is not an imposition or a construction, but rather a public explication, a making clear of what is inherent in the very nature of man. Spelling out the cultural biases and assumptions, and indeed acknowledging that many of these assumptions are Western in origin and nature, does not however vitiate it any more than acknowledging the Arabic and Indian contribution to mathematics in the West disqualifies them from normative consideration. Historical contingency and cultural diversity are brute facts, not answers to normative questions.

Anticipating the concerns of organizations like the American Anthropological Association and the thrust of the above-mentioned questions, UNESCO (United Nations Educational, Scientific, and Cultural Organization) recruited some of the leading thinkers and philosophers of the day for a committee to investigate the theoretical bases of human rights. As I have explained earlier in this chapter, the general approach of the committee and subsequently of the drafters of the declaration was to distinguish sharply between the practical and the theoretical. In response to the question, "How is agreement conceivable among men and women who come not only from different cultures and civilizations, but also from sometimes antagonistic schools of thought?"[6] The philosophers concluded that even people who seemed to be far apart in theoretical and cultural outlook could agree on a few practical norms. As they put it, such people can agree "that certain things are so terrible in practice that no one will publicly approve them, and that certain things are so good in practice that no one will publicly oppose them." Torture, rape, child prostitution, and blatant racism, for example, were thought to be universally abhorred, while survival, liberty, security, personal integrity, and equality were seen as universally commended. Of course, this argument was pitched at the level of ideals, not of political reality. Even as the drafting committee was at work, the Cold War between the United States and the Soviet Union was starting and the blockade of Berlin was instituted by Stalin, tensions simmered in Palestine over the creation of the state of Israel, and conflict broke out in Greece, Korea, China, India, and Pakistan.

This "solution" to the problems of cultural diversity and relativism, of opting for a universalism at the practical level, while allowing for pluralism at the theoretical, was nonetheless made possible by an ethical idealism that might be considered utopian today. In order to show this, I want to contrast two answers to the central philosophical question of how to understand the "human" of human rights, the *humanum*. Charles Malik, perhaps the deepest philosophical mind on the drafting committee and one who exerted considerable influence on the final form of the declaration, proposed four principles to guide the work of the commission. First, the human person is more important than any national or cultural group to which he may belong. Second, a person's mind, conscience, and inherent dignity are his most sacred and inviolable possessions. Third, any pressure from the state, church, or any other group aimed at coercing consent is unacceptable. Fourth, since groups as well as individuals may be right or wrong, the individual's freedom of conscience must be supreme.

Compare that conception of the human being with this one taken from the contemporary human rights thinker Michael Ignatieff:

> What it means to be a human being, what defines the very identity we share as a species is the fact that we are differentiated by race, religion, ethnicity, and individual difference. These differentiations define our identity, both as individuals and as a species. No other species differentiates itself in this individualized abundance. A sense of otherness, of distinctness is the very basis of the consciousness of our individuality, and this consciousness, based in difference, is a constitutive element of what it is to be a human being. . . . In this way of thinking we understand humanity, our common flesh and blood, as valuable to the degree that it allows us to elaborate the dignity and honor that we give to our differences.[7]

We have here two moral and idealistic definitions of a human being, but the abstractness of the first stands in marked contrast to the concreteness of the second. Human rights, like many other moral questions of our day, are balanced, stably at some times and unstably at others, between the two poles of an abstract universalism and concrete particularism, tilting in one direction or the other. In the 53 years of its existence, the UDHR has unquestionably changed our moral landscape, bringing in its wake a great number of covenants, treaties, and protocols. At the start of the 21st century, there is not a single nation, culture, or people that is not in one way or another involved with questions of human rights.

But the UDHR is not a finished or a frozen document. Charles Malik believed that over time, the declaration's principles would "either bring to light an implicit agreement already operative, perhaps dimly and unconsciously, in the systems and ways of life of the various peoples, or consciously and creatively advance further the area of agreement."[8] The UDHR serves as a framework for such ongoing cross-cultural conversation, which is its very lifeblood. And how such conversation might most fruitfully be conducted is presented in the final section.

THE CHALLENGES OF CROSS-CULTURAL DIALOGUE

Ignatieff's dialectical notion of human identity based on difference rather than sameness points to what cross-cultural conversation entails. Rights are after all social constructs, so that it is futile to think that we can bypass the challenge of cultural difference by opting for a biological or naturalistic notion of humanness. It is appropriate in this context to remind ourselves of Hegel's teaching on this point. For Hegel, the very self-consciousness that individualizes human beings simultaneously socializes them and links them to other self-conscious beings in an organized community. As he says in a famous passage from *The Phenomenology of Spirit:* "Spirit is the absolute substance, which is the unity of the different independent self-consciousnesses, which in their opposition enjoy perfect freedom and independence. An 'I' that is a 'we' and a 'we' that is an 'I.' "[9] A system of rights, says Hegel, can only be worked among persons, a social concept standing in marked contrast to isolated individuality. And to be a person means at a minimum to be a "self," i.e., to possess self-consciousness. Self-conscious persons must recognize one another as selves, or to put it differently, there must be a correlation between rights claimed by one person and the potential duties imposed on other persons. In mutual recognition (*Anerkennung*), there arises the awareness that the capacity of one person to claim rights depends on his ability to accord all others the same status as rights holders. Human rights, therefore, are inseparable from integral membership in a collectivity composed of free and independent persons, united by relationships and obligations to one another.

That idea of sociality suggests three models of cultural exchange that I want to distinguish—the supracultural, the supercultural, and the intercultural. The supracultural model, as exemplified in the earlier natural rights tradition, for example, attempts to rise above or transcend the realm of the cultural by invoking some divine or natural essence that is alleged to be the true mark of our humanity. Quite aside of the category mistake involved in thinking that a theological construct can do the work of a political one, there is the problem that even a divine essence has to be mediated through human and cultural understanding with all its context of boundedness. There is thus no escaping the challenge of culture. The same argument applies *a fortiori* to an attempt to define the human at some purely biological level. The derivation of social norms from biological data is also culturally mediated.

If the supracultural model is unviable, the temptation is to go to the supercultural, which is, in fact, very often done. This consists in the assertion that human rights thinking represents an advanced state of cultural evolution, which not all cultures have achieved. In actuality, it is Western culture alone that is alleged to have done so, and what the universality of human rights means is that non-Western cultures now have to embark on the same journey and path of modernization as the West. Just as, for example, the West moved "beyond" its religious heritage to arrive at a "mature" secular outlook that can serve as the proper basis for human rights, other cultures must be expected to do the same, if human rights are to be truly universal. Universality, in other words, in this model is seen as an emulation, a mimesis, of the West that provides the universal standards. Universality is here confused with uniformity.

Sometimes, this conclusion is argued not in terms of cultural evolution but in terms of normativity. The example of Newtonian physics is used to claim that the Western origin of human rights should not be used to invalidate its universal applicability. It is true that one should not confuse genesis with validity, or the context of discovery with the context of justification. But a stronger claim is being made in the supercultural model and that is that the notion of human rights, as it is understood in the West, provides the only notional understanding on which universality should be achieved. This is no longer a *descriptive* assertion about origins, which are after all historically contingent, but a *prescriptive* claim that is debatable.

It is debatable because the universalizability of the Western notion of human rights is an attempt to universalize what is in fact a very particular idea, which has meaning and validity within a particular cultural context. The underlying ideas of the individual, of individual autonomy, of human dignity separate from solidarity with all of life, and of rights isolated from duties—all the ideas that are used to ground human rights in the West—are not only not shared in the non-Western world by and large, but are also seen as highly problematic. Here, for example, was Gandhi's reply to the inquiries from the UNESCO philosophers' committee when they sought responses to initial drafts of UDHR: "All rights to be deserved and preserved come from duty well done. Thus the very right to live accrues to us only when we do the duty of citizenship of the world. From this one fundamental statement, perhaps it is easy enough to define the duties of Man and Woman and correlate every right to some corresponding duty to be first performed. Every other right can be shown to be a usurpation hardly worth fighting for."[10]

It is not just that the supercultural model represents a form of cultural imperialism, of imposing a particular ethnocentric standard on the rest of the world and assuming a universality that in fact is not present and has yet to be achieved, but also a form of epistemological blindness, where one lacks the imagination or the will or both to recognize that the dominant Western way of conceiving human rights represents only *one way* of looking at things, one particular language and understanding, and that there are other ways that need at least to be considered. Truth is indeed universalizable, or else it would be no different from opinion. But the expression of truth in specific concepts and symbols is ineluctably perspectival. No one and no one culture has direct access to the universal range of human experience, a stance that the English ethicist Henry Sidgwick once called "the point of view of the universe." We can only indirectly and through a necessarily limited perspective come to know what we believe to be the truth. To say this is not necessarily to agree with Nietzsche that truth is reducible to interpretation. It is rather to point to the inevitable partiality of interpretation and to suggest that truth emerges out of the encounter and dialogue of different interpretations.

It is this dialogic encounter that opens up the space for the third model—the intercultural one. Here one starts from the humble premise that one's culture is not only one among many with diverse strengths and achievements, but also with partialities and blind spots. This model that I am advocating attempts neither to transcend cultural differences (as in the case of the supracultural model), nor to finesse these differences by making one culture superior and normative for the others. It rather takes the other cultures as seriously as it takes itself and attempts an open-minded, meaning-and-truth-seeking dialogue.

This is not the occasion for spelling out the methodology of this cross-cultural hermeneutic, which I have done elsewhere, a hermeneutic that attempts to cross epistemological and ontological boundaries. Let me rather conclude this chapter by suggesting how such a model might actually work in the area of human rights dialogue. In order to do this, I am going to adopt a distinction made by Charles Taylor. He distinguishes in human rights discourse between moral norms, legal forms, and background philosophical and religious justifications:

> What we are looking for, in the end, is a world consensus on certain norms of conduct enforceable on governments. To be accepted in any given society, these would in each case have to repose on some widely acknowledged philosophical justification, and to be enforced, they would have to find expression in legal mechanisms. One way of putting our central question might be this: what variations can we imagine in philosophical justifications or in legal forms that would still be compatible with a meaningful universal consensus on what really matters to us, the enforceable norms?[11]

This tripartite distinction between norms, legal mechanisms, and justification provides the framework within which cross-cultural dialogue proceeds and in this context, how it may be possible to move beyond Western ethnocentrism. It allows for the recognition and acceptance of the fact that there are many human rights cultures around the world, even if human rights is not necessarily the term these cultures would use in self-description. In many of them, the relations between morality, positive law, and worldviews are differently articulated than in the West. For instance, the classical Indian moral universe is pervaded by the notion of *dharma*, a concept that some Indians invoke in the context of human rights discussion. *Dharma* is a multivocal concept, signifying morality, religion, truth, justice, and much else. But it does not start with the individual, whose rights it is concerned to protect from the encroachments or oppression of society and the state. From the dharmic standpoint, human reality is not incarnated in the individual only but in the social whole also, and the social whole in turn is an expression of a cosmic order whose integrity *dharma* tries to protect. From such a perspective, many of the assumptions underlying Western human rights discourse would be disputed. In addition to a critique of individualism, the tradition of *dharma* would also criticize the idea of rights being separated from responsibilities and the idea of rights applying to humans alone.

I am not concerned, in adducing this example, with conducting a full-fledged dialogue between these two moral universes, which would require a presentation unto itself. I only wish to suggest that each tradition might have something to contribute to the other and to the development of a global human rights culture. The further evolution of human rights discourse needs to go beyond the limits of its original Western-oriented formulation.

CONCLUSION

The 53 years of the UDHR have indeed revolutionized our moral thinking to the point where as U.N. Secretary General Kofi Annan has suggested it may have become the "yardstick by which we measure human progress." The Nobel Laureate Nadine Gordimer goes even further in describing it as the "essential document, the touchstone, the creed of humanity that surely sums up all other creeds directing human behavior."[12] Archbishop Desmond Tutu, talking about the South African struggle against apartheid, says, "We who have suffered under injustice where the most fundamental rights were flagrantly violated give thanks for the existence of this Universal Declaration of Human Rights for serving to inspire us to be subversive of that injustice and oppression. We must all, everywhere, commit ourselves to work for an ordering of society where the contents of the Declaration are embodied and also to remain forever vigilant against a violation of those rights."[13]

I have tried in this chapter to provide a context and a history for this remarkable document. In assaying a selective critique of it, I am by no means insensitive to its signal importance. On the contrary, precisely because I am convinced of its importance and the urgency of its more widespread implementation, I have tried to provide some constructive proposals for the broadening and deepening of the consensus upon which the future of human rights depends. It seems to me that this can best be done by, on the one hand, looking for and strengthening the internal discourse of local cultures around human rights and, on the other, by promoting intercultural conversation, engaging in the cross-cultural hermeneutic I have outlined. In that way, one can hope to move toward the universality that the UDHR proclaims, but whose actual achievement still lies in the future.

NOTES

1. Jacques Maritain cited in Mary Ann Glendon, *A World Made New: Eleanor Roosevelt and the Universal Declaration of Human Rights* (New York: Random House, 2001), p. 77. This article is heavily dependent on this fine book, especially for the historical sections.

2. See, for example, Edith Wyschogrod, *Spirit in Ashes: Hegel, Heidegger, and Man-Made Mass Death* (New Haven, CT: Yale University Press, 1990).

3. Lee Kwan Yew cited in Charles Taylor, "Conditions of an Unforced Consensus on Human Rights" in Joanne Bauer and Daniel Bell, eds., *The East Asian Challenge for Human Rights* (New York: Cambridge University Press, 1999), p. 126. Taylor in turn is citing an interview conducted by Fareed Zakaria with Yew, "Culture Is Destiny: A Conversation with Lee Kwan Yew," *Foreign Affairs,* March/April 1994, 111.

4. See C. B. MacPherson, *The Political Theory of Possessive Individualism: Hobbes to Locke* (Oxford: Clarendon Press, 1962).

5. Taylor, "Conditions of an Unforced Consensus on Human Rights," p. 130.

6. Glendon, *A World Made New,* p. 222.

7. Michael Ignatieff, "Lemkin's World," *The New Republic,* February 26, 2001, 27, 28.

8. Glendon, *A World Made New,* pp. 222, 223.

9. Georg Wilhelm Friedrich Hegel, *Phenomenology of Spirit* (New York: Oxford University Press, 1977), p. 110. This is paragraph 177 in the A. V. Miller translation.

10. Glendon, *A World Made New,* p. 75.

11. Taylor, "Conditions of an Unforced Consensus on Human Rights," p. 129.

12. Nadine Gordimer, "Reflections by Nobel Laureates" in Yael Danieli, Elsa Stamatopoulou, and C. J. Dias, eds., *The Universal Declaration Human Rights: Fifty Years and Beyond* (Amityville, NY: Baywood, 1999), p. vii.

13. Desmond Tutu, "An Available Instrument of Subversion: The Universal Declaration of Human Rights as Source of Inspiration for South Africans," *U.N. Chronicle* 35, no. 4 (December 1998): 1.

Chapter 12

The Concept of Religious Freedom[1]

Arvind Sharma

I

The expression "religious freedom" is frequently invoked in contemporary discourse. For instance, the U.S. Commission on International Religious Freedom (USCIRF) was constituted in 1998 in the United States, as part of the International Religious Freedom Act. Thus, the concept of religious freedom is no longer merely a matter of theory but has also acquired the status of a policy, for the commission's "primary responsibilities are to make foreign policy recommendations to the President and the Congress related to the status and impact of freedom of religion or belief around the world." According to a recent announcement, the USCIRF, "a bipartisan independent federal commission created by Congress in 1998, is the only independent governing body in the world focused primarily on monitoring and advancing the internationally recognized freedom of thought, conscience, religion or belief and related human rights. It is also the only international human rights commission in the United States government."

It is clear, therefore, that the concept of religious freedom plays a vital role in human rights discourse and has even been institutionalized in the form of the USCIRF. Closer home, the recent controversy surrounding the presence of the Bengali author Taslima Nasreen in India, whose writings have provoked the wrath of Muslims in Bangladesh and now in India, may also be couched in the idiom of religious freedom. Her freedom to express her religious views constitutes one side of the debate and how its exercise impinges on the freedom of other Muslims pursuing their faith, without having it impugned (at least in their own perception), constitutes the other. It is not my intention to either examine the working of the USCIRF nor is it my intention to debate the case for or against Taslima Nasreen. I have alluded to them to draw attention to the importance and contemporary relevance of the exercise we are engaged in at the moment, namely, that of interrogating the concept of religious freedom. It seems to me that the intellectual attention bestowed so far on this concept is hardly commensurate with its importance, and it is my fond hope that this chapter will contribute its mite toward rectifying this state of affairs.

II

What is religious freedom? When the issue is framed and probed in this way, then the answer usually put on the table is in the form of the provisions pertaining to it, as found in the documents relating to human rights. One such key provision is Article 18 of the Universal Declaration of Human Rights, which was adopted by the United Nations on 10 December, 1948. The United Nations had close to 60 members at the time, of which half a dozen abstained. The key provision runs as follows:

> *Article 18*
> Everyone has the right to freedom of thought, conscience and religion; this right includes freedom to change his religion or belief and freedom, either alone or in community with others and in public or private, to manifest his religion or belief in teaching, practice, worship and observance.[2]

The fact that Saudi Arabia abstained on account of the fact that this provision allowed one to change one's religion is not unexpected, because according to the classical legal tradition in Islam, the penalty for apostasy is supposed to be death. But while the response of Saudi Arabia may not have been unexpected, that response possesses an unexpected theoretical significance, for it highlights the fact that our *concept of religious freedom cannot be divorced from our concept of religion.* For the Wahhabi school of Islam, as for almost all Muslims, Islam is the final and perfect religion. In the face of such a position, religious freedom could hardly consist of giving up such a religion. It could possibly consist of allowing other religions to exist alongside Islam, but in view of Islam's self-perception of itself as the final perfected religion, it could hardly include the freedom to give it up This is one important theoretical point that emerges from examining the Saudi case: that our concept of religious freedom cannot be divorced from our concept of religion. The second important point pertains to the light the Saudi case sheds on the nature of the relationship between the theory and practice of religious freedom. The Universal Declaration of Human Rights embodies general aspirations, which are meant to be given concrete shape in the form of covenants to which the member states of the United Nations are signatories. For various reasons, two sets of covenants were developed on the basis of the Universal Declaration of Human Rights, namely, the International Covenant on Civil and Political Rights[3] and the International Covenant on Economic, Social, and Cultural Rights.[4] Article 18 of the Universal Declaration of Human Rights that appears in the International Covenant on Civil and Political Rights is as follows:

1 Everyone shall have the right to freedom of thought, conscience, and religion. This right shall include freedom to have or to adopt a religion or belief of his choice, and freedom, either individually or in community with others and in public or private, to manifest his religion or belief in worship, observance, practice, and teaching.
2 No one shall be subject to coercion that would impair his freedom to have or to adopt a religion or belief of his choice.
3 Freedom to manifest one's religion or beliefs may be subject only to such limitations as are prescribed by law and are necessary to protect public safety, order, health, or morals or the fundamental rights and freedoms of others.
4 The states parties to the present Covenant undertake to have respect for the liberty of parents and, when applicable, legal guardians to ensure the religious and moral education of their children in conformity with their own convictions.[5]

It is worth noting that the freedom to "change" one's religion now appears as the right to "have or adopt a religion." Please note that the expression "to change" is stronger in its connotation as implying a break with the previous religion one was following, than "to have or adopt." This latter formulation is more acceptable in Islamic terms, in the sense that it is *giving up of the religion* that attracts the charge of apostasy in Islam rather than adopting something alongside. For one can *adopt* without abandoning what one has, but one cannot change without abandoning what one has. For example, one can adopt another child without giving up one's own, but if one changes, i.e., exchanges one child for another, then one has to give up one's own.

This modification makes it clear that religious freedom is not something static but dynamic and takes on new shape under the influence of forces that impinge on it. In the following sections, I would like to build on these two insights: (1) that the concept of religious freedom cannot be divorced from that of religion and (2) that the concept of religious freedom is something dynamic and not static.

III

If the discourse on human rights claims to be universal, then it must take concepts of religion and the corresponding concepts of religious freedom other than the Western into account, in order to be truly universal. There are two ways in which universality may be achieved: either by suppressing diversity or by acknowledging it. Thus, one way to achieve universality is through uniformity. It could be argued that this was the route taken in the Universal Declaration of Human Rights, which privileged one's understanding of religion, a secular Western one—according to which one can only belong to one religion at a time, although one could change this one religion to which one belonged. This arrangement appears isomorphic with serial monogamy—according to which one can only have one legally wedded partner at a time, although one could change the partner over time. Another way of achieving universality, however, is through identifying commonality rather than imposing uniformity. The difference between the two may be illustrated as follows in terms of religious freedom. If only, for instance, Article 18 ran as follows: "Everyone has the right to freedom of thought, conscience and religion . . . and the right . . . either alone or in community with others and in public and private, to manifest his religion or belief in teaching, practice, worship and observance"—i.e., if the clause "this right includes freedom to change his religion or belief" had been excluded, then hardly any religion would have objected, for it would have confirmed universal religious freedom for everyone, in their common acceptance of their own individual religion. It is the clause that pertains to the right to "change," which opens up the possibility of a different kind of universalism: everyone changing their religion so that they all adhere to the same religion.

But let us take this matter as it exists now into account. If we adhere to the commonality approach, then the concept of religious freedom, which undergirds Article 18 as we know it now, should be such as accommodates, as far as possible, the different concepts of religious freedom generated by different concepts of religion within the framework of its provisions.

Such differences in concepts of religion, and the corresponding concepts of religious freedom, can be identified if we review the religions of the world in terms of their approaches to (1) religious conversion and (2) religious participation.

IV

The various religions of the world can be classified broadly into two categories in terms of their attitude to religious conversion, on the basis of whether they actively seek, or do not seek, converts. According to this criterion, those religions that actively seek converts may be called missionary religions; the term "nonmissionary religions" being reserved for those who do not do so. Buddhism, Christianity, and Islam would then qualify as missionary religions, in terms of this classification, and Judaism, Zoroastrianism, and Hinduism would fall in the nonmissionary category. This is well known. It needs to be recognized that the primal religions of the world, whose followers constitute approximately 4 percent of the world's population, also belong here, as noted by John Mbiti. He uses the term "universal" in the Western sense of the term. This is what he says:

> Traditional religions are not universal: they are tribal or national. Each religion is bound and limited to the people among whom it has evolved. One traditional religion cannot be propagated in another tribal group. This does not rule out the fact that religious ideas may spread form one people to another. But such ideas spread spontaneously, especially through migrations, intermarriage, conquest, or expert knowledge being sought by individuals of one tribal group from another. Traditional religions have no missionaries to propagate them; and one individual does not preach his religion to another.
>
> Similarly, there is no conversion from one traditional religion to another. Each society has its own religious system, and the propagation of such a complete system would involve propagating the entire life of the people concerned. Therefore a person has to be born in a particular society in order to assimilate the religious system of the society to which he belongs. An outsider cannot enter or appreciate fully the religion of another society. Those few Europeans who claim to have been "converted" to African religions—and I know some who make such fantastic claims!—do not know what they are saying. To pour out libation or observe a few rituals like Africans, does not constitute conversion to traditional religions.[6]

Thus, the concept of religion in primal religions does not also involve conversion. Therefore, in these religions as well, religious freedom would consist of the freedom of not having to change one's religion. One should be free not to convert, and one should remain free from any pressure to convert. In other words, freedom of religion consists as much of the freedom to retain one's religion as to change it, although only the latter is specifically mentioned in Article 18 of the U.N. declaration. In the light of the fact that so many religions of the world are nonmissionary, the relevant part of Article 18 should have read:

> Everyone has the right to freedom of thought, conscience and religion; this right includes freedom to retain or to change his religion or belief.

This suggestion is not as contrived as one might be inclined to think. Section 147 of the Penal Code of the People's Republic of China (PRC) reiterates Article 26 of the 1982 PRC Constitution (still in force) and also refers to Article 4 of the Constitution in affirming: "each nationality has the freedom to retain or change its customs and habits." The Chinese intuition here is salutary, although presented not in terms of religion but customs and habits, and not in relation to individuals but rather nationalities.[7]

It is true that Article 18, as it appears in the International Covenant on Civic and Political Rights, uses the expression to "have or adopt" rather than "change," and I leave it to you to decide whether this phrasing suffices to cover the point being made here. It seems to me that the expression "have or adopt" does not convey the point with the required clarity and force the way word "retain" does.

This, then, is one way in which the concept of religious freedom may have to be revisited, in the light of the insight that our concept of religious freedom cannot be divorced from our concept of religion. A second way in which it may have to be revisited is suggested by an examination of the concept of religious participation embedded in a particular concept of religion. A distinction may be drawn in the context of religious participation between *exclusive religious participation* and *multiple religious participation.* Some religions insist on exclusive adherence and prominent among these are Judaism, Christianity, and Islam—the so-called Abrahamic religions. One cannot be a Jew, a Christian, and a Muslim at the same time, notwithstanding such groups as "Jews for Jesus." Other religions such as Hinduism, Buddhism, Jainism, Sikhism, Confucianism, Taoism, Shinto, and the primal religions, by and large, allow for dual or multiple religious participation. It is when the religions of the world are arranged in this fashion that the real significance of the Article 18 of the Universal Declaration of Human Rights comes into view, when it elaborates that the right to religious freedom "includes freedom to change" one's religion or belief. For it is in order to follow Judaism, Christianity, and Islam that one must change "one's religion." One does not have to "change" one's religion to belong to Hinduism, Buddhism, Jainism, Sikhism, Confucianism, Taoism, Shinto, or primal religions. Here "initiation" should not be confused with "conversion." One could be initiated into these religions if one wanted, but it does not involve conversion in the sense of having to consciously abandon one's previous religious connections. It is here that the Western bias of this article may be said to stand out rather starkly, for Judaism, Christianity, and Islam are Western religions.

The point can be developed further in the light of the distinction introduced earlier between missionary and nonmissionary religions. "Religious freedom" is often invoked, the current discourse on human rights, to castigate nonmissionary religions for resisting the conversion of their members by the missionary religions, as compromising religious freedom. The pressure point comes to rest on the nonmissionary religions and on their reluctance for allowing "conversion" to take place because they are used to multiple religious participation and do not see the need for such conversion from two points of view. They see no need to change one's religion as most of them are not missionary religions themselves, nor do they feel the need for anyone to "convert" to the missionary religions if such a religion appeals to one, on account of their acceptance of multiple religious participation. If these nonmissionary religions became more assertive, then the pressure point would come to rest on the missionary religions, for then some nonmissionary religions, in keeping with their acceptance of multiple religious participation, could demand that they have full access to the rites and rituals of the missionary religions without having to convert to them as part and parcel of the exercise of their own religious freedom. In such a case, *not* offering the bread and wine in the Eucharist to unbaptized Hindus or Buddhists would be seen as compromising the religious freedom of these Hindus and Buddhists, and so on. This discussion leads one to propose the following addition to the Article 18: "without discrimination." The whole article would then read as follows:

> Everyone has the right to freedom of thought, conscience and religion; this right includes the freedom to change his religion or belief and freedom, either alone or in community with others and in public and private, to manifest his religion or belief in teaching, practice, worship and observance *without discrimination* (i.e. *without discriminating against others*).

V

I have so far investigated one element in the expression "religious freedom" in some detail, namely, "religious," by examining the implications our changing understanding of the term "religion" has for religious freedom. It is now time to interrogate the term "freedom" itself. What is freedom? What constitutes freedom? May I be so lowbrow as to cite the definition of this term from the Merriam-Webster's Collegiate Dictionary? I think the reader will be pleasantly surprised by the outcome. The good book defines freedom as follows:

1: The quality or state of being free: as

a) the absence of necessity, coercion, or constraint in choice or action
b) liberation from slavery or restraint or from the power of another
c) the quality or state of being exempt or released usually from something
d) onerous
e) EASE, FACILITY
f) the quality of being frank, open or outspoken
g) improper familiarity
h) boldness of conception or execution
i) unrestricted use

2:

a) a political right
b) FRANCHISE, PRIVILEGE[8]

If we analyze these statements, it soon becomes clear that the concept of freedom involves the twin concepts of minimization of restriction and the maximization of options. These are in fact two sides of the same coin. If an animal is bound to a pole, then the less the restriction on the movement, the longer the rope, i.e., the freer the animal may be said to be. Thus, as restriction is minimized, freedom is enlarged. Similarly, let us think of a patient who has just had surgery, which involved abstention from food. The patient is first allowed to drink liquids. Then, as a next step, the patient is allowed to eat fruits. Earlier on the patient had only one dietary option, now the patient has two options. When the patient is allowed to eat light food, the range of the patient's options is enlarged further. In other words, the greater the number of options, the greater the degree of freedom. When finally the patient is allowed to eat any item of food the patient likes, the patient's options are maximized and so is the patient's freedom.

The concept of religious freedom, as it prevails in human rights discourse, arguably represents the understanding of freedom that emphasizes freedom as freedom from restraint or restriction Thus, a person is allowed to change his or her religion, thereby removing any restriction that might have hindered such an exercise of freedom in the past. If, however, we look upon freedom as involving the maximization of the range of options available to a person, then a slightly different perspective begins to emerge. Normally, we are aware mainly of the existence of our own religion and perhaps of a few allied ones. Thus, a Muslim will possess a certain amount of knowledge about his own religion and may also possess a nodding acquaintance with Judaism and Christianity. Similarly, a Hindu may possess some knowledge about his own tradition and may also be acquainted in some measure with the allied religions of Buddhism and Jainism. In such a scenario, the choices open to both the Muslim and the Hindu are rather restricted, because neither of them possess an adequate knowledge of other world religions for these other religions to appear as live options before them. If, however, both the Muslim and the Hindu became better acquainted with the other religions of the world, then the range of religious options available to them will be considerably extended. This is how our perspective shifts if we think of freedom as consisting of providing maximum choices, rather than as merely minimizing restrictions.

Under this revised concept of religious freedom, religious freedom would be maximized if every human being became acquainted with the religious traditions of humanity reasonably well to consider all of them as live options. Such an understanding of religious freedom would then involve providing all members of humanity with the knowledge of either all or at least as many religions of the world as possible, so that the options available to a human being, any human being, are maximized. According to the logic of this argument, a course in world religions in the curriculum around the world would maximize religious freedom by enlarging the range of religious options available as far as possible. If one wanted to maximize religious freedom, then this would be the way to go.

VI

It was recognized, earlier in this chapter, that religious freedom is a dynamic concept. If we approach the matter in this spirit, then we can offer two conclusions to the academic and faith communities as a result of the exercise we are engaged in now. The first is that a revised version of Article 18 of the Universal Declaration of Human Rights could be proposed on the basis of the insight that the concept of religious freedom cannot be divorced from the concept of religion. Article 18 would now read as follows:

> Everyone has the right to freedom of thought, conscience and religion, this right includes freedom *to retain* or to change one's religion or belief, and freedom, either alone or in community with others and in public and private, to manifest his religion or belief in teaching, practice, worship and observance *without discrimination.*

This is the first conclusion. The second is that if we wish to maximize religious freedom, then a course in world religions should be included in the curriculum of every country around the globe wherever religion is taught in any form. The study of world religions, in the same spirit, should also be included as a part of the secular curriculum around the world.

NOTES

1. Parts of this chapter have been previously published by the author in "The Possibility of Religious Freedom" in *Studies in Global Justice,* Volume 9, *Problematizing Religious Freedom,* Part 1 (Dordrecht, etc.: Springer, 2011), pp. 85–93.

2. See Ian Brownlie, ed., *Basic Documents on Human Rights* (Oxford: Clarendon Press, 1992), p. 25.

3. Ibid., p. 125.

4. Ibid., p. 114.

5. Ibid., p. 132.

6. John S. Mbiti, *African Religions and Philosophy,* 2nd ed. (Oxford, etc.: Heinemann, 1969), p. 4.

7. Sumner B. Twiss, "Religious Intolerance in Contemporary China, Including the Curious Case of Falun Gong," *Chinese Studies Forum* 4 (2003): 46.

8. *Merriam-Webster's Collegiate Dictionary,* 10th ed. (Springfield, MA: Merriam-Webster, 2002), p. 464.

Chapter 13

Vietnam Central Highlands at the Crossroads: Globalization, Development, Sustainability, and Cultural Identity

Tran My-Van

Globalization cannot be easily and consistently defined despite a massive literature on the subject.[1] It has also become a controversial topic. This is partly due to its consequences. It can indeed facilitate many positive things in human society, providing people with the means to connect with others from different backgrounds, cultures, and ideologies around the world. It creates new opportunities for trade, advances in technology, and improvements of living standards. The list of benefits can go on. In the case of Asia Pacific, it has unleashed its force, especially with Foreign Direct Investment (FDI) and greater economic integration. Indeed, in 2007, "this region" remained the top one for FDI, attracting US$ 395 billion of investment. While this ushers in new opportunities for business and growth, it raises many challenges. A few pressing and serious challenges are the issue of development sustainability, corporate social responsibility, inequality within society, and cultural identity.

Vietnam, a multiethnic and multireligious country, also known as the Socialist Republic of Vietnam (SRV) since 1975, is no exception. What is more interesting is that although it remains a socialist state, governed by the Communist Party of Vietnam (CPV) , it is fervently playing the catch up game with its fast-globalizing Asian neighbors. Its admission as 150th member of the World Trade Organization (WTO), on January 11, 2007, heralds a new chapter in its economic history. It marks the full integration of Vietnam with the rest of the world and, more or less, with the capitalist economic system. Its Communist leaders are reportedly treating the event as "a major victory" to the extent they "became consumed with the elixir of triumph, and embraced grandiose plans in disregard of reality."[2]

This chapter offers a critical overview of contemporary Vietnam where, under the influence of economic reform and globalization, major economic and social developments have taken place during the past two decades. The focus is the Central Highlands of Vietnam, the home of more than 20 ethnic minorities known collectively as Montagnards, where the intensification of commercial activities is already felt. In the past three years, the determination of the Communist leaders to implement a "master plan" to develop a bauxite and aluminum industry involving the People's Republic of China's state-owned companies has given rise to severe criticism and protest in Vietnam and overseas. The most serious concern lies with the impact on the environment, the livelihood, and cultural identity of the Montagnards, with Chinese expansion into Vietnam, using it as a strategic gateway to Southeast Asia and the South China Sea to enhance their global power. This chapter concludes by noting that the Central Highlands is under serious threat. Its social, political, and commercial transition has been painful for the Montagnards, especially for Dega protestant people. ("Dega" is a term derived from a Rhadé ethnic minority phrase "Anak Ede Gar," meaning "sons of the mountains.") It urges the Vietnamese authorities, in the national interest, to address issues of sustainable development and human rights, including religious rights for its local ethnic minorities.

VIETNAM SINCE ECONOMIC REFORM (DOI MOI) IN 1986

In the decade following "reunification" in 1975, the SRV's economy faced stagnation, with deep inflation reaching 500 percent in 1986 and a serious shortage of FDI. A great number of people, especially southerners, endured starvation and suffering in various new economic zones or reeducation centers. Some took to sea in flimsy boats in search for freedom. To help salvage Vietnam, the Communist Party at its sixth Congress (1986) approved a reform package, which became known as "Doi Moi" (Renovation). The package introduced market-oriented economic reforms along Chinese lines.

On account of Doi Moi, the business environment of Vietnam steadily changed. Economic growth was recorded on average at 7.5 percent per year. Inflation dropped sharply to 34.7 percent (1990) while FDI rose sharply. Twenty years later, 84 countries and territories are committed to invest in Vietnam.[3] In 2008, "the foreign invested sector has accounted for 29.8% of the country's total investment, 40.2% of industrial output, 40% of the national export, and 22% (2007) of the GDP of Viet Nam."[4] Overseas Vietnamese remittance to their homeland reached US$ 6 billion in 2008, indicating "160 times bigger than it was in 1991—an annual growth rate of over 35%."[5] These economic changes have been hailed by the SRV as "bringing about prosperity and happiness to the entire people and creating more favourable conditions for them to enjoy the fundamental human rights enshrined in the UN Charter."[6] Indeed, by 2007, Vietnam was regarded as the next Asian "tiger." Seemingly, a new page of Vietnam's history had been turned.

However, these striking words have failed to capture the reality in the Central Highlands, one of the three main terrains (fields) for the tribal people. They were worse off, having experienced marginalization, poverty, and human rights abuses, including religious freedom violations during the period of growth.

CENTRAL HIGHLANDS (TÂY NGUYÊN) OF VIETNAM SINCE DOI MOI

According to official sources, Vietnam has 54 nationalities of which 53 belong to ethnic minorities. These minorities account for 14 percent of the total population, which stands at 86 million. Ethnic Vietnamese (Kinh people) and Chinese account for the remaining 86 percent. They inhabit the Red River delta, the Central Coastal delta, the Mekong delta, and major cities. The ethnic minority groups are scattered in mountainous provinces in the North, in the Central Highlands, and in the Western provinces of the Mekong delta. The Central Highlands Montagnards population was estimated to be 1 million out of 4 million mostly ethnic Vietnamese inhabitants.[7]

The Central Highlands, called Tây Nguyên by the authorities, officially consist of four provinces of South Central Vietnam: Kon Tum, Gia Lai, Dak Lak, and Dak Nong, although bordering areas, including Lam Dong province, are also often included. Much of this region is mountainous and occupied by ethnically diverse indigenous tribes, known collectively as Moi (meaning "savages") by the Vietnamese (Kinh) lowlanders. During French colonization, from the mid-19th century, these tribal people have been referred to as Montagnards (mountain dwellers). Currently, there are 21 different ethnic groups numbering about 2 million inhabitants; the largest being the Jarai, Rhadé, Bahnar, Sedang, Koho, Mnong, Raglai, Hre, Raglai,

Mnong, Stieng, and Bru-Van Kieu, belonging to two language families: the Austronesian (Malayo-Polynesian) and Austro-Asiatic (Mon-Khmer). To a large extent, they still maintain social organization of clannish and tribal character, while following animistic and/or pantheist beliefs.

In terms of established religions, in the wake of French colonialism, Catholicism was propagated in Vietnam, including the Central Highlands. In 1977, it was estimated there were 100,000 Catholic followers in the Central Highlands.[8] However, a majority of the Montagnards have been converted to Protestantism. This was first introduced to Vietnam in the late 19th century by the Christian and Missionary Alliance (CMA). During the period from 1954 to1975, the Vietnam War years, there was more effort from the U.S.-based CMA, Vietnamese General Protestant Church, and foreign Protestant organizations to spread their religion far and wide among these ethnic minorities. In 1975, the General Protestant Church had 61,500 believers. Since the 1990s, protestant followers have been growing in number. The Government Committee on Religious Affairs recorded their number reached 393,546 in 2004.[9]

"Dega Protestanism" (Tin Lanh Dega), which is a form of evangelical Christianity, was formally founded in 2000, when the Dega Protestant Organization (DPO), also known as Dega Protestant (House) Church, broke away from the Evangelical Church of Vietnam South, which was authorized by the Communists authorities. DPO members were against both governmental assimilationist policies and registering their religious organization with the Vietnam Fatherland Front. Furthermore, they are not in tune with the so-called state sanctioned motto of "living the gospel, serving God, the Fatherland and the Nation." Since then, Dega Protestantism has been banned by the government for being "illegal." Followers and supporters have been suppressed. Thus, Dega Protestantism, as a part from Montagnard Protestantism in general, has developed on the margins of the Montagnard culture. It should be noted that while they had been converted before and during the Vietnam War, it was only after the withdrawal of the U.S. forces when they had been left to face the Vietnamese Communists alone, that they turned to Christianity as an integral part of their ethnic identity. In Pearson's words, "Dega" and Christianity then became "two faiths . . . intimately linked."[10]

During the Vietnam War between Communist forces of the North and non-Communist forces of the South, the Central Highlands suffered much devastation as fierce battles, including heavy aerial bombardment, took place. This was due to the Ho Chi Minh Trail that traversed it. After the Communist takeover of South Vietnam in 1975, the CPV changed the name of the Central Highlands to Tây Nguyên (meaning "Western plateau"). Many Montagnards, who had fought with the Republic of Vietnam (South Vietnam) and U.S. Special Forces, were sent to "reeducation" camps. Many of their religious leaders, who had been converted to Protestant Christianity by U.S. missionaries during the Vietnam War, were also interned, while their religious institutions were closed down. Worse still, the Communist leaders' earlier promise of autonomy for the Montagnards was not kept. Instead, a fixed cultivation and sedentarization program and modern agricultural methods were introduced. Large tracts of land were designated as new economic zones for setting up agricultural cooperatives, state farms, and state forest enterprises, to resettle overcrowded lowlanders. Partly to "civilize" the Montagnards, the government forced them to relocate to fixed residences.[11] In addition, "Red Books" were issued to households, which were to be used to "transfer, assign, lease, inherit, and mortgage" land-use rights.[12] The state farms also leased out land to households for cash crop production on a sharecropping 60/40-percent basis.

During the coffee boom of the 1990s, the Central Highlands witnessed an increasing and uncontrolled in-migration. It was estimated up to 46 percent of new settlers cleared "unclaimed" land, used by the Montagnards for shifting cultivation, with the authorities turning a blind eye.[13] This influx of migrants has marginalized the Montagnards further and caused land ownership disputes, in which often the latter were losers.

Squeezed between a corrupted and authoritarian regime and more aggressive, skillful, and calculating ethnic Vietnamese, the Montagnards suffered adverse effects during this period of economic growth. In population terms, by 2001, their collective population was no more than 1.7 million, accounting for only 33 percent of the Central Highlands' total population.[14] Development in the Central Highlands has become less and less inclusive. On the economic front, it has turned the Montagnards into minorities in their own land, with most of them lacking the necessary skills and capital to be successful in "cash crop," resource-intensive production.[15] On the social front, their cultural identity, which is closely associated with their ancestral lands and lifestyle, is fast diminishing. The establishment of the DPO reflects the Montagnards' rejection of ethnic Vietnamese domination over their religious domain and their reluctance to submit themselves to the authorities.[16]

UNREST IN THE CENTRAL HIGHLANDS IN 2001 AND 2004

Tensions between ethnic minorities and ethnic Vietnamese and the government in the Central Highlands came to the surface at the turn of the 21st century. Due to communication technology, the world caught a glimpse of an unprecedented and violent unrest, which was unleashed by 10,000 Montagnards from different ethnic tribes in the region that lasted 4 days in March 2001. They demanded respect for and return of their traditional lands and customs, and expressed resentment over their ancestral forests being turned into coffee plantations. Unrest was harshly crushed by the government, with the help of elite military units. Ethnic Vietnamese in civilian clothing were reported brandishing crude weapons such as metal bars, shovels, chains, machetes, and clubs with nails in them, to intimidate the Montagnards further.[17] The unrest resulted in nine deaths and many protesters being wounded and thrown in jail; a majority of them trekked their way to Cambodia for asylum.

To stem further unrest, the government reinstated a five-year socioeconomic development plan with a budget of US$ 2.36 billion for the Central Vietnam region. This was to help boost existing programs such as the Hunger Eradication and Poverty Reduction (Program 133) and Socioeconomic Development of Especially Difficult Communes in Mountainous and Remote Areas (Program 135). The government's effort yielded some good result, as poverty did fall in Central Vietnam from 51.8 percent in 2002 to 32.7 percent in 2004. However, the poverty of the Montagnards remained very steep. This is confirmed by the Danish government, one of the main aid donors to Vietnam:

> Inequalities are also widening between the majority Kinh people, who constitutes 86 per cent of the total population, and the 53 ethnic minority groups. While the poverty rate for the Kinh majority fell from 54 to 23 per cent during the period 1990–2002, the poverty rate among ethnic minorities was only reduced from 86 to 69 per cent during the same period. The severity of poverty among ethnic minorities is illustrated by the fact that their share of the extreme poor increased from less than 30 per cent in 1993 to 53 per cent in 2002.[18]

On Easter weekend (April 10–11, 2004), an estimated 30,000 Montagnards including women and children, with the majority of them being Protestants from Dak Lak, Gia Lai, and Dak Nong provinces, staged a series of bigger and more coordinated demonstrations against the government. Their list of grievances included land theft, lack of social services and economic aid, and intensifying religious persecution. This showed that their problems were far from resolved. For once, the government accepted that there was large-scale highlands unrest, but blamed it on the U.S.-based Montagnard Foundation Inc. (MFI). Like the previous time, official repression was swift. The protestors, whom the government regarded as separatists, were harshly crushed, with many more arrested and wounded. Since then, their voices have been muted. However, concerns have been raised. Part of a report by Amnesty International criticized the Vietnamese authorities, stating that "to blame 'outsiders' for the unrest avoids addressing fundamental and underlying problems including land rights' pressures from internal migration and differences of religion and culture."[19] Kok Ksor, chairman of MFI, has stated:

> As an indigenous people, our people only ask the government of Vietnam to respect our rights to our ancestral lands, according to our customs, tradition and culture and as human beings we ask the Vietnamese government to respect our human, civil and political rights and to stop sterilizing our women.
>
> The existence or promotion of a new denomination . . . is what is called "the freedom of religion" and we do not want to be part of a "government controlled religion" with "Government appointed religious leaders." I cannot see anything wrong with wanting to be free of "government controlled religions."[20]

NEW DEVELOPMENT FOR THE CENTRAL HIGHLANDS: BAUXITE MINING AND THE CHINESE CONNECTION

Despite the Central Highlands problems, Vietnam has attracted increasing FDI. In 2007, Vietnam remained one of the top 10 nations receiving global FDI. On December 31, 2006, Vietnam was recorded to have 4,220 FDI enterprises, 2.77 times higher than in 2000: 79.2 percent (3,342 enterprises) were foreign owned and 20.8 percent (878 enterprises) joint ventures. During the same period (2000–2007), the Central Highlands received 34–64 enterprises. Most of them were of small scale; on average, each project was estimated at US$ 6.2 million, as compared with US$ 9.7 million per enterprise nationwide. Even so, it seems the Montagnards failed to benefit from these projects.

Bauxite Mining

For the past two years, the Central Highlands has once again been in the spotlight. It has received headlines such as "Vietnam Bauxite Plan Opens Pit of Concern,"[21] "Development-Vietnam: Government Bauxite Plan Stirs Public Worries,"[22] "Foreign Donors Caution Vietnam on Bauxite Mining,"[23] and "The Government Chooses Economic Growth over Xenophobia and Greenery."[24] This has occurred due to a much-debated and publicized new development plan for the Central Highlands, which holds rich bauxite reserves estimated at 8 billion tons—approximately the third largest in the world. This master plan, which the government is determined to adopt against all criticism, originally envisioned the exploitation of 5.4 billion tons of bauxite ore in six projects in the region until 2015. It has now called for investments in mining and refining bauxite of around US$ 15 billion by 2025, to tap Vietnam's rich bauxite reserves. Prime Minister Nguyen Tan Dung, who was appointed in 2007, has called bauxite exploitation "a major policy of the party and the state."[25] He has approved several big mining projects for the Central Highlands. Already, the state-run Vietnam National Coal & Mineral Industries Group (Vinacomin) has worked in earnest with Chinese state-owned enterprises, in particular with China Aluminium International Engineering Co. (Chalieco), a subsidiary of Aluminum Corp of China Ltd., to develop the bauxite industry. A mining deal to build a US$ 460-million alumina plant on pristine land in Lam Dong was signed in April 2008, despite lack of transparency, consultancy, and feasibility study.[26] The event unleashed harsh criticism and protests in Vietnam and overseas, which fell on deaf ears. This is partly because of the visit of Prime Minister Nguyen Tan Dung to China (October 2008) "to promote China–Vietnam strategic partnership of cooperation." The mining deal was regarded as "a gift to China," when Dung met President Hu Jintao to begin "a new phase of comprehensive development."[27] Amid mounting protests and fear that more similar deals with the Chinese would come, Vinacomin president Doan Van Kien stated: "Each project will produce 600,000 tonnes of aluminium, creating some 2,000 jobs and earning 150 to 200 million U.S. dollars per year."[28]

The Central Highlands has in the past produced 80 percent of Vietnam's coffee production. It has also other products including cocoa, tea, and cashew. These productions are now under threat. "Hills that used to be plantations of tea have already been bulldozed into a 50-hectare site to locate the bauxite project," reported the state-controlled *Tuoi Tre* newspaper from Lam Dong province, the location of one of the planned mines. "The same thing has happened to the coffee hills in Dak Nong province, but on a larger scale—the construction site may stretch over to 200 hectares."[29]

Chinese Connection

While the development of the Central Highlands to meet the special needs of the locals, especially for the ethnic minorities, is greatly needed, the Chinese factor in the master plan for bauxite development is a cause of great concern. Firstly, China, the world's most populous nation, has always tried to exert its influence on its neighbors. Vietnam, in the more distant past, was regarded as a Chinese province and the country underwent 1,000 years of Chinese domination; anti-Chinese feeling resulted. In the 20th century, the Sino–Vietnamese relationship has had its ups and downs. During the Vietnam War, North Vietnam relied on Chinese military, financial, and moral support. Yet, Vietnam's invasion of Cambodia in 1978–1979 was met with Chinese military retaliation along its northern border "to teach Vietnam a lesson." Sino–Vietnam relations got back on track in 1991, but with some tensions arising from the Spratly Islands dispute and the Vietnam–China boundary demarcation dispute. The latter was only settled in December 2008, but, over time, there has been systematic resettlement of ethnic Chinese and other indigenous people from China in Vietnamese populated areas.

Today, Vietnam has a huge trade deficit with China. It reached US$ 3.8 billion in 2006, US$ 9 billion in 2007, and US$ 13 billion in 2008. Vietnam has no choice but to bring down this deficit. Part of the answer is to expand economic relations with China. Indeed, Prime Minister Nguyen Tan Dung expressed his desire to expand bilateral trade with China, from US$ 20 billion in 2008 to US$ 25 billion by 2010. However, with China being at the forefront of bauxite development in the Central Highlands, a serious threat to the environment, the security, and the stability of Vietnam looms large. This is due to China's poor track record on environment, development sustainability, governance, transparency, and human rights. In recent times, China has had to close many of its own factories on account of safety standards. It has also shut down several bauxite mines due to serious environmental problems. It can now shift these problems to Central Vietnam. What is more, the Chinese government is encouraging powerful Chinese companies to look for bauxite overseas, so as to ease domestic supply tensions. In 2008, China had 73 investment projects worth US$ 334 million in Vietnam. What worries Vietnamese critics is the asymmetry in relations between China and Vietnam; the worst being the way the Communist leaders of Vietnam have kowtowed to China's wishes and whims. Vietnam's recent anti-Chinese protest over the bauxite deal and Chinese encroachment on Vietnam's territory was suppressed by the authorities. Many Internet sites, where people posted their anger, were shut down.

China and its transnational companies are significant global actors. The Hanoi government is also calling for their investment. The huge trade deficit with China does not allow Vietnam bargaining power. As the *Economist* eloquently stated, "in straitened economic times, beggars cannot be choosers."[30] So, the Central Highlands zone is under threat to its environment, strategic position, and, most significantly, the livelihood and culture of its ethnic minorities. With ongoing bauxite and aluminum projects, with more to come, the Central Highlands will suffer ecological consequences. It happens that "bauxite is extracted from open-pit mines, requiring the replacement of topsoil before the land can be reforested or used for agriculture. The refining process creates large amounts of caustic red slurry which must be contained so as not to pollute water sources."[31] The SRV's proposed bauxite and aluminum projects in Dak Nong alone would involve seven complexes, collectively covering an area equivalent to nearly one-third of the province's entire land surface, or 1,910 km2.[32] Experts have pointed to soil degradation, deforestation, the destruction of wildlife habitats, water effluents and polluted waterways, fluoride dust emissions, "red mud" (contaminated with caustic soda), flooding, and wind erosion from uncovered topsoils.[33]

Most Venerable Thich Quang Do, the current patriarch of the outlawed Unified Buddhist Church, added another dimension. He is not only concerned for the environmental degradation, but also believes Vietnam is "under threat of invasion" because of Chinese workers who have mushroomed on the plateau, and 10,000 more Chinese settlers are expected in the coming year. Others share his concern judging from the volume of bloggers, Facebook posts, and writings by environmentalists, scientists, and cultural experts. Popular writer on the Central Highlands, Nguyen Ngoc, has written: "If the land and forest base of the western highlands disappear, its culture will be broken, its society will be unstable, and these ethnic minorities will no longer exist."[34]

The fiercest critic on bauxite mining with the Chinese is the well-respected 97-year-old General Vo Nguyen Giap, a founding member of the CPV and a top war hero and military strategist. In one of three open letters to the leaders, he raised his concern about allowing the Chinese access to Central Vietnam, as this would give them de facto control and a strategic position over the most crucial military position in Vietnam. Giap's point has gained attention as more people have questioned the role of thousands of Chinese workers, soldiers, and technicians, who have been on the ground for the past two years, supposedly for bauxite excavation. Their activities include exploring, setting up recreation centers and restaurants, Chinese street signs, and construction of residences and buildings with high walls to fence themselves off from local scrutiny. This gives rise to a new fear that bauxite mining is only a pretext for the Chinese to explore and control uranium resources in Vietnam.[35]

CHALLENGES AHEAD

Leaving the Chinese influx and strategic positioning aside, development to date in Central Vietnam, in the form of bauxite or uranium mining, has not proved profitable for the locals. Nguyen Van Thu, the chairman of Vietnam's Association of Mechanical Industries, confirmed: "They eat up everything and leave nothing. . . . Chinese contractors bring everything here, even the toilet seats! . . . These are materials Vietnam can produce, and work that Vietnamese can do."[36] Neither is it compatible with the sustainable development theme as expounded by the World Commission on Environment and Development, according to which "humanity has the ability to make development sustainable—to ensure that it meets the needs of the present without compromising the ability of the future generations to meet their own needs."[37] Agenda 21 of the Rio Summit noted: "While promotion of economic growth in developing countries is important, such growth must be both sustained and sustainable and must strengthen employment and income-generating programmes."[38] Chinese involvement in bauxite projects of Central Vietnam, as approved by the government, has not resulted in more employment, nor generated more income for locals. This cannot be brushed aside. In fact, the Norwegian ambassador to Vietnam, Kjell Storlokken, has already cautioned the Vietnamese authorities on behalf of international donors, by asking for a "careful stewardship" to ensure that the people of the Central Highlands benefit "fully and fairly."[39] He also urged: "Equally, it is important that every effort must be made to limit the environmental cost of mining and minimize the impact on the natural surroundings to protect the legacy for future generations."[40]

In 2000, Vietnam committed to the implementation of the U.N. Millennium Development Goals (MDGs). More specifically, the government aimed to reduce poverty, including food poverty, and to increase life expectancy. Vietnam has also committed itself to "growth with equity" in its strategy of development. Yet, the deteriorating situation of the Central Highlands, especially that of the Montagnards, poses a serious challenge for the government to tackle. There is no denying that the country has achieved high economic growth, with annual GDP growth rates of around 7 percent over the past 10 years, and that poverty rates have declined remarkably in urban areas. However, to leave the full development of bauxite projects in the hands of the Chinese, without a definite feasibility study and due response to serious criticism and allegations, seems extremely unwise. The government behavior is not in the national interest. On sustainable development grounds alone, questions remain. How and when can the Vietnamese government prevent exploitation, implement long-term plans, and strengthen local businesses? How will the development benefit the inhabitants, the Montagnards, and future generations? Most importantly, how can the government prevent further large-scale Central Highlands unrest? These questions are yet to be answered.

CONCLUSION

"The marriage of political socialism and economic capitalism poses a number of challenges for the Vietnamese Government and the people of Vietnam."[41] More seriously, with China gaining an upper hand in bilateral business with Vietnam, the Central Highlands, the home of the Montagnards, is at the crossroads: There is a long path ahead to secure a sustainable future for them. Their fields and their identity have to a large extent been destroyed in the name of development. This is also true of their religious freedom, on account of the government's increasing effort to control and manage religious affairs. What is more, the attempt to justify their severe persecution of Montagnard Christians, in particular Dega Protestants and their supporters on ground that they undermine national unity under Article 87 of the penal code, does not bear scrutiny.

Under the authoritative, Communist regime of Vietnam, voices of protest have been muted, dissidents thrown in jail, and freedom of press absent. As for the fate of the Montagnards, Amnesty International reported that in 2008, at least 250 of them were still serving long prison terms in connection with protests in 2001 and 2004 over landownership and religious freedom. As Prime Minister Phan Van Khai said in an interview with the *Washington Post,* on his official visit to the United States in June 2005 to lobby U.S. support for Vietnam entry to the WTO, "Political reforms and economic reforms should be closely harmonized." But this has not become a reality. In this context, globalization, development, and economic growth in Vietnam have led neither to democracy or freedom, nor to improvement in the life expectancy for the Montagnards.

The government is facing an uphill battle to combat rampant corruption, which comes from the top. In terms of transparency, Vietnam is ranked 121st out of 180 countries in Transparency International's Corruption Perceptions Index.[42] Despite these serious constraints, the authorities must act quickly and precisely to salvage the situation in the Central Highlands, before it is too late. In the first instance, perceived economic results from bauxite mining, without hard proof, cannot be the only "priority of the state and party." The leaders should focus on pressing social and environmental issues. They must pay more than lip service to the commitment to the Five-Year Socio-Economic Development Plan (2006–2010). Part of this highlights the need for a coherent and integrated approach to sustainable development. While emphasizing economic growth, this plan also identifies the need to enhance social equity and environmental sustainability.[43] Furthermore, the 2009 World Bank report titled "Country Social Analysis Ethnicity and Development in Vietnam" "provides a timely recognition of the need for social inclusion to foster real sustainability now and into the future" for minority groups. This need is pressing as Vietnam has aspired to join the ranks of developed nations by 2020, with a knowledge-based economy and stable and secure livelihoods for all sections of society.

Last but not least, Vietnam is currently a member of U.N. Security Council, and will assume presidency of Association of Southeast Asian Nations and its Intergovernmental Human Rights Commission from next year. It should set an example by improving its human rights practices. Indeed, the European Parliament, while passing its resolution condemning religious persecution and human rights violations in Vietnam and Laos (November 26, 2009), has suggested that "The government [of Vietnam] could start by releasing the hundreds of peaceful government critics, independent church activists, bloggers and democracy advocates imprisoned on groundless national security charges in violation of international law for expressing peaceful dissent."[44]

Globalization and economic development are vital and unstoppable but not sustainable without rule of law and all citizens' livelihood being taken into serious consideration. For this, Vietnam leaders must act fast. This means, they must improve the Montagnards' fast-deteriorating situation, in accordance with the U.N. MDGs and their own undertakings.

NOTES

1. For example, see David Held and Anthony McGrew, *Globalisation/Anti-Globalisation* (Cambridge: Polity, 2002); Gennady Chufrin, ed., *East Asia between Regionalism and Globalism* (Singapore: ISEAS, 2006); Chamsy El-Ojeili and Patrick Hayden, *Critical Theories of Globalization* (New York, Palgrave Macmillan, 2006); Alex MacGillivray, *A Brief History of Globalisation* (London: Robinson, 2006); David A. Kelly, Ramakishen S. Rajan, and Gillian H. L. Goh, *Managing Globalisation: Lessons from China and India* (Singapore: World Scientific Publishing Co. Pte. Ltd, 2006); Mark Beeson, *Religion and Globalization in East Asia* (London: Palgrave, 2007); Nick Bisley, *Rethinking Globalisation* (New York: Palgrave Macmillan, 2007); Alastair Greig, David Hulme, and Mark Turner, *Challenging Global Inequality: Development and Practice in the 21st Century* (New York: Palgrave Macmillan, 2007); and Manfred B. Steger, *Globalization: A Very Short Introduction* (New York: Oxford University Press, 2009).

2. Vu Quang Viet, "Vietnam's Economic Crisis Policy Follies and the Role of the State-Owned Conglomerates," *Southeast Asian Affairs* 2009 (2009): 389.

3. Ministry of Planning and Investment, *Vietnam Investment Guide* (Hanoi: Foreign Investment Agency, 2009), p. 20.

4. Ibid., pp. 21, 22.

5. VietNamNet Bridge, "2008 May See Biggest Overseas Remittance so Far," *Look at Vietnam*, December 3, 2008, http://www.lookatvietnam.com/2008/12/2008-may-see-biggest-overseas-remittance-so-far.html.

6. Ministry of Foreign Affairs, *Achievements in Protecting and Promoting Human Rights in Vietnam* (Hanoi: Foreign Investment Agency, 2005), pp. 46, 47.

7. Gerald C. Hickey, "Montagnard Land Ownership and Area Defense," in *Accommodation and Coalition in South Vietnam* (Santa Monica, CA: Rand Corporation, 1970).

8. Nguyen Thanh Xuan, "Religions in the Areas of Ethnic Minority Compatriots in Vietnam," *Religious Studies Review* 1, no. 2 (May 2007): 67.

9. Ibid.

10. Thomas Pearson, *Missions and Conversions: Creating the Montagnard—Dega Refugee Community* (New York: Palgrave Macmillan, 2009), p. 75.

11. United Nations High Commissioner for Refugees (UNHCR), *Vietnam: Indigenous Minority Groups in the Central Highlands* (Centre for Documentation and Research, January 2002), pp. 13, 14 and *Vietnam: Situation of Indigenous Minority Groups in the Central Highlands* (Status Determination and Protection Information Section, June 2006), p. 29.

12. David Koh, "The Politics of a Divided Party and Parkinson's State in Vietnam," *Contemporary Southeast Asia* 23, no. 3 (December 2001): 546; Vuong Xuan Tinh 2001, p. 268. "Changing Land Policies and Its Impacts on Land Tenure of Ethnic Minorities in Vietnam," Enabling Policy Frameworks for Successful Community Based Resource Management Initiatives: Eighth Workshop on Community Management of Forest Lands (Honolulu, HI: East-West Center, 2002), http://www2.eastwestcenter.org/environment/CBFM/Tinh2.pdf.

13. Oscar Salemink, *The Ethnography of Vietnam's Central Highlanders: A Historical Contextualization, 1850–1990* (Honolulu, HI: University of Hawaii Press, 2003), p. 13 and UNHCR, *Vietnam: Situation of Indigenous Minority Groups*, p. 30.

14. UNHCR, *Vietnam: Indigenous Minority Groups*, p. 5 and *Vietnam: Situation of Indigenous Minority Groups*, pp. 2, 3.

15. Salemink, *The Ethnography of Vietnam's Central Highlanders*, pp. 12, 13; Dang Dinh Trung, "Coffee Production, Social Stratification and Poverty in a Vietnamese Central Highland Community" in Rodolphe de Koninck, Jules Lamarre, and Bruno Gendron, eds., *Understanding Poverty in Vietnam and the Philippines: Concepts and Context* (Laval, QC: Localized Poverty Reduction in Vietnam (LPRV) Project, September 2003), p. 111; and UNHCR, *Vietnam: Indigenous Minority Groups*, pp. 13–15.

16. Tran My-Van and Allan Shane Noble, "Dega Protestantism in Vietnam: Syncretic Religion or Political Movement?," paper presented in the *3rd Conference on South and Southeast Asian Association for the Study of Culture and Religion*, June 6, 2009, Denpasar, Bali.

17. "Vietnam: Open Central Highlands to International Observers," *Human Rights Watch*, April 22, 2004, http://www.hrw.org/english/docs/2004/04/22/vietna8478.htm.

18. Danida, *Vietnam-Denmark Partnership: Strategy for Development Cooperation (2006–2010)* (Copenhagen: Ministry of Foreign Affairs of Denmark, 2006).

19. Amnesty International, *Socialist Republic of Viet Nam: Renewed Concern for the Montagnard Minority* (London: International Secretariat, April 2004), http://www.unhcr.org/refworld/pdfid/412a08864.pdf.

20. UNHCR, "Montagnard Foundation president replies to the government of Vietnam," *DEGAR—Indigineous People of Indochina*, September 12, 2007, http://cih07.wordpress.com/2007/09/12/montagnard-foundation-president-replies-to-the-vietnamese-government/.

21. Duy Hoang, "Vietnam Bauxite Plan Opens Pit of Concern," *Asia Times Online*, March 16, 2009, http://www.atimes.com/atimes/Southeast_Asia/KC17Ae01.html.

22. Tran Dinh Thanh Lam, "Development-Vietnam: Government Bauxite Plan Stirs Public Worries," *Newsmekong*, May 29, 2009, http://www.globalissues.org/news/2009/05/29/1657.

23. Stephen Denney, "Foreign Donors Caution Vietnam on Bauxite Mining," *Asia Pacific News*, Wednesday, June 10, 2009.

24. "Bauxite Bashers: The Government Chooses Economic Growth over Xenophobia and Greenery," *The Economist*, April 23, 2009.

25. Ibid.

26. "China Inks $460 mln Alumina Deal in Vietnam," *Ministry of Natural Resources and the Environment*, July 17 2008, http://www.monre.gov.vn/v35/default.aspx?tabid=675&CateID=57&ID=46970&Code=KGHFF46970.

27. "Vietnam, China Become Comprehensive and Strategic Partners," *Viet NamNet*, June 3, 2008, http://english.vietnamnet.vn/politics/2008/06/786348/.

28. Ibid.

29. Cited in Tran Dinh Thanh Lam, "Development-Vietnam."

30. Denney, "Foreign Donors Caution Vietnam on Bauxite Mining."

31. "Vietnam Prime Minister Backs Controversial Aluminium Project," *Earth Times*, August 19, 2009, http://www.earthtimes.org/articles/show/281931,vietnam-prime-minister-backs-controversial-aluminum-project.html.

32. Asia Indigenous People Pact Foundation (AIPP), "Bauxite in Vietnam," *Mekong Communities Networking Workshop on Extractive Industries, Agri-business, and Hydro Power,* Chiang Mai, Thailand, September 27–28, 2007, p. 26.

33. Clarita Muller-Plantenberg, "Social and Ecological Consequences of the Bauxite-Energy-Aluminium Product Line: Steps Towards Sustainable Metal Management," in Arnim von Gleich, Stefan Gössling-Reisemann, and Robert U. Ayres, *Sustainable Metals Management* (Dordrecht: Springer, 2006), p. 451, table 19.1, http://www.bauxitevietnam.info.

34. Cited in "New Opposition to Mine . . .," *Radio Free Asia,* April 2, 2009, http://www.queme.net/eng/news_detail.php?numb=1186.

35. Mai Thanh Truyet, "Ven Man Bi Mat tai Vietnam," *Nam Uc Weekly,* no. 708, August 21, 2009.

36. Quoted in Martha Ann Overland, "In Vietnam, New Fears of Chinese Invasion," *Vietnam Today,* April 22, 2009, http://calvin-chong.blogspot.com/2009/04/vietnam-today.html.

37. World Commission on Economic Development, *Our Common Future* (New York: Oxford University Press, 1987), p. 8.

38. See "Agenda 21," *Division for Sustainable Development,* http://www.un.org/esa/dsd/agenda21/res_agenda21_01.shtml.

39. "Denmark and Norway Caution Vietnam against Bauxite Mining," *Vietnam Aujourd'hui,* June 14, 2009.

40. Ibid.

41. Lyndall J. Stoyles, *View on Vietnam: Briefing Series* (Sydney: Uniya, November 2004), http://www.uniya.org/research/view_vietnam.pdf.

42. "Corruption Perceptions Index 2008," *Transparency International,* http://www.transparency.org/policy_research/surveys_indices/cpi.

43. Ministry of Planning and Investment, *The Five Year Socio-Economic Development Plan 2006–2010* (Hanoi: Foreign Investment Agency, March 2006).

44. European Parliament, "European Parliament Resolution of 26 November 2009 on the Situation in Laos and Vietnam," *Viet Tan,* November 27, 2009, http://www.viettan.org/spip.php?article9265.

Chapter 14

Religion as a Possible Impediment to Environmental Discourse

Bidisha Kumar and George James

With the emergence of the relatively new subfield of religion and ecology, much attention has been focused upon the ways in which various religious traditions have enhanced and supported, or might enhance and support, a viable relationship between human beings and the environment. Many scholars have found neglected insights in texts from the great religious traditions that support the environment and that have been overshadowed by the prevailing instrumentalist valuation of nature. Some scholars, however, have contested these insights and argued that some religious traditions have fostered and supported at best the neglect of nature. In the case of the Hindu religious tradition, scholars like Ranchor Prime, O.P. Dwivedi, Chris Chapple, and others have argued that the attitude of the Hindu religious tradition to nature has been a positive one.[1] Others like Lance Nelson, John Passmore, and J. Baird Callicott argue that Hinduism has instilled attitudes hostile to the environment and to environmental protection.[2] More recent scholarship has begun to acknowledge that it is hardly possible to make a general statement concerning the ecological assets or liabilities of an entire tradition, especially one as extended in time as Hinduism. Reflection of the events of September 11, 2001 brings into focus another nuance in the question of the relationship of religion to the environment: the danger that the positive contribution to environmental consciousness from a particular religious tradition can be used to promote a sectarian communalist agenda. This chapter examines how the tendency to evoke nature, religion, and identity can steer away from a fluid and egalitarian ethos to propound a divisive and exclusivist identity politics detached from the socioeconomic and ecological concerns. We present here three cases in which religious mobilizations have evaded, discredited, or undermined the legitimate environmental insights derived from and supported by the religious tradition it invokes.

THE AMARNATH LAND DISPUTE

With more than a 2000-year-old history and the gift of an enchanting landscape, the Kashmir valley is an attractive destination for tourists from around the world. Yet, years of military repression, victimization, and violence in the name of national security has rendered this region ecologically devastated, economically stressed, and culturally impoverished. Along with social suffering, widened inequalities, and conflicts that have claimed some 70,000 lives since the 1990s, the valley has the distinction of being the most militarized zone in the world.[3] Largely, because of the violence between Indian security forces and militant separatists over the past two decades, today the region is reckoned as one of the slowest growing economies of South Asia.[4] The alienation from the Indian state and political resistance articulating the right of self-determination or *tehreek* cannot be divorced from the struggle of the indigenous population to break free from oppression, disenfranchisement, and exploitation.[5]

The conflict over Kashmir is intertwined with long-standing communal strife between Hindu nationalists on one hand and Islamic separatist communities on the other. A recent controversy over the transfer of forestland to a Hindu shrine board in Kashmir brought environmental concerns into the political debate in the state of Jammu and Kashmir. Yet, the debate quickly turned into a communal and political storm that polarized religious communities evading the environmental, socioeconomic, and common cultural concerns of the region.

At an altitude of 3,952 meters (12,962 feet), a natural cave formed of limestone and calcareous rocks, locally called Amarnath (the Immortal One, the name of Hindu god Shiva), is one of the most important sacred sites of this region. The cave contains an ice stalagmite, formed annually by melting snow seeping through the ceiling and then freezing at a particular spot on the floor of the cave. This feature of nature is deified as the *lingam* or symbol of the Hindu deity, Lord Shiva. Until recently, owing to weather conditions, it was open to pilgrims for only a short period in July and August every year. Normally, devotees have to brave an arduous 5-day, 40-mile trek across inhospitable terrain to visit the cave and worship the *lingam.* Besides the difficulty of the terrain and weather conditions that often threaten the life and safety of the devotees, the shrine that is located at the center of the conflict ravaged Kashmir valley is under constant military vigilance. For centuries, this Hindu pilgrimage (*yātrā*) was looked upon as a meeting ground of people from the plains and the Kashmiris, and reflected a symbiotic relationship between two different cultures in the 18th century. [6] It was a Muslim shepherd who discovered the shrine. The pilgrimage would hardly be conceivable without the cooperation, goodwill, and fraternity of the local Muslim community, who play an integral role in the pilgrimage economy. Muslims support the *yātrā* as porters, guides, horsemen, and palanquin bearers, carrying the aged and ailing to the shrine. They take care of the pilgrims, arrange free food from *langars* (community kitchens), and provide shelter, sometimes in their own homes, in the case of severe and threatening weather.[7]

More recently, an increasing number of pilgrims have become a concern for state authorities. The authorities have focused their efforts on the improvement of security and expanding services for the influx of worshipers. Among the local people, the drive to provide better amenities like proper shelter and toilet facilities for the pilgrims, who have had to deal with such primitive amenities as open trench toilets separated by gunny sacks, initially received sympathy and attention. But the exponential rise in the number of pilgrims, in an ecologically fragile environment, did not. In May 2008, the ruling Congress-led government of Jammu and Kashmir issued a notice to transfer 100 acres of forestland in the Baltal and Domail region of the Sindh forest division to the Shri Amarnath Shrine Board (SASB), the management trust for the *yātrā.* The purpose of the transfer was the construction of basic facilities for the pilgrims.

In the past, local people have resented and protested the transfer of land for central developmental projects, army camps, and schools run by the Indian army.[8] The new land transfer unleashed a long-standing public suspicion about land grabs and settlements. Along with support from separatist groups, the All Parties Hurriyat Conference undertook peaceful demonstrations in Kashmir in protest.[9] Fearing escalation of protests and tension, on July 1, 2008, the state government rescinded the land transfer. With the support of the leading Hindu nationalist groups, Bharatiya Janata Party (BJP), the Vishwa Hindu Parishad (VHP) and the Bajrang Dal, radical Hindus in Jammu then led a counter agitation demanding the land back for the SASB, and resorted to an economic blockade of the valley.[10] Over half of Kashmir valley's population lives off the land, where the biggest economic sector remains agriculture and fruit-growing in particular, which employs more than half a million people.[11] The blockade precipitated an economic crisis that victimized the people of the valley with acute shortages of food, medicine, and other basic necessities. As the valley's rich fruit harvest began to perish, the fruit-growers grew desperate. In response, the activists in the valley resorted to various methods of nonviolent civil disobedience.[12] A nonviolent mass march was called by the fruit-growers union and the separatist groups to open another trade route through Pakistan-held Kashmir. As the unarmed protestors began advancing toward the cease-fire line, the Indian troops opened fire, killing about 15 people.[13] The agitation led by the Hindu communal forces in Jammu—who were responsible for violence, arson, and killings—stands in glaring contrast with the peaceful protests of Hurriyat in the valley protesting the blockade. The Hindu rights were culpably involved in stepping up political unrest and deepening the communal divide within the region as well as without.[14]

While armed conflict in the Kashmir valley has declined since insurgency began in 1989,[15] the valley residents now eager for the realization of their own self-determination look upon the proliferation of pilgrim inflow less enthusiastically. Scholars and analysts interpret their indifference as the response to what they see as an aggressive religio-political statement by an increasingly Hindu state and its ideological and institutional creed of *Hindutva*. The ideological strain of Hindu nationalism and its assimilative identity that focuses on "Hinduizing" the polity as well as the nation has disturbed the long-standing interaction and exchange of shared interests and aspirations between local culture and the people of the plains. Today, the proliferation of pilgrims from 12,000 in 1989 to between one-third and half a million in recent years has augmented this tension.[16] While the ice *lingam* of Shiva has a material life of only 15 days per year, the SASB has extended the pilgrimage to a period of two and a half months. To save the time of the pilgrims, they also opened a new and shorter route to the site though the geologically fragile mountains of Baltal. For those who could afford it, they also added the attraction of helicopter service to the cave. It appears that the press of people now attending the site is actually endangering the formation of the ice lingam for which they are coming.[17] But the response of the SASB is to "harness science to preserve the lingam," by running electric air conditioners to prevent the ice lingam from melting.[18] Nevertheless, the surge in religious pilgrimage seems to be elevated to the heights of a patriotic enterprise of Hindu nationalism. Navlakha observes that this ideological propaganda is expressed in a Press Information Bureau release during the 1999 Kargil War:

> [The] Yearning For Moksha (Salvation) Can Move The Devotees To The Challenging Heights Of Kashmir And Will Be A Fitting Gesture Of Solidarity With Our Valiant Soldiers Who Have Been Fighting The Enemy To Defend Our Borders.[19]

Initially, the rationale behind the protests in the Kashmir valley following the allotment of land to the SASB was an ecological concern. It was feared that the construction of temporary shelters might affect the delicate ecology of the region and threaten a nearby wildlife sanctuary. An environmental report, by the J&K State Pollution Control Board in 2006, stressed that the amounts of waste (about 55,000 kg) generated per day and the absence of waste disposal sites constituted a threat to the Lidder River, impairing its aquatic diversity and endangering the health of downstream users.[20] In addition, vehicular air pollution as well as the sheer mass of people could threaten the stability of the fragile ecosystem, including the glaciers. Indiscriminate flow of a large number of pilgrims beyond the carrying capacity of the fragile mountain ecosystem is also a threat to the primacy of access and rights of local residents to natural resources, and to their livelihood. But the agitation against the land transfer lacked a persuasive focus on the region's pressing ecological and social justice issues. Instead of questioning the aggressive developmental agendas, and threat of the destruction of a fragile Himalayan ecology, the leaders of the valley's separatist organizations raised their arguments on communal grounds. The protestors argued that land allotment would lead to an intrusion of Hindu culture, that it would cause further alienation of Kashmiri land, and change her demographics.[21] While communalizing the land transfer issue suits the agendas of separatists and the Hindu nationalists, the separation of people into oppositional forms of a majoritarian "Kashmiri Muslim" community versus the "Hindus" does not do justice to the disparate, diverse, and shared interests of entire Kashmir's populace. For the Hindu nationalists, these diverse and shared interests seem peripheral and secondary to the central agenda of an assimilative religious ideology and the exclusionary narrative framework of *Hindutva.*

The fact that the environmental and social impact of the *yātrā* was never seriously considered is an indication that SASB's project to encourage an unrestricted flow of pilgrim traffic in Kashmir is oriented more to the promotion of a communal ideology than to matters of spiritual or moral concern.[22] It could be argued that such aggressive promotion of pilgrimage as commercial tourism, especially in an ecologically sensitive region, undermines the true spirit of pilgrimage. Traditionally, the pilgrimage is a struggle in the interest of penance, humility, and sacrifice. In fact, the traditional virtue of Hindu pilgrimage arises as much from the sacred character that is attached to the place as from desire to honor the deity of the shrine. The desecration of the aesthetic and spiritual beauty of nature clearly violates the most basic teachings of Hindu religious scriptures. While their argument that the use of prefabricated structures for camping might offer some check on the widespread pollution from garbage and sewage generation by hundreds of thousands of pilgrims, it cannot be a solution to the growing ecological crisis of the region. The need is to prioritize the carrying capacity of the land and equity issues in terms of a ceiling on pilgrim flow as well as on duration of the pilgrimage, along with cost effective and organic measures for reducing pollution during the pilgrim period. Without full consideration of the above, the *yātrā* will remain a blatant show of political religious rhetoric rather than a holy and spiritual undertaking.[23] The Hindu nationalists' involvement and support for the struggle against the Tehri Dam is another illustration of this point.

THE PROTEST AGAINST THE TEHRI DAM: HINDU NATIONALIST IDEALS AND THE ENVIRONMENT

There was perhaps no name more widely associated with the protest against the Tehri Dam than that of Sunderlal Bahuguna. Initiated at the age of 13 into Gandhi's constructive program, his thought and activism presents an integrated philosophy of nature rooted in the spiritual traditions of India and informed by modern ecology. The movement that Bahuguna led was against a controversial high dam on the headwaters of the sacred river Ganga in the northern Himalayan state of what is today Uttarakhand. It was one of the most active antidam campaigns in the world. For Bahuguna, the Tehri Dam was inappropriate for the Himalayan region because it was a temporary solution to the permanent problem of water shortage. It was socially unjust because it imposed the unfair burden of displacement upon 100,000 people of the hills. It was also unsafe because it was to be located on a seismically active site, only 15 kilometers from the meeting of the Indian plate and the Eurasian plate. Supporting these ideas was Bahuguna's view that the divine reality is not to be found in temples and in images alone but also in nature: in mountains, in rivers, in birds, in beasts, and in all of humanity. To abuse nature is to abuse the divine reality it represents. He maintained as he does today that his ecological vision of a harmonious relationship with nature is rooted in the soil of Indian spirituality and the humanism of Gandhi.

After the terrorist attacks on the World Trade Towers in New York of September 11, 2001, Professor T. Shivaji Rao, the director of the Department of Environmental Studies at the College of Engineering, Gandhi Institute of Technology and Management in Visakhapatnam, visualized another threat to the Tehri Dam and to the population below it. As a member of the Environmental Appraisal Committee of the Union Ministry of Environment in 1989–1990, he had studied the design of the dam and the plans for disaster management. His committee had unequivocally rejected the proposal for the Tehri Dam. In 1992, he had published a book entitled *Tehri Dam is a Time Bomb*. But after the events of September 11, 2001, he published an abstract of this book in which he pointed out that the Tehri Dam would be an easy target for terrorists, and that such an attack should be anticipated because it would be an inexpensive bid for them to destroy the life and culture of India. Because it is made of earth, sand, and gravel, an attack by means of a bomb conducted by the agents of enemy countries would easily cause the dam to collapse, killing millions of Indians and destroying temples, sacred towns, and cities.[24]

The thought of an attack by enemies of India infused an element of nationalism into the discourse, concerning the viability of the dam. It also gave support to those concerned with the Ganga for its religious significance. Among the groups for whom the religious significance of the Ganga was especially pronounced were members of what has been called the Sangh Parivar or "family of parties or organizations." British scholar Emma Mawdsley explains that the principal constituents of this family includes the political BJP that, with its leader Prime Minister Atal Behari Vajpayee, was until 2004 the main party of the central Government of India; the Rashtriya Swayemsevak Sangh, a cultural organization founded in 1925, that among other things promotes paramilitary and martial arts training; and the VHP or World Hindu Council set up in 1964 to bring together the diverse elements of Hindu belief and practice. Mawdsley adds that the youth wing of the VHP, called the Bajrang Dal, is largely made up of disaffected Hindu youth "who can be called upon to intimidate and threaten opponents." She explains that the core ideology of the Sangh is that of "Hindutva," meaning Hinduness, but she indicates that it has come to refer to the more narrow agenda of Hindu nationalism. "Essentially, Hindutva represents a 'blood and soil' vision of the sacred land of Hindustan for the Hindus."[25]

The Sangh Parivar, and the VHP in particular, was especially occupied with the sanctity of the Ganga River, which they saw as compromised by being dammed. The VHP also recognized the safety hazard of the project and argued that the two issues together presented a strong case against continuing with the dam construction, a view that presented a challenge to its ally, the BJP, that supported construction of the dam. However, issues concerning the safety of the dam soon became equated with an apparent "threat" to Hindutva. The specter of a terrorist attack invoked and instilled fears of a Muslim threat to a Hindu nation, categorizing the Muslims as outsiders and as problems surrounding the dam. The VHP and their allies, therefore, metaphorically imagined the damming of the Ganga as "imprisoning the Ganga" and as "an organized conspiracy to demolish" Hindus and their culture.[26] The most blatant form of this categorization was reflected in the president of the VHP, Ashok Sinhal's attempt to save the purity of the Ganga by launching an "Ayodhya-type movement,"[27] in case the government continues to construct the dam.[28]

The religious and mythological importance of the Ganga and her symbolic value can also be consciously used to generate ethno-religious divides and exclusions and to promote and consolidate the notion of an *akhand bharat* (undivided India) or *aryavarta* (Hindu culture). This alters the ecological and social context of the movement to the vantage of a conservative religious ideology. After visiting areas in Gujarat devastated by the earthquake of January 2001, Singhal pointed out that an earthquake in the area of the Tehri Dam would cause colossal cultural loss, wiping out the Hindu holy cities located downstream. He also pointed out that the damming of the Bhagirathi would result in the loss of the purity of the Ganga.[29] Yet, the issue of the safety of the dam was quickly eclipsed, when he later declared to his followers during the Sri Ganga Rakhsha Yatra (Ganga Protection March) in July 2000, "I am not here to talk about the seismic condition of the dam site or about the cost-benefit analysis of the project. I am talking about Gangatva. Gangatva is Hindutva. Hindutva is Rashtratva." Translated, the rhetoric implies: "Ganga is the essence of Hinduism, which in turn is the essence of (Hindu) Nationalism."[30] Much public apprehension concerning the safety of the dam now seemed to have support in the concerns of the VHP. Typically, the *yātrā* became projected as a Hindutva brigade to protect the "purity" of the Ganga, which on the one hand attempted to unite some, while demonizing and disregarding others. In response to a question asked about why the Muslim population was singled out of the movement, one campaigner responded thus: "Ganga is our mother. How can those people accompany us who do not consider Ganga their mother? They are unworthy bad sons."[31] This demonstrates how a boundary-defying ecological entity like the Ganga can be transformed into a boundary-producing one.[32]

For Bahuguna, the Tehri Dam was not only an ecological issue, but also a social, a cultural, and a spiritual issue. He, thus, recognized the support of those concerned with the religious significance of the river as an appropriate religious concern. In an interview at the Kumbh Mela in 2001, when Bahuguna was told that the VHP had passed a resolution that condemned the proposed Tehri Dam, Bahuguna stated that he was glad of the support. He stated that he had read that Swami Chinmayananda, another leader of the VHP, had spoken against the dam and commented that it was good that such persons were opposing the project. But he also pointed out that he had never met Swami Chinmayananda nor had he ever exchanged any ideas with him.[33] Bahuguna's concern was for a comprehensive Himalayan policy to save the hills. "The Himalayas," he said, "are a mountain of emotion, not rocks and boulders. We must preserve and nurture it to save our culture, to save our souls." Unlike the VHP's polarized opposition against the dam, which was to raise fear of a Muslim threat to a Hindu nation and to demarcate and exclude specific religious "others," Bahuguna's approach was one that understands the River Ganga in terms of a complex network of relationships between environmental justice, spirituality, and culture. The Ganga is, therefore, not for the Hindus alone, as it binds the whole country into one unit, historically, culturally, and spiritually. Thus, while using Hindu myths, Bahuguna describes how the river through her natural course benefits all, "irrespective of caste, creed, color, poverty, or wealth," but that when she is dammed, she "becomes the possession of the privileged and powerful who can dispense her blessings on a partisan basis."[34] In a speech at the Kumbh Mela, Bahuguna pointed out that rituals that are performed in a living stream cannot be the same when they are performed in stagnant water. This articulates his ecological concern that water flowing along a turbulent course is alive with high oxygen content, but turns dead once it is impounded.[35] The damming of the Bhagirathi River will therefore mean, he says, "that the river will lose its sanctity." In summary, Bahuguna's concern was to relate river ecology to spirituality and to culture. The concern of the VHP, on the other hand, was to relate the sanctity of the river to religion and to nationalism.

On March 26 of that year, Ashok Singhal announced that he would undertake an indefinite fast "in defense of the Ganges," to begin at the end of the month, to protest the construction of the Tehri Dam. But the interest of the VHP in the protest against the Tehri Dam provoked little notice among the people of Tehri. Angry shop owners in the market area were dismayed that Singhal had not spoken a word about their demand, if the dam should be completed, for fair compensation and an adequate plan for resettlement.[36] Ashok Singhal finally called off his threatened fast when the Prime Minister Atal Behari Vajpayee assured him that a new committee of experts would be constituted to consider, among other things, the impact of the dam on the sanctity of the river! Journalists now suggested that the critical issues concerning the project were being co-opted by the VHP to further its nationalist agenda. Journalists and academics seized upon Bahuguna's approval of VHP opposition to the dam and began to interpret his concern for the religious aspects of the Ganga as an alliance with the political objectives of the VHP. This conflation is misleading and flawed. Eva Saroch clarifies the difference between VHP's and Bahuguna' s approaches succinctly: "What VHP shares in common with environmentalist like Sunderlal Bahuguna . . . . is that the dam construction be stopped, but for altogether different reasons."[37] Mukul Sharma, a Delhi-based environmental journalist, pointed out that those opposed to the dam not only spoke the language of ecological politics, but also invoked certain metaphors to engage with religious practices and mythical beliefs. He states: "In their use of these metaphors and myths, the environmentalists often come close to the beliefs of conservative Hindu forces and their chosen communal path."[38] He states that especially in the later part of the movement, the antidam politics were persistently "constructed through a conservative Hindu imagery, often in partnership with Hindutva politics. Ganga becomes holier and holiest. The ecological reasoning is blurred and goes beyond logic, eliciting Hindu support, patriotism and xenophobia."[39] Writing about the hazards of VHP's involvement in the protest against the Tehri Dam, Emma Mawdsley states that while Bahuguna had fought all his life for the wider goals of social and environmental justice for the people of the hills, to many secular and Gandhian activists, he was by this time "disturbingly compromised by his ties with the VHP."[40] While Mawdsley failed to demonstrate any ties at all between Bahuguna and the organization of the VHP, its personnel, or its nationalist objectives, his concern for the spiritual significance of the Ganga tended nevertheless to undermine his credibility and attenuate the effectiveness of his movement.

For the record, when questioned about the VHP's concern for the preservation and promotion of Hindu traditions and its opposition to the Tehri Dam, Bahuguna pointed out that there is a critical difference between spirituality and sectarian religion. "They [the VHP] had made it a political thing in order to get support of the people, in order to arouse their emotions." Adding that there was no ethical content to their protest, he stated:

> You know in (the) practical, if one follows Hindu traditions then there should be austerity. They should use less and less things. And austerity should be practised not only in private life but in the public life also, and again with respect for nature. The modem civilization converts nature into cash. This is the trouble with the present day society.[41]

When asked whether he considered Ashok Singhal and his followers to be a part of the anti–Tehri Dam movement, he replied emphatically that Singhal was not a part of his movement but that Singhal has a movement of his own.[42]

PROTECTING THE RAMA SETHU: AMBIVALENT GOALS IN A COMMUNALIZED LANDSCAPE

The Rama Sethu (Adam's Bridge) is a natural underwater formation composed of a 48-km long chain of limestone shoals located in the shallow water of Palk Strait between India and Sri Lanka. In July 2005, the Government of India inaugurated an ambitious project to dredge a 152-km long, 300-m wide, and 12-m deep shipping canal cutting through this geological formation for the purpose of shortening the journey between India's eastern and western seaboards. The project was originally planned by the British, but was never implemented. The reviving of colonial projects is not new in independent India. Several proposals were put forward for a channel that would cut across or bypass the Rama Sethu. Like the many developmental projects, the shipping canal was pursued for inflated economic benefits that seriously downplayed ecological, economic, and social costs. The project that would cost nearly US$ 850 million had questionable economic benefits and unknown, potentially huge environmental costs that could impoverish both present and future generations.[43] From the inception of the project, objections came from economists, environmentalists, and from Tamil Nadu's local fishermen. Some of the concerns included the vulnerability of the region, because of unpredictable cyclones, the possible adverse impact of dredging the seabed, and the dumping of dredged material on coastal fisheries. This latter was also considered to have a negative impact on the delicate ecohydrological balance and biodiversity of the Marine Biosphere Reserve of Gulf of Mannar, lying in the vicinity of the project.

For many Hindus, however, the Rama Sethu is valued for its mythological and religious significance. It is argued that the *Sethu* is an object of cultural heritage and therefore, it cannot be demolished for the purpose of excavating a shipping canal. The "cultural" significance of the Sethu can be traced back to the canons of Valmiki's *Rāmāyaṇa,* one of the versions of the Hindu epic composed circa 300 BCE. According to the epic, there was a bridge engineered by the Hindu god-king Rama with help from his army of monkeys and men. The bridge was made to cross over the ocean to reach Lanka (present day Sri Lanka) and rescue Rama's wife Sita, who was abducted by the demon-king Ravana. It was this particular aspect of Hindu mythology that inspired the VHP in the summer of 2007 to launch a nationwide agitation against the project. Following a series of writ petitions that were filed to stop the destruction of the mythological bridge, the Supreme Court ordered a temporary halt, though not an end, of the construction work for the proposed canal.

The issue of protecting the Rama Sethu became a matter of political strategy on the part of those who became mobilized in the name of faith and those who reacted to it. Interestingly, this time, the usual opponents in the movement were not the demonized "foreigners" and "out-groups" like the Muslims or the Christians, but the state itself, and the lower-caste Hindus of South India. Mobilizing public opinion against the Sethu, therefore, became a more complex issue and was not as simplistic as invoking anti-Muslim rhetoric and polarizing the society along communal lines. The first problem surfaced when in response to the writ petition in the Supreme Court to preserve Rama's heritage, the Archeological Survey of India (ASI) came up with a counter affidavit questioning the historicity of the text of the *Rāmāyaṇa* and the existence of Rama, as well as arguing that the Sethu is not a man-made structure but a natural geological formation caused by tidal action and sedimentation.[44] While from the perspective of archaeology and history, such questioning of historical evidence for the existence of Rama or the bridge may appear right, conflating its significance with that of belief and faith of millions of people precipitated an unproductive controversy. The BJP and its ally VHP raised a strong campaign of countrywide agitation against the affidavit. Polemists from the Indian diaspora described the act as a "subjection" of Hindu beliefs and history to "allegedly superior investigative forensic science." It was further labeled as an "Islamo-Christian conspiracy" that "threatens to subjugate Hindus politically . . . . that will impale them on the beliefs of their imperialist conquerors."[45] Portraying the issue in terms of an anti-Hindu conspiracy, the agitation alienated itself from the cause, the community, and the creed.

The Rama Sethu protection movement estranged itself from the sacred nature of the Rama Sethu and its mythopoeics rooted in the local culture of South India. While, in North India, Rama is a popular symbol among all caste groups, he is not quite so in the South. In contrast to Valmiki's *Rāmāyaṇa* or its Hindi rendering *Rāmcaritmānas,* which is dominant in the North, in South India, it is the *Rāmāyaṇa* of Kamban composed in Tamil in the 11th century that is the most popular. In fact, the Rama story has countless variations and retellings throughout tropical Asia. Each has its own local flavor, some even contradicting one another. Those who believe in the "Sanskrit" Valmiki version might object to or dismiss these other "vernacular" versions, as they are different and conflicting. This creates a problem for others who believe that their version is the correct and legitimate one. It could be stated that the traditions of the *Rāmāyaṇa* is as much traditions of contestation as of canonicity.[46] In fact, the Sethu is not an essential part of every version of the story of *Rāmāyaṇa.* Instead of imaging the regional versions of the story and the evolutionary nature of the epic as an invitation to social solidarity in the common cause of ecological and cultural conservation, the Sangh risked alienating the Hindus of South India by focusing on the Sethu as a "pan-Hindu" identity symbol. Furthermore, the Sangh shifted from a focus on the religious significance of the Sethu to an effort to demonstrate its historical authenticity, conflating mythology with the historicity of the bridge itself.[47] In attempting to provide "scientific" evidence of the historicity of the Sethu, it took mythology to be false and history to be true.

What it missed was the relationship between folk culture of the people and the environment. The *Rāmāyaṇa* is a morality tale based on the story of Rama that represents a fascinating layering of folk history. It relies on oral narratives, poems, and the retelling of events because of their relevance to the present, not merely to the past. Such retelling happens in active association and partnership between religion, morality, and the environment. The Sangh's agitation, though successful in annulling of ASI's counter affidavit, could not properly articulate this end.

A singular focus on the historicity of Rama and the Sethu paid little or no critical attention to the central teaching of the *Rāmāyaṇa,* the spiritual and moral values encoded in *dharma,* its appeal to human conscience, and hence its relevance to the present world. *Dharma* is duty and righteousness, upholding the right attitude and relationship toward people and all of nature. In the *Kacchit Sarga* of *Rāmāyaṇa,* Rama asks his brother Bharata about his *dharmic* duties and responsibilities concerning respect for and conservation of nature, the nonpatronization of high-caste Brahmins for their conceit, and the protection of the interests of the lower castes and women. The narration depicts such values as that of a dutiful king, his asceticism, and his forest life, all of which reconcile the ethical and spiritual qualities of responsibility, self-control, and temperance. Evading these *dharmic* injunctions, the Sangh Parivar's movement did not support responsibility for preserving ecology or the environment, or for protecting local peoples' livelihood. The Sangh did not protest the project because it was bound to devastate a marine biosphere reserve containing some 3,600 species, including the endangered marine turtles, the globally endangered *dugong* (sea cow), or stress the loss of sea grass and coral reefs that would directly affect the marine life flourishing beneath the reef. Neither were the activists interested in the adverse effect of dredging on the livelihood of one third of a million fisherfolks living in the 138 villages and towns of coastal Tamil Nadu.[48] The overwhelming right-wing protests did not grow out of a genuine concern for conservation, but for a singular obsession with the protection of the Rama Sethu. Hence, the movement lobbied for a dredging route that would not physically affect the Sethu. A statement by the BJP spokesperson Ravi Shankar Prasad clearly asserts this linear focus: "We are not against the Sethusamudram project but we want a realignment to protect the Rama Sethu."[49] Such an attitude reflects a poor understanding of the significance of the ecological message reflected in the *Rāmāyaṇa*'s graphic portrayal of forest flora and fauna, the rich *araṇya* (forest) culture, and the role of animals as an important part of Rama's adventures.[50]

During the agitation to stop the project, Ashok Singhal declared, "We are preparing for a massive andolan (movement) if anyone attacks the Ram Sethu. . . . They have declared a war on Hindus and we will not stand by."[51] Exclusionary visions like this fail to engage with the intuitionist, ethical, and spiritual dimensions of Hindu religion, and downplay the interests of the poor, low-caste people, women, and other minorities affected by the project. Concern for ecology, equity, and justice thus never received serious consideration in the agenda of the Sangh to save the Rama Sethu.

RELIGIOUS DISCOURSES ON ECOLOGICAL PRESERVATION—CAN THERE BE A DIALOG?

Discussion of the problematic relationship between right-wing religious organizations in India and the environment informs us about the potential obstacles to faith-based environmental discourses. It is helpful in two ways. First, it provides an understanding of how environmental and livelihood struggles over resources are stifled within a communal framework. It reveals the emerging power of mainstream religious ideologies to "absorb, co-opt and alter the views of an environmental movement."[52] Secondly, such obstacles undermine the legitimate ecological and moral insights derived from and supported by the Hindu religious tradition, and preclude opportunity for constructive intercultural dialogue with the scientific and the decision-making domain.

The modern construction of Hinduism, its upper-caste Brahmin identity, and its homogenizing discourse on one hand, and its demarcating of specific religious "others" on the other, can be best described in the words of historian Romila Thapar, as an "imagined religious community."[53] It represents a "syndicated, semiticized Hinduism, a Hinduism of one God, one book, one place, one people, a religion resembling exclusivist versions of Judaism, Christianity and Islam."[54] Such an ideology suffers from serious descriptive and historical flaws. It not only departs from the history of religious groups involved by ignoring the shared narratives, memories, and iconographic resources, but also fails to consider the essential differences that interact and intersect in socially and culturally significant ways. Consider, for instance, the interplay of folk culture and history, rituals, emotions, and economy in the pilgrimage to Amarnath. The discovery of the shrine by a Muslim, the local Muslims' participation in the pilgrimage economy, as well as their selflessness in the welfare of the pilgrims highlight shared identities and memories that enrich and complement the identities of both Hindus and Muslims. The shrine and its environs together form a spiritual domain defined by pilgrimage behavior and evolved from collective memories. It also highlights the central place of worship of nature, and how the sacred hill shrine and the surrounding nature are traditionally intertwined. Indifference toward environmental impact caused by the unbridled flow of pilgrims in the valley runs counter to the tradition severing the interrelationship between human and natural landscapes. On the other hand, the growing religious bifurcation into "Muslim" versus "Hindu" and "us" versus "them' discourse stifles the communicative space and shared expressions of all regional and religious aspirations of a diverse community. The failure to acknowledge differences as well as accommodate religious "others" has ruled out the possibility of constructive dialogue and mutual enrichment on issues of harmonious coexistence between sustainability, humanity, culture, and nature.

Discourse with the larger historical, social, and cultural mindset that shapes shared memories and interests can rekindle new meaning and perspectives on nature in public imagination. One way to do this is to open up constructive dialogue not only between and amongst the worldview of religious leaders and activists of different traditions, but also between environmentalists, scientists, journalists, and policy-makers for a shared ecological future. For this to happen, there is a critical need to recognize the true ecological insights of the Hindu religious tradition. This would mean (1) to reject the attitudes of religious absolutism, as well as attitudes that proclaim that there is nothing left to learn since their tradition "already possesses the full truth, which is only partially available elsewhere,"[55] and

(2) to acknowledge the ecological insights of other traditions and communities. These must endorse transformative and prophetic insights from within traditions as well as without, empathetic appreciation of other traditions, and a creative revisioning of one's own. This poses existential, intellectual, and ethical questions that trace back to the very source of what faith is about. It brings us back to the original concern of how religion can help us deal with the harsh ecological, social, and economic problems of our time. We argue that the answer to both questions lies in the way Mohandas Gandhi defined religion.

A GANDHIAN APPROACH TO CONNECTING RELIGION WITH ENVIRONMENTAL PRESERVATION

To Gandhi, religion as an idea transcends all formal and organized religions and their practices. Though it "transcends," it does not "supersede" institutional or organized religions, but constitutes their common foundation. The difference between the two is that the organized institutional religions aim to realize the idea of religion in time. Religion as an idea is beyond any sectarian bias. It simply implies the belief that the universe is pervaded and governed by the supreme cosmic, and the moral imperative of living and ordering one's life accordingly.[56] His notion of religion as an idea is perhaps no better expressed than in his own words:

> Let me explain what I mean by religion. It is not the Hindu religion, which I certainly prize above all other religions, but the religion which transcends Hinduism, which changes one's very nature, which binds one indissolubly to the truth within and which ever purifies. It is the permanent element in human nature which counts no cost too great in order to find full expression and which leaves the soul utterly restless until it has found itself, known its Maker and appreciated the true correspondence between the Maker and itself.[57]

For Gandhi, the function of religion is its transformative potential: its adherence to truth and its capacity to purge the ego of its passions. It establishes a true correspondence and relationship between the individual, the collective self, and the cosmic spirit. Its purpose is the transcending of the bounds of all institutional religions and dogmas.[58] According to Gandhi, it was in this interrelationship with nature and the reality around us that truth or God is revealed. Seeking and discovering this reality of all existence prepares the ground for dialogue and learning from each other.

Gandhi's perspective on religion prepares the ground for a genuine religious pluralism by providing an objective basis for recognition of the equality of all religions (*sarva-dharma-samabhāva*) and the foundation for genuine interreligious dialogue. Gandhi reasoned that since man is imperfect, any religion promulgated by his limited mind will be imperfect as well. From this, Gandhi drew the conclusion that there can be "no one religion higher than any other."[59] Gandhi's view is different from an attitude of mere "toleration" and "respect" for religions other than one's own. Instead, he inculcates a deep "spiritual humility" or a sense of "equimindedness" toward all faiths. Acknowledgment of imperfections of one's own as well as other religions invites a spirit of interreligious dialog as a process of understanding one another and offering and receiving from others. The religion of Gandhi, as Bhikhu Parekh once put it, "placed the individual at the centre of the religious search, liberated religion from the stranglehold of traditionalism and literalism, encouraged fresh readings of scriptures, and made space for an inter-religious dialogue."[60] Gandhi's understanding of his own religion was not creedal. His interpretations engaged with the pluralistic strand within Hinduism, which is inclusive of the "other" and sought not only to tolerate but also to "define, propagate, and celebrate differences."[61] Gandhi's concept of *sarva-dharma-samabhāva* frees religion from dogmatic encapsulation, sectarian pride, and fanaticism, posing a challenge to the exclusivist approaches of the proponents of *Hindutva* in modern India.

Gandhi's view of the equality of religions clarifies the role of religion in environmental and social discourse. Gandhi knew how to integrate intersubjective perspectives through constructive social representations that open up communicative space.[62] Constructive renderings of tradition mobilized public opinion against the rule of the British on one hand and broke through social barriers on the other. Familiar symbols came to convey revolutionary ideas. Gandhi evoked the mythology of Sita (the consort of Rama) as the epitome of simplicity, sacrifice, self-reliance, and nonviolent power that stands in sharp contrast to the stereotype of a submissive, obedient woman. This image fired the imagination of thousands of homebound, socially segregated women to join India's freedom struggle on an equal footing with the men. His innovative renderings of the ancient religious concepts of *aparigraha* (nonpossession) and *asteya* (nonstealing) continue to be relevant for their ethical and spiritual content. In postcolonial India, Gandhians in the famous Chipko movement organized folk plays from the *Bhagavata Purana* to raise spiritual and ecological consciousness amongst the people, hundreds of whom took the pledge to save the forests, if necessary, at the cost of their lives. In the context of the Rama Sethu debate, a viable application of Gandhi's approach would be to reappropriate the shared moral and iconographic resources embedded in the tradition and to motivate people for the cause of the environment. In that way, the tradition of *Rāmāyaṇa* would remain relevant to the needs of the entire population. Conscious and creative spreading of an ecological message through shared narratives, group memories, local history, and through traditional idioms and symbols creates positive linkages between nature and existing scriptural representations. It prepares the ground for new collective perspectives that overcome community divides and put one in an active relationship and dialogue with society, environment, and reality. Present and continuing obstacles to Hindu environmental discourse can be overcome by realizing Gandhi's idea of religion on one hand and contributing to the attainment of the ultimate end of all religions by engaging in the collective search for truth through the practice of *sarva-dharma-samabhāva* on the other. Efforts to conserve environment and the cultural relations tied to it must evolve as a path of dialogue between traditions that represent genuine religious pluralism and that support humility, openness, cooperation, and respect.

NOTES

1. Ranchor Prime, *Hinduism and Ecology: Seeds of Truth* (London: Cassell, 1992); Onkar Prasad Dwivedi, "Vedic Heritage for Environmental Stewardship," *Worldviews* 1, no. 1 (1997): 25–36; and Christopher Key Chapple, and Mary Evelyn Tucker, eds., *Hinduism and Ecology: The Intersections of Earth, Sky and Water* (Cambridge, MA: Harvard University Press, 2000).

2. Lance E. Nelson, "The Dualism of Non-Dualism: Advaita Vedanta and the Irrelevance of Nature" in Lance E. Nelson, ed., *Purifying the Earthly Body of God: Religion and Ecology in Hindu India* (New York: SUNY Press, 1998) and J. Baird Callicott, *Earth's Insights: A Multicultural Survey of Ecological Ethics from the Mediterranean Basin to the Australian Outback* (Berkeley, CA: University of California Press, 1994).

3. Haley Duschinski, "Destiny Effects: Militarization, State Power, and Punitive Containment in Kashmir Valley," *Anthropological Quarterly* 82, no. 3 (2009): 691–718.

4. Shahid Javed Burki, *Kashmir: A Problem in Search of a Solution,* Peaceworks No. 27 (Washington, D.C.: U.S. Institute of Peace, March 2007), http://www.usip.org/files/resources/PWmarch2007.pdf.

5. Duschinski, "Destiny Effects."

6. Shashi Mehta, "A Yatra That Is an Affirmation of Faith," *The Sunday Tribune,* August 31, 2003, http://www.tribuneindia.com/2003/20030831/spectrum/travel.htm.

7. Sarwar Kashani, "Amid Amarnath Land Row, Pilgrimage Keeps Its Peace," *Hindustan Times,* August 14, 2008, http://www.thaindian.com/newsportal/uncategorized/amid-amarath-land-row-pilgrimage-keeps-its-peace_10083857.html and Indo-Asian News Service, "Muslims Holding Makeshift Kitchens for Stranded Amarnath Pilgrims," *Hindustan Times,* July 1, 2008, news.oneindia.in/2008/07/01/muslims-holding-makeshift-kitchens-stranded-amarnath-*1214906700.html.*

8. Gautam Navlakha, "Kashmir: State Cultivation of the Amarnath Yatra," *Economic & Political Weekly* 43, no. 30 (July 2008): 17, 18.

9. Indo-Asian News Service, "Curfew in Kashmir as Hurriyat Calls for Peaceful Protests," *Sulekha News,* September 1, 2008, http://newshopper.sulekha.com/curfew-in-kashmir-as-hurriyat-calls-for-peaceful-protests_news_957423.htm and

Purav Goswami, "Price of Peace," *The Viewspaper,* September 9, 2008, http://theviewspaper.net/price-of-peace/.

10. A.G. Noorani, "Why Jammu Erupts," *Frontline* 25, no. 19 (September 13–26, 2008), http://www.hinduonnet.com/fline/fl2519/stories/20080926251907800.htm.

11. Alexander Evans, "Kashmir: A Tale of Two Valleys," *Asian Affairs* 36, no. 1 (March 2005): 35–47.

12. Nagesh Rao, "Kashmir Repression Rewards Hindu Far Right," *Socialist Worker.org,* August 14, 2008, http://socialistworker.org/2008/08/14/kashmir-repression.

13. Yaroslav Trofimov, "A New Tack in Kashmir: Peaceful Protest Gains in Separatist Flight," *The Wall Street Journal,* December 15, 2008, http://online.wsj.com/article/SB122930169820005503.html.

14. Nagesh Rao, "Kashmir Repression Rewards Hindu Far Right"; "Amarnath Row: BJP-VHP Bandh Turns Violent, 2 Killed," *Zee News,* July 3, 2008, http://www.zeenews.com/Nation/2008–07–03/452826news.html; and "VHP Bandh over Amarnath Land Transfer Issue Today," *Express India,* July 3, 2008, http://www.expressindia.com/latest-news/vhp-bandh-over-amarnath-land-transfer-issue-today/330769/.

15. Trofimov, "A New Tack in Kashmir."

16. Gautam Navlakha, "Jammu and Kashmir: Pilgrim's Progress Causes Regression," *Economic & Political Weekly* 41, no. 27 (July 8, 2006): 2975–77.

17. "Shiva Lingam Melts at Amarnath," *The Tribune,* July 17, 2008.

18. "Amarnath Cave Shrine to Go AC," *Merinews,* August 30, 2007.

19. Navlakha, "Kashmir: State Cultivation of the Amamath Yatra," 17, 18.

20. Peerzaada Arshad, "Polluted Lidder River Casts Cloud over Pilgrimage," *Down to Earth* 15, no. 8 (September 15, 2006) and "Faith's Filth: Waste of Pilgrims Threatens Pahalgam's Ecology," *Down to Earth* 13, no. 6 (August 15, 2004).

21. Madhur Singh, "A Perilous Religious Game in Kashmir," *Time,* August 6, 2008.

22. While there is no effort at restricting the number of pilgrims at Amarnath, the BJP is conscious of the ecological impact of unchecked tourist inflow at Gomukh, another pilgrimage of the Hindus in the (Uttarakhand) Himalayas. The government led by the BJP in the state issued a notification on May 2008, restricting the number of pilgrims to only 150 a day to protect the environment around Gangotri glacier. See Noorani, "Why Jammu Erupts."

23. Ibid.

24. Shivaji T. Rao, *Tehri Dam Is a Time Bomb* (New Delhi: Vani Printers, 1992), http://ganga-ahvaan.blogspot.com/2008/09/like-their-attacks-on-usa-if-terrorists.html.

25. Emma Mawdsley, "The Abuse of Religion and Ecology: The Vishva Hindu Parishad and Tehri Dam," *Worldviews* 9, no. 1 (2005): 7, 8.

26. Mukul Sharma, "Nature and Nationalism," *Frontline* 18, no. 3 (2001), http://www.frontlineonnet.com/fl1803/18030940.htm.

27. Here Singhal is referring to the planned demolition of a 16th-century mosque in Ayodhya by militant Hindu activists in 1992—an event that gravely affected the political landscape of India.

28. Eva Saroch, "Hydro Borders in South Asia: Geopolitical Imaginations and Contestations" in Eiki Berg and Henk van Houtum, eds., *Routing Borders between*

Territories, Discourses and Practices (Burlington, VT: Ashgate Publishing Company, 2003).

29. "Singhal Threatens Fast against Tehri Dam," *The Hindu*, March 24, 2001.

30. Sharma, "Nature and Nationalism."

31. Mukul Sharma, "Down with the Dam," *The Express Magazine*, August 20, 2000.

32. Saroch, "Hydro Borders in South Asia."

33. Prem Panicker, "Bahuguna at Kumbh, Sounds Alarm over Damming Ganga," *Rediff News*, www.rediff.com/news/2001/jan/20kumbh.htm#top.

34. George A. James, "Tehri Dam" in Bron R. Taylor, Jeffrey Kaplan, Laura Hohgood-Oster, Adrian Ivakhiv, and Micheal York, eds., *The Encyclopedia of Religion and Nature*, Vol. 2 (London: Thoemmes Continuum, 2005), pp. 1626, 1627.

35. A. Bahuguna, *Tehri Dam over Bhagirathi (Ganga)—A Threat to Ecology, Economy and Security* (Amritsar: Pingalwara Charitable Society, 2002).

36. T. K. Rajalakshmi, "A Saffron Twist: The Vishwa Hindu Parishad's Opposition to the Tehri Dam on Religious Grounds Sidesteps the Real Issues Involved in the Matter," *Frontline* 18, no. 8 (April 14–27, 2001).

37. Saroch, "Hydro Borders in South Asia."

38. Mukul Sharma, "Saffronising Green," *Seminar* 516 (August 2002): 3, http://www.india-seminar.com/2002/516/516%20mukul%20sharma.htm.

39. Ibid., 6.

40. Mawdsley, "The Abuse of Religion and Ecology."

41. Sunderlal Bahuguna, interviewed by George A. James, Old Tehri, June 14, 2002.

42. Ibid.

43. Priyanka P. Narain, "Ram Setu Project Faces Cash Crunch," *Hindustan Times*, September 27, 2007, http://www.hindustantimes.com/special-news-report/News-Feed/Ram-Setu-project-faces-cash-crunch/Article1-249840.aspx and Srinivasan Kannan, *Socio-economic Impact of the Sethusamudram Project*, MPRA Paper No. 13828, March 6, 2009, http://mpra.ub.uni-muenchen.de/13828/1/MPRA_paper_13828.pdf.

44. R. Ramachandran, "Myth vs. Science," *Frontline* 24, no. 19 (September 24–October 5, 2007) and Prashant K. Nanda, "ASI Turns 'Ravan' in Ram Sethu Controversy." *Indo-Asian News Service*, September 15, 2007, news.monstersandcritics.com/india/news/article_1356129.php/ASI_turns_Ravan_in_Ram_Sethu_controversy_blame_game_begins.

45. Gautam Sen, "An Attempt to Orphan an Entire Civilisation by Denying the Wellsprings of Its Foundation," *Organiser* 59, no. 18 (November 11, 2007): 4, http://organiser.org/archives/historic/dynamic/modulesd4c1.html?name=Content&pa=showpage&pid=209&page=4.

46. Sheldon Pollock, "Ramayana and Political Imaginations in India" in David N. Lorenzen, ed., *Religious Movements in South Asia 600–1800: Debates in Indian History and Society* (New York: Oxford University Press, 2004), p. 194.

47. Ram Madhav, "Ram in Hindu Belief?: Immortality Is Historicity," *Organiser* 59, no. 18 (November 11, 2007): 15, http://organiser.org/archives/historic/dynamic/modules4b6c.html?name=Content&pa=showpage&pid=209&page=15.

48. Srinivasan Kannan, *Socio-economic Impact of the Sethusamudram Project.*

49. Bhadra Sinha, "Ramayana No Basis for Ram *Setu* Debate," *Hindustan Times*, September 12, 2007, http://www.hindustantimes.com/spccial-news-report/News-Feed/Ramayana-no-basis-for-Ram-Setu-debate/Article1-247568.aspx.

50. David Lee, "The Natural History of the Ramayana" in Chapple and Tucker, *Hinduism and Ecology*.

51. Priyanka P. Narain, "Verdict on Sethu Samudram Project Unlikely Today," *Live Mint*, March 4, 2008, http://www.livemint.com/Politics/jMUX5ff6Mejh13N6chCcVP/Verdict-on-Sethu-Samudram-project-unlikely-today.html.

52. Mukul Sharma, "Passages from Nature to Nationalism: Sunderlal Bahuguna and Tehri Dam Opposition in Garhwal," *Economic & Political Weekly* 49, no. 8 (February 21, 2009): 41.

53. Romila Thapar, "Imagined Religious Communities" in Lorenzen, *Religious Movements in South Asia 600–1800*, p. 355.

54. Susanne Hoeber and Lloyd I. Rudoplh, "Modern Hate," *New Republic* 208, no. 12 (March 22, 1993): 26.

55. Ian G. Barbour, *Religion and Science: Historical and Contemporary Issues* (San Francisco, CA: HarperCollins, 1997), p. 154.

56. Bhikhu C. Parekh, *Gandhi* (New York: Oxford University Press, 1997).

57. M.K. Gandhi, *The Collected Works of Mahatma Gandhi*, Vol. 44 (New Delhi: Publication Division, Ministry of Information and Broadcasting, 1958), p. 167.

58. Anthony Parel, *Gandhi's Philosophy and the Quest for Harmony* (Cambridge: Cambridge University Press, 2006).

59. M.K. Gandhi, "Equality of Religions," *Gleanings Gathered at Bapu's Feet by Mira* (Ahmadabad: Navjeevan Publishing House, 1949), p. 4.

60. Parekh, *Gandhi*, p. 37.

61. Sudarshan Kapur, "Gandhi and Hindutva: Two Conflicting Visions of Swaraj" in Anthony J. Parel, ed., *Gandhi, Freedom and Self-Rule* (Lanham, MD: Lexington Books, 2000), p. 132.

62. Ragini Sen and Wolfgang Wagner, "Gandhi, Secularism and Social Capital in Modern India," *Psychological Studies* 54, no. 2 (June 2009): 133–41.

Chapter 15

Acculturation of the Tribals in North India during the British Colonial Period: An Ethnographic Perspective

Radha Madhav Bharadwaj

A study of the festival-related material from the north and central part of Northern India as given in the *British District Gazetteers* of the 19th and early 20th centuries makes startling revelations. The picture that emerges from the ethnographic data related to *Brāhmaṇic*/Hindu religious festivals shows that they are of mixed nature and are a product of the long process of acculturation and interaction between the dominant *Brāhmaṇic*/ Hindu and Hinduized minor tribal traditions. That this process of acculturation continued even during the British period is amply clear from the *British District Gazetteers* of North and Central India and other contemporary books. Of particular interest is the fact that there have also been cases of vehement opposition by the tribals to thwart attempts at acculturation, which aimed at imposing *Brāhmaṇical* culture on them, and make them and their culture subservient to the culture and the religion of the *Brāhmaṇ as*. My proposed study of the acculturation of the tribals in North India in the light of the ethnographic sources may prove to be significant in the sense that it will bring into focus the social and religious conditions of the tribals who remained on the fringes of the mainstream *Brāhmaṇic*

Hinduism even during the British period, despite hundreds of years of acculturation by the cultural forces of the latter. But we cannot do justice to the name and theme of the topic, unless we explore the festivals related to the deities of tribal background in some detail and also back it up with the reasons with which it actually began in history.

The intermixing and acculturation of the tribals with the core *Brāhmaṇic* region and religion took place in a transitional phase of Indian history, marked by regional state formation and an unprecedented agrarian expansion based on reclamation and settlement of new tracts of land by the social and political elites in the peripheral tribal regions roughly between the 4th and the 12th centuries AD. We have ample references to this in the contemporary literary and epigraphic sources.[1]

Ram Sharan Sharma says that interaction and intermixing between different ethnic elements was a continuous process, and once the class-based and state-based agricultural society was established (roughly the end of the later *Vedic* period around 6th to 5th centuries BC), attempts were made to extend its frontiers by absorbing the forest-living aborigines (called by the omnibus term *Dasyus*) in it.[2] Vijay Nath has said that the processes of agricultural expansion and acculturation took place during the period when the *Purāṇas* were being composed roughly during the first millennium AD, but during the later *Vedic* times also, the processes had become relatively accelerated.[3] This process of intermingling and acculturation began to take place on a much bigger scale from the Gupta period (4th–5th centuries AD) onward, because of the rise of a number of nascent regional kingdoms in the wake of the pressure from foreign intrusions that led to the proliferation of land grants to individual *Brāhmaṇas* and temples, and the rise in the number of rural settlements in the peripheral tribal regions of North and Central India like Bengal, Orissa, Brahmaputra valley in Assam, Rajasthan, Madhya Pradesh, Chhattisgarh, Jharkhand, and the modern Himachal Pradesh.[4] Between c. AD 400–650, about 50 kingdoms surfaced in eastern Madhya Pradesh (central part of Northern India), Orissa, Bengal (Northeastern India), Maharashtra, and Andhra Pradesh.[5] The emergence of state societies in prestate tracts is a marker of transition in rural landscape and sociopolitical organization.

AGENCIES OF ACCULTURATION

Religion played an important role in the acculturation and worked through various agencies. R.S. Sharma quotes the *Mahābhārata* (*Śānti Parva* 131.14) that advises the king to treat the tribals with respect and give them gifts.[6] The religious myths in the *Purāṇas* played an important role in the absorption and acculturation of the tribal people. An extended version of a religious myth was the performance of the *Purāṇic Hiraṇyagarbha* (Golden Womb) ceremony (*Matsya-purāṇa* 275.1–23) for some ambitious chiefs who wanted a higher caste for themselves. In this, the priest would insert the chief into a golden pot "womb" and perform the rituals for a pregnant woman and child birth, and then the chief would step out from his contracted position with a high caste, usually *Kṣatriya,* with the *gotra* (common descent) of the *Brāhmaṇa* priest. This was not the caste of the rest of the tribe when they were absorbed into the caste society.[7] Some tribal priests were also allowed to be metamorphosed into *Brāhmaṇas* during this period.[8] Many *Brāhmaṇas* even married into the tribe giving birth to new tribal *Brāhmaṇas,* which ultimately led Indian society to be formed out of diverse elements.[9]

The institution of *Tīrthas* (pilgrimage centers) also proved to be an effective tool in the dissemination of *Brāhmaṇic* culture in the peripheral regions. Giving recognition to so many *Tīrthas* in outlying areas was in fact a tactical move of the *Purāṇa* writers to bring local cultic shrines within the sphere of influence of the major *Brāhmaṇic* religion, of which we have numerous references.[10] A factor that contributes toward making *Tīrthas* an effective mechanism of acculturation is its liminal character. According to Victor Turner, the *Tīrthas* act as an expression of "antistructure," where it transforms itself into a state in which social distinctions disappear leading to the free-mixing of the people of different cultural backgrounds.[11]

An equally important agency of religion was the *Vratas* (religious vows) and *Utsavas* (religious festivals). A perusal of the *Purāṇic, Dharma Śāstric* (theological), inscriptional, and ethnographic sources show that the *Vratas* and *Utsavas* also played a very important role in the integration and acculturation of the tribal people.[12] The incorporation of *Tāntric* elements in the *Purāṇic Vratas* also indicates the liberality of the *Purāṇa* writers, as *Tantra* is widely believed to be an admixture of the classical and the tribal traditions. A major reason for the wide prevalence of *Śakti-pūjā* (worship of female energy as a goddess) was the integration of many tribal communities into *Brāhmaṇical* society. Hemadri, a medieval *Nibandha* (treatise writer on religious and social rites) of 13th century AD, quotes the *Bhaviṣyottara* in saying that the goddess *Durgā* (*Devī* or *Śakti*) is worshiped by various groups of *Mlecchas* and *Dasyus.*[13] This is also important to note that the *Kirātas* (forest tribes) are given concession regarding food in worshipping the goddess *Caṇḍikā* (a form of *Durgā*). They could worship the goddess with wine and meat, and without *Vedic japa* and *mantra* (chantings).[14] Through the cult of "*Śakti*" or "*Devī,*" a maximum number of local/tribal deities represented as mother goddesses or as titular household/village (kula/*grāma*) deities (*devtā/devtī/ṭhakurānī*) could enter into the Brāhmaṇical pantheon. From the 4th–6th centuries AD onward, a large number of epigraphic records bear references to female deities having tribal associations such as *Araṇyavāsinī, Khimlatā,* and *Vaṭayakṣiṇī Devī.*[15] The serpent goddess *Manasā* was originally worshipped by primitive people, but gradually found a place in the orthodox Hindu pantheon.[16] The induction of

Śītalā Māi (*Śītalā,* the goddess of smallpox) into the *Purāṇic* pantheon is the same as that of *Manasā.*[17] The ethnographic data collected from Madhya Pradesh as early as 1907 also say that *Śītalā,* called *Mātāmāi,* is one of the seven sisters of the tribal pantheon.[18] The integration of the tribals into the *Brāhmaṇical* tradition was also achieved by assigning to the members of these tribes some important roles in the temple festivals, which helped create a common cultural milieu where the tribals and the nontribals could interact and relate to each other.[19]

Now the pertinent question that arises is that was the process of acculturation always smooth and welcome? It will be worthwhile to examine it in the light of the facts arising from the epics *Mahābhārata* and the *Rāmāyaṇa* and the *Purāṇic* literature. We will see that it was not always without violence and clash of interests, which led to tension and physical clashes between the two opposite cultural groups. It is this moot point that has led us to trace its history in the ancient past, which continued during the medieval and the modern period, as will be clear from the modern ethnographic materials.

D.D. Kosambi opines that a *Brāhmaṇa* being a peaceful witch-doctor, his ritual and way of life was imposed quite easily upon the savages. The *Brāhmaṇas* could peacefully reduce the tribes to castes. No doubt the *Brāhmaṇas,* through various subtle means, were able to penetrate the tribal territories with better success than others, but Kosambi's view represent only the partial truth as he has seen only the success part. A critical examination of the facts presents a different story. We have several instances that point toward the fact that the process of acculturation was beneficial only for the caste and class society people, and not the poor tribals who exhibited their resistance through various means. R.S. Sharma quotes the *Mahābhārata* (*Śānti Parva* 131.11) that even the *Dasyu*'s conscience revolts against acts of cruelty.[20] This statement proves that the *Dasyus* revolted against the occasional cruelty meted out to them. Devraj Chanana says that the term "*Raksasa*" in the *Rāmāyaṇa* may have been used for the tribals, as they are shown to have been the masters of the forest territories around *Daṇḍaka, Mithilā,* and *Mathurā.* There were always clashes and bloody violence between them and the *Brāhmaṇa* and *Kṣatriya* sages and rulers. *Tāḍakā,* the widow of the slain *Rakṣasa Sunda,* destroyed two human settlements that might have cropped up in her territory.[21] The process of setting up of *Tīrtha* in the peripheral regions was not always smooth and peaceful, and the indigenous people living there might have occasionally put up some resistance against what must have appeared to them as blatant attempts at landgrabbing under the garb of religion.[22] We have numerous literary references where Brahmahatyā (Brāhmaṇa Murder) and the seizing of the land of the Brāhmaṇas are considered a great sin, and this is a recurrent theme.[23] The tension and conflict between the two culturally opposite groups is proved through various *Purāṇic* mythological stories also, such as the one related to king *Veṇa,* an archetypal king in so many *Purāṇas.* In the *Bhāgvata-Purāṇa* (IV.13)—which, according to Hazra, was composed in the 6th century AD,[24] and according to P. V. Kane, was composed as late as 9th century AD[25]—King *Veṇa* puts a ban on the *Vedic* sacrifices and gifts to the *Brāhmaṇas.*[26] There are references to monarchical expeditions against such tribal groups as the "*Śabaras, Pulindas,* or *Bhīls,*"[27] which must have created friction. The efforts of local dominant castes to extend agriculture were resisted by the local tribals. The *Bhīl* revolts in the history of *Mewar* point to the complexities in the sociocultural integration of a region.[28] This way we see that the process of acculturation in ancient and early medieval India had to face resistance, revolt, and violence by the tribals, who must have felt that the advancing agrarian economy and society was eating into their space and cultural identity.

Our proposed study of the acculturation of the tribals in different pockets of North Central India, in the light of ethnographic sources, may prove to be significant as it will bring into focus the diverse nature of Indian society,[29] and that the social and religious conditions of the tribals could only become semi-Hinduized despite hundreds of years of acculturation. The tribals, their territories, their deities, and their cultural practices, all underwent change due to acculturating forces during the 5th–12th centuries AD, but the tribal culture could never be subsumed and fully *Brāhmaṇized*/ Hinduized. They had shown resistance during the ancient period, which continued even during the medieval and the British colonial period. This will become clear when we begin scanning the ethnographic data regarding festivals as collected in the *British District Gazetteers* of the late 19th and the early 20th centuries. Since the tribals could not be fully Hinduized, they exhibited their tribalness and carried on many of their cultural traits like tribal rituals in festivals, tribal priesthood, and non-*Brāhmaṇic* offerings such as pigs and buffaloes to the deities. They also continued to put up resistance against attempts at acculturation and subjugation as in the case of clash between the cult of god *Raghunāth* and the tribal god *Jamlū,* which we shall shortly be discussing. This poses a serious question whether the process of acculturation could ever become complete, because we see that a great number of tribals in North and Central India remained on the fringes of the *Brāhmaṇic* Hindu culture. The social and cultural relationship of a great number of them remained a little different vis-à-vis the *Brāhmaṇical* tradition; because apart from acculturation, there never was any attempt on the part of the *Brāhmaṇical* forces to also address to the socioeconomic concerns of the hapless tribals, and hence, we see sporadic cases of resistance by them against political and cultural subordination in the backdrop of acculturation. Let's now examine what the festival related data from the North Central India has to say.

Himachal Pradesh

1. *Raghunāth Yātrā* at Kulu: The institution of festival operates as a type of religious network and is a sure means of diverting tradition by providing a substitute focus in the newly won areas. The *Raghunāth Yātrā* (the car festival of god *Raghunāth*) at Kulu in modern Himachal Pradesh provided that substitute focus in that area. This, the greatest festival in honor of god *Raghunāth,* an incarnation of god *Viṣṇu,* is observed on the last day of the *Dussehra* festival. Once a year, there is a parade of all the local tribal deities of Kulu valley in honor of god *Raghunāth* at Sultanpur, the capital of Kulu state. From olden times, the local deities have been brought in by the express command of the king of Kulu. All the followers come from the mountain villages along with their own deities to escort *Raghunāth* in his *Rath Yātrā.* On the last day of the festival, which lasts for seven days, the triumphal car of *Raghunāth* is again brought into requisition to carry his idol escorted, as on the first day, to celebrate his triumph and bring him back to the temple in the palace of the king. By an early hour the next morning, all the local deities with their followers get dispersed to their hamlets.[30] This ritual of the coming of the minor village deities for escorting the chief god *Raghunāth* in his *Rath Yātrā* serves as a great example of subordination of local deities to the cult of *Raghunāth* of orthodox Hinduism and thereby of the local tribal people to the king—the political master. But one local god *Jamlū* refused to submit to the authority of the all-encompassing god *Raghunāth.*
2. Festival of minor god *Jamlū:* A festival in honor of the local god *Jamlū* takes place twice a year in *Phālgun* (February–March) and in *Śrāvaṇa* (July–August) at *Malānā* and other adjoining villages. *Malānā* is a small village at a very deep and narrow glen, extending from the inaccessible mountain forming the tri-junction of the rivers—Beas, Chenab, and Spiti watersheds. This is extremely isolated, and one of the causes of its isolation is the use of an unintelligible language by its people, other than that prevalent in Kulu. This village contains the buildings sacred to the worship of god *Jamlū.* The chief buildings are a granary for storing the grain rents of the land assigned to the god, a house entered only on the occasion of one of the annual festivals. There is thus no temple in the proper sense of the term at *Malānā,* though there are temples dedicated to *Jamlū* in many villages throughout Kulu. The following fact is specially significant and is to be noted down:

> *Jamlū* was much feared in older kings' times and he neither paid tribute to the *Raghunāth* temple at Sultanpur nor attended at the temple to escort and pay respects to *Raghunāth* on *Dussehra* as, all of the

Kulu deities were compelled to do. Again, the *Malānā* men who were under his special protection were allowed great license; they used to say that the other gods' temples were their *Deo*'s (god's) *Dogris* (outhouses). In his fight against the chief god *Raghunāth, Jamlū* forged an alliance with other powerful local deities as it is said that *Jamlū* is the brother of *Devī Hirmā* and, of *Gyephen,* the god of a snowy peak in Lahul.[31]

This alliance must have gone a long way in making him stronger and helping him retain his independence from the commanding nature of the all-pervading royal cult of *Raghunāth,* and saving his followers from the ideological and political subjugation of the king of Kulu.

Rajasthan

Although Hinduized to a great extent, the animists did exist in Rajasthan, who were either *Bhīls* or *Girasiyās,* whose religion may be said to be a mixture of animism and Hinduism. They worshipped different *Mātājis* (mother goddesses) like *Piplād Mātā* and *Mokal Mātā* at Bikaner, *Namdā Devī* and *Sachiā Mātā* at Jodhpur, and *Khokhrī Mātā* and *Kaivāsa Mātā* at other places.[32] They are worshipped by other castes also. Nowhere in the classical Hindu religious texts do we have goddesses bearing such names, but here in Rajasthan, all the above mentioned *Mātājis* and *Devīs* are but the different manifestations of goddess *Durgā* and have temples dedicated to them. It appears that in the course of the expansion of Rajput states, these tribal deities were absorbed into the Hindu-fold along with the Hinduization of the local aboriginals, which suited the social and political elites of the region.

Central India

1. Despite the long process of acculturation, and metamorphosis of the tribal gods and goddesses into the Hindu pantheon, we see that the tribals still maintain the names of their deities, and offerings of their tradition, and have not allowed the *Brāhmaṇas* to take over the priestship of the worship of their deities.
2. *Marhāi Devī:* A festival in honor of *Marhāi Devī* (goddess *Marhāi*) is observed by the *Gonds* and *Baigā* tribals who worship her as the goddess of cholera and offer pigs to propitiate her. The tribals have a pantheon of their own and, as such, *Marhai* is one of the seven sisters: *Mātāmāi* (goddess of smallpox), *Khokhlī* (coughing), *Jarhāi* (fever), and three others.[33]
3. *Bijā Sen:* She is in reality a *Gond* goddess, but has been transformed into an incarnation of *Durgā.* Fasts are observed in her honor in the

same manner as that of *Durgā*. She is also one of the seven sisters—who are all incarnations of *Devī* and who are supposed to preside over different diseases. She resides in *neem* (*Melia indica*) tree.[34]

4. *Mātāmāi* (another name for *Śītalā*): A festival is observed in her honor as a goddess of smallpox. She is represented by a number of rough stones with smallpox signs placed under the neem tree.[35]
5. *Baḍī Sanjorī:* This is a festival in honor of all the village gods for the well-being of the village every three years. A *Gond* priest is necessary for the worship of the village gods on this occasion.[36]
6. *Bara Deo* (great god): The *Gonds* and *Baigās* hold a religious festival in honor of their great god, *Bara Deo,* whom they worship as the pervading spirit of nature and the woods, once in three years. They offer pigs and liquor to propitiate him.[37]
7. *Āsandhī Pūjā:* This is festival in honor of a tribal god *Thākur Deo* in *Āṣāḍha* (July–August) when the tribal cultivators—*Gonds, Baigās,* and others—give the *Baigā* priest a handful of grain to sow a portion beneath the tree sacred to the god and to keep the rest as his fee.[38]

Jharkhand

1. *Dhartīmāi* (Mother Earth): The Paharia Santhali tribals worship *Dhartīmāi,* her servant, or, as some say, sister, *Garāmi* and *Siṃhabāhinī* (*Purāṇic* goddess *Durgā*), who rule over tigers, snakes, and other beasts. To the goddess *Siṃhabāhinī,* goats, pigs, and fowls are offered in the month of *Māgha* (January–February) and *Āṣāḍha* (June–July), and buffaloes at the time of *Durgā-Pūjā* (September–October). The village *Māñjhī* (tribal) officiates as the priest.[39]
2. *Worship of local spirits:* In Hazaribagh district, even where the landlords and the majority of the tenants are Hindus, it is still customary to employ as the *Pahān* (the tribal priest as sacrificer) one of the race of the aboriginal clearers of the village, at least of an earlier dispossessed race, for propitiating the local spirits. The *Brāhmaṇa* grantee or the purchaser of a jungle village considers it a matter of mere common sense to retain, by the attraction of rent-free land, the *Muṇḍāri* or *Bhogtā Pahān,* whose brethren have long since been expelled.[40]
3. *Worship of local spirits in Palamau:* Same as in Hazaribagh, here also, the *Baigā* (or the *Pahān*) is the village priest who propitiates the tutelary deities of the village to keep away evil spirits. Persons of aboriginal descent are preferred for the post, the belief being that as they are the oldest inhabitants, they are best acquainted with the habits of the local spirits, and that *Brāhmaṇas* and other Hindus could only offer a divided allegiance to the sylvan deities and would, therefore, not be acceptable to them. *Dosādha* and Bhuiya tribals are often *Baigās,* and the person preferred is a member of the tribe that first

cleared the jungle, but *Kahārs, Brāhmaṇas,* and even Muhammedans are, though rarely, found holding the office of the *Pahān.*[41] The *Baigās* are also appointed by the whole village as the priest for propitiating the chief deity, the village god, and whole rent-free land for that. All castes from *Bhuiyas* to *Brāhmaṇas* join in his worship.[42]

Bengal

1. *Manasā Pūjā:* This is a festival in honor of the goddess *Manasā* who is worshipped by the *Bāgḍis* and *Bauris*—the two Hinduized aboriginal tribes, who, although they worshipped *Śiva, Viṣṇu, Durgā,* and other Hindu gods and goddesses, declare that there favorite goddess is *Manasā.* She is worshipped for immunity from snakebite on the Hindu religious festival of *Nāga Pañcamī* on the fifth of the bright half of *Śrāvaṇa. Bāgḍis* or *Dom* priests called *Dharam Pundits* preside over *Manasā Pūjā.*[43]
2. *Śītalā Pūjā:* It takes place in Bengal in honor of Śītalā—the goddess of infectious diseases, such as measles, chicken pox, smallpox, and cholera. This festival traditionally falls on the eighth day of the second half of *Phālguna* (February–March), but one more occasion is the *Śītalā Saptamī,* on the seventh day of the bright half of *Māgha.*[44] Although *Śītalā* is very much a Purāṇic deity today, it has been so since the time of the *Skanda-Purāṇa,*[45] and is worshipped by all castes; but there are a number of pointers to the fact that she was originally a tribal deity.[46] Field data, collected as late as during the Census of 1951 by Ashok Mitra for Bengal, show that the traces of its being an offshoot of the lower tradition can still be found. This is quite interesting to note that in Midnapur, Brāhmaṇas did not assist in the worship of *Śītalā.*[47]In Howrah, the goddess is called *Basant-caṇḍī* and a Brāhmaṇa officiates as a priest among the higher castes, but the *Kaibarttas* (fishermen) and members of other low castes officiate for the caste to which they belong.[48]
3. *Dharmarāja Pūjā:* This is the most popular festival in honor of *Dharmarāja* or *Dharma Thakur,* who represents the village god (*grāma devatā*) in a large region of West Bengal, in the months of *Vaiśākha, Jyeṣṭha,* and *Āṣāḍha* on the full moon day, and in some places, on the last day of *Bhādra* (August–September). There are many deities known by the name of *Dharmarāja* in various parts of Bankura, but the most ancient is said to be *Briddhākṇa* (the one with old eyes), enshrined in the town of Bishnupur. The god is represented by a piece of stone covered with vermillion and having metal eyes. The priests are a family of *Karmākaras,* or blacksmiths known as *Dharma Pundits.* It is said that its worship goes back to the days before the establishment of Bishnupur Raj, i.e., over 1,100 years, and that the

ancient kings of Mallabhum gave the idol endowments of land, some of which are still held by the priest. *Dharmarāja* has other representations also. *Bankur Rāi* of Indas is represented by a stone, with some carvings interpreted as representing as one of the 10 incarnations of god *Viṣṇu*. This idol is in the house of a *Sūtradhāra* or carpenter, who acts as the priest, and its festival is observed on the (*Purāṇic*) festival of *Makara Saṅkrānti*, when *Khichri Bhog* (cooked food of mixed rice and pulses) prepared by the *Brāhmaṇas* is offered to the deity. *Rantak Rāi* of Bansi Chandpur is a stone emblem, said to be the tortoise incarnation of *Viṣṇu*, in the house of an *Aṇgūrī* (held to be of low caste). But the priest is a Brāhmaṇa, and the festival in his honor takes place on the (Purāṇic) festival of *Akṣaya Tṛtīyā*. *Baṅsīdhara* of Sias is another tortoise emblem in the house of a *Nāpita* (barber), who also acts as its priest, and its worship falls on the festival of *Makara Saṅkrānti*. The origin of the names of the deities is unknown, but it has been suggested that they were the names of persons who inaugurated the *Dharma* worhip. Mahamahopadhyaya Har Prasad Shastri has been quoted as saying that "*Dharma* worship remained confined to the lowest classes of the people—the dirtiest, meanest and the most illiterate. All the lowest forms of worship, rejected by the *Brāhmaṇas*, gradually rallied round *Dharma* and his priests, throughout Bengal, enjoy a certain consideration which often excites the envy of their highly placed rivals, the *Brāhmaṇas*, who though hating them, yet covet their earnings wherever these are considerable and there are instances in which the worship of *Dharma* has passed into *Brāhmaṇa* hands, and has been, by them transformed into a manifestation of either *Śiva* or *Viṣṇu*." Shastri goes on to say that "the *Dharma* worshippers are fully aware that *Dharma* is not an inferior deity; he is higher than *Viṣṇu*, *Śiva*, *Brahmā* and even *Pārvatī* (the powerful consort of *Śiva*).To this may be added that at the present day the image of *Dharma Thakur* is generally found in the house of low caste men but at the same time *Dharma* is offered cooked food even by a *Brāhmaṇa*."[49]

Orissa

1. The cult of *Grāma Devatī* or *Thakurānī* (village goddess): The cult of *Grāma Devatī* and festivals related to her are the most prevalent among the common populace and has been reported from all over Orissa. At the present time, twofold worship coexists throughout Orissa. The common people have their shapeless stones or blocks before which they make their simple offerings in the open air, while side by side with it is a temple to one of the *Aryan* (*Vedic-Purāṇic*)

gods with its carved image and elaborate rites. Every village pays homage to the *Grāma Devatī,* as these stones and blocks are called, and revere her as the tutelary goddess of their community. Besides the generic name *Grāma Devatī,* each goddess has a separate specific name, which is commonly one of the thousand names of the *Purāṇic* goddess *Kālī.* Clay horses, elephants, and other animals are placed before her, as she is supposed to wander about at night. The most noticeable feature of this worship is the nonpriestly caste of men who conduct it—the *Bhaṇḍārī, Mālī* (flower growers), and *Dhoba* (probably, washermen) being usually the priest. They hold small free grants called "*Māfī Grāma Devatī,*" lands that are left unassessed for her worship at the time of the first regular settlement, and they receive doles from the rich and the peasants for the village. Her worship is conducted on the *Mahāṣṭamī* (great eighth day of the bright half of the month of *Āśvina*—September–October), the day of the *Durgā Pūjā.* It seems hardly open to question that this worship of the malevolent spirit, in the form of shapeless stones, is an offshoot of the fetishism of the aborigines. It still includes animal sacrifices—one of the most characteristic features of aboriginal worship, like the offering of the fowls—detested by class Hindus. The restriction of the priestly function to the *Śūdra* (fourth) castes is another link in the chain of circumstances that indicates the aboriginal origin of this form of worship.[50]

2. *Festival of Saru Penu:* It is observed in honor of *Saru Penu,* the god of the hills, a jealous god who doesn't like people to trespass on his domain. The chief object of his worship is to induce him to protect from fever and the attack of wild animals, and also to secure a full yield of the forest products that the *Khond* tribals so largely use for food. They engage their own priest, called *Dehurī,* and offer goat, fowl, rice, and drink to the god through the priest.[51]
3. *Festival of Tana Penu:* It is observed in honor of *Tana Penu,* the earth goddess, believed to be very vindictive and who vents her anger upon those who neglect her worship, afflicting them with various diseases and making their land unfruitful. To avoid them, the *Khonds* offer pigs and goats to her every year, and a buffalo at irregular intervals. Her priest is called *Guru,* whose office is hereditary, and is usually filled by the *Khonds,* but *Kumhārs* (potters) are sometimes also accepted as priests.[52]
4. *Festival of Dharma Penu:* It is celebrated in honor of *Dharma Penu,* a personification of the sun, by the *Khonds.* They regard this deity as the supreme god and the creator of the universe. There is no fixed time for the observance of this festival, as we find in the case of the *Vedic-Purāṇic* festivals.[53]

In conclusion, we can say that ethnographic details found in the brief survey of religious festivals in the *British District Records* and *Gazetteers* of the late 19th and early 20th centuries throw ample light on the diverse composition of the Hindu society and religious culture. That the process of acculturation that was unleashed during the first millennium of the Christian era continued even during the British period, and despite hundreds of years of acculturation, the tribal people could not be fully integrated into the Hindu society. Although the tribals and their culture underwent great change under the influence of the major *Brāhmaṇic*/Hindu tradition over the last 2,000 years, the former could never be subsumed and fully Hinduized. The *Vedic-Purāṇic* Hinduism could never fully integrate them and bind them in its fold because, along with acculturation, there never perhaps was any serious attempt on the part of the acculturating forces to give them equal role in religion and to address the social and economic concerns of the hapless tribals. Hence, we see sporadic cases of resistance by them against political and cultural subordination under the garb of acculturation. The tribals not only showed resistance to ward off their subordination through acculturation, but also continued to maintain their cultural identities and individuality, by maintaining some of their own deities and festivals with tribal rituals, offerings of pigs, fowls, buffaloes, and liquor, and priesthood along with celebrating the festivals in honor of the *Vedic-Purāṇic* gods and goddesses.

NOTES

1. Radha Madhav Bharadwaj, "Vratotsavas and Acculturation: A Preliminary Enquiry into the Role of Vratotsavas as a Force of Acculturation between the Fourth and the Twelfth Centuries A.D.," *Proceedings of the Indian History Congress,* Part I, Millennium (61st) Session, Kolkata, 2000–2001, pp.155–64 and Vijay Nath, *Purāṇas and Acculturation: A Historico-Anthropological Perspective* (New Delhi: Munshiram Manoharlal, 2001). For dissemination of Sanskritic culture and attendant acculturation through the spread of rural settlements in the tribal regions, see Krishna Mohan Shrimali, *Agrarian Structure in Central India and the Northern Deccan (c. A.D. 300–500)* (New Delhi: Munshiram Manoharlal, 1987), pp. 22–28; K.V. Ramesh and S.P. Tewari, eds., *A Copper-Plate Hoard of the Gupta Period from Bagh* (New Delhi Archeological Survey of India, 1990); Brajadulal D. Chattopadhyay, *The Making of Early Medieval India* (New York: Oxford University Press, 1994), Introduction; also see his *Aspects of Rural Settlements and Rural Society in Early Medieval India* (Calcutta: K.P. Bagchi & Co., 1990), pp. 28, 29; and Nayanjot Lahiri, *Pre-Ahom Assam: Studies in the Inscriptions of Assam between the Fifth and the Twelfth Centuries A.D.* (New Delhi: Munshiram Manoharlal, 1991), pp. 106, 107.
2. Ram Sharan Sharma, *Material Culture and Social Formations in Ancient India* (New Delhi: Macmillan, 1983), p. 146.
3. Vijay Nath, "King Veṇa, Niṣāda and Pṛthu: A Recurrent Purāṇic Myth Reconsidered," *The Indian Historical Review* 29, nos. 1 and 2 (January–July 2002): 48–65 and *Purāṇas and Acculturation*, pp. 34–35.

4. Bharadwaj, "Vratotsavas and Acculturation," pp. 155–64 and Brajadulal D. Chattopadhyay, "Historiography, History and Religious Centres: Early Medieval North India, c. A.D. 700–1200" in Vishakha N. Desai et al., eds., *Gods, Guardians and Lovers: North Indian Temple Sculptures, c. A.D. 700–1200* (Ahmedabad: Mapin Publishing House, 1996), pp. 8–27.

5. Ram Sharan Sharma, *Urban Decay in India (c. A.D. 300–1000)* (New Delhi: Munshiram Manoharlal, 1987), p. 168. For the rise of new states like Kamarupa (Assam), see Dineschandra Sircar, *Select Inscriptions Bearing on Indian History and Civilization,* Vol. I (Calcutta: University of Calcutta, 1965), p. 265; for Jejakbhukti in Bundelkhand, U.P. and M.P. boarder, see Sisirkumar Mitra, *The Early Rulers of Khajuraho,* 2nd ed. (Delhi: Motilal Banarsidass, 1977), pp. 1–11; and for Rajasthan, see Dasharatha Sharma, ed., *Rajasthan through the Ages,* Vol. I (Bikaner: Rajasthan State Archives, 1966), pp. 11–19.

6. Sharma, *Material Culture and Social Formations in Ancient India,* p.154.

7. Damodar Dharmanand Kosambi, *An Introduction to the Study of Ancient Indian History* (Bombay: Popular Prakashan, 1990), p. 318 and also see his *The Culture and Civilization of Ancient India in Historical Outline* (Delhi: Vikas Publishing House, 1990), p. 171.

8. Kosambi, *An Introduction to the Study of Ancient Indian History,* pp. 318, 319.

9. Ibid., p. 319 and Kosambi, *The Culture and Civilization of Ancient India in Historical Outline,* p. 172.

10. Vijay Nath, "Purāṇic Tīrthas: A Study of Their Indigenous Origins and Transformation," *The Indian Historical Review* 34, no. 1 (January 2007): 5 and for tribal affiliations of the Tīrthas, see, Sadashiv Ambadas Dange, *Encyclopedia of Purāṇic Beliefs and Practices,* Vol. III (New Delhi: Navarang, 1987), pp. 761–865.

11. Victor Turner, "The Center Out There: Pilgrim's Goal," *History of Religion* 12, no. 3 (1973): 191–230.

12. Bharadwaj, "Vratotsavas and Acculturation," p. 155 and Nath, "*Purāṇic* Tīrthas," 24.

13. Hemādri, *Caturvarga Cintāmaṇi by Hemādri,* Vol. II, Part 1, *VrataKhaṇḍa* (Calcutta: The Asiatic Society of Bengal, 1978), p. 910.

14. Bharadwaj, "Vratotsavas and Acculturation," p. 162.

15. Nath, "Purāṇic Tīrthas," 37.

16. Pranabanand Jash, "A Hermeneutical Coalition between Archeology and Literature: The Cult of Manasā" in Amita Ray and Sameer Mukherjee, eds., *Historical Archeology of India: A Dialogue between Archeologists and Historians* (New Delhi: Books and Books, 1990), pp. 312, 313.

17. Pandurang Vaman Kane, *History of Dharmaśāstra,* Vol. V, Part 1 (Poona: Bandarkar Oriental Research Institute, 1974 [1962]), p. 5.

18. R. V. Russell, ed., *Central Provinces District Gazetteers* (Bombay: Chindawara Times Press, 1907), pp. 43, 44.

19. James J. Preston, "The Goddess Sarala: Evolution of an Orissan Goddess Temple," *Folk Culture,* Vol. II, p. 116; also see Lewis Sydney Steward O'Malley, ed., *Bengal District Gazetteers: Puri* (Calcutta: Bengal Secretariat Press, 1918), pp. 104–6.

20. Sharma, *Material Culture and Social Formations in Ancient India,* p. 146.

21. Devraj Chanana, "Expansion of Agriculture in North India" in D. N. Jha et al., eds., *Prachin Bharat* (in Hindi) (New Delhi: Macmillan, 1978), pp.102, 108.

22. Nath, "Purāṇic Tīrthas," 36 and V.S. Aggarwal, *Matsya* Purāṇa*: A Study* (Varanasi: All India Kashiraj Trust, 1963).

23. Radha Madhav Bharadwaj, "Vratas and Utsavas in North and Central India: A Study of the Literary and Epigraphic Sources between the Fifth and Twelfth Centuries A.D." (Ph.D. thesis, University of Delhi, New Delhi, 2007), pp. 42, 69, 70, 130–34, 163, 176, 196, 198, 199, 206, 207, 219, 224–26.

24. Rajendra Chandra Hazra, *Studies in the* Purāṇic *Records on Hindu Rites and Customs* (Delhi: Motilal Banarsidass, 1975), p. 55.

25. Pandurang Vaman Kane, *History of Dharmaśāstra,* Vol. V, Part 2 (Poona: Bandarkar Oriental Research Institute, 1962), p. 899.

26. Nath, "Purāṇic Tīrthas," 30–54 and "King Veṇa, Niṣāda and Prthu," 54.

27. F. Kielhorn, "Two Chandella Inscriptions from Ajaygadh," *Epigraphia Indica,* Vol. I (New Delhi: Archaeological Survey of India, 1971[reprint]), p. 337 and D.R. Bhandarkar, "Ghatyala Inscriptions of Kukkuka: Samvat 918," *Epigraphia Indica,* Vol. IX, pp. 277–81.

28. Nandini Sinha, "State and the Tribe: A Study of the Bhīls in the Historic Setting of Southern Rajasthan," *Social Science Probings* 10, nos. 1–4 (1993): 55–67 and also see her "Rural Society and State Formation in Early Medieval South-Western Rajasthan," *Proceedings of the Indian History Congress,* 55th Session, Aligarh, 1994, pp. 123–31.

29. Kosambi, *The Culture and Civilization of Ancient India in Historical Outline,* p. 172 and for diverse nature of Indian society and religion of Bengal during the ancient and medieval Bengal, see Kunal Chakravarty, *Religious Process: The* Purāṇa *and the Making of a Regional Tradition* (New York: Oxford University of Press, 2001), pp. 234–81.

30. P.D. Agnew, *Punjab District Gazeteers: Gazetteer of Kangra District—Kulu, Lahul and Spiti* (Lahore: Indus Publishing Company, 1899), pp. 41, 42.

31. Ibid., pp. 49–53.

32. Keith David Erskine, ed., *The Gazetteer of Western Rajputana States* (Ajmer: Scottish Mission Industries, 1904), pp. 178–94.

33. R.V. Russell, ed., *Central Provinces District Gazetteers: Damoh* (Allahabad: Pioneer Press, 1906), p. 36.

34. R.V. Russell, ed., *Central Provinces District Gazetteers: Narasinghpur* (Bombay: Times Press, 1906), pp. 49–53.

35. R.V. Russell, ed., *Central Provinces District Gazetteers: Chindwara* (Bombay: Times Press, 1907), pp. 43, 44.

36. Charles Ernest Low, ed., *Central Provinces District Gazetteers: Balaghat* (Allahabad: Pioneer Press, 1907), p. 85.

37. Francis Reginald Rider Rudman, ed., *Central Provinces District Gazetteers: Mandla,* Vol. A (Bombay: Times Press, 1912), pp. 32, 33.

38. Ibid., p. 33.

39. Lewis Sydney Steward O'Malley, ed., *Bengal District Gazetteers: Santhal Pargana* (Calcutta: Bengal Secretariat Press, 1910, pp. 83, 84.

40. Edward Lister, ed., *Bihar and Orissa District Gazetteers: Hazaribagh* (Patna: GPO, 1917), p. 76.

41. Phillip Cubitt Tallents, ed., *Bihar and Orissa District Gazetteers: Palamau* (Patna: GPO, 1926), p. 46.

42. Ibid.

43. Lewis Sydney Steward O'Malley, ed., *Bengal District Gazetteers: Bankura* (Calcutta: Bengal Secretariat Press, 1908), p. 57 and *Bengal District Gazetteers: Parganas* (Calcutta: Bengal Secretariat Press, 1914), p. 71.

44. Lewis Sydney Steward O'Malley, ed., *Bengal District Gazetteers: Midnapu* (Calcutta: Bengal Secretariat Press, 1911), p. 82 and *Bengal District Gazeteers: Parganas,* p. 71.

45. M. Monier Williams, *Sanskrit-English Dictionary* (Delhi: Motilal Banarsidass,1979 [reprint]), p. 1078.

46. Pandurang Vaman Kane, *History of Dharmaśāstra,* Vol. I (Poona: Bhandarkar Oriental Research Institute, 1975), p. 43.

47. Ashok Mitra, ed., *District Census Handbook—1951: Midnapur* (Calcutta: Government of India Publication, 1953), see subsection on festivals.

48. Ashok Mitra, ed., *District Census Handbook—1951: Howrah* (Calcutta: Government of India Publication, 1953), see subsection on festivals.

49. Lewis Sydney Steward O'Malley, ed., *Bengal District Gazetteers: Bankura,* pp. 59–62; *Bengal District Gazetteers: Nadia* (Calcutta: Bengal Secretariat Press, 1910), p. 56; and *Bengal District Gazetteers: Birbhum* (Calcutta: Bengal Secretariat Press, 1910), pp. 32, 33.

50. Babu Jamini Mohan Das, "Note on the Grāma Devatī or Tutelary Village Deity of Orissa," *Journal of Asiatic Society of Bengal* 72, part III, no. 2 (1903) and O'Malley, *Bengal District Gazetteers: Puri,* pp. 76, 77, and 189.

51. Lewis Sydney Steward O'Malley, ed., *Bengal District Gazetteers: Angul* (Calcutta: Bengal Secretariat Press, 1908), p. 38.

52. Ibid.

53. Ibid.

Chapter 16

Ecological Cosmology in Hindu Tradition for the 21st Century

Rana P.B. Singh

Much has of course been written about ecology, environment, and their cultural interlinings during the last quarter of the 20th century, but little attention has been paid to its intrinsic roots that lie deeply embedded in human thought. The Second World War tells us the sad story of the consequences of industrial revolution and the heavy destruction caused by human greed. In the span of time, human beings realized that they failed to follow the right track of progress. This resulted in raised consciousness among individuals and organizations concerned with research and reflection about the deteriorating environmental situation. The Club of Rome, a group of concerned people and scientists, met in 1968 in Rome and produced a report on the predicament of mankind titled *The Limits of Growth*.[1] This book reminded the world that the resources of the earth were not unlimited; they recommended "the limit to growth." The report stated that five basic factors determine and limit growth on this planet: population, agricultural production, natural resources, industrial production, and pollution.

Contrary to this report, the Hudson Institute, the internationally recognized think tank, had a different view: the sky is the limit to growth. They refuted all the arguments of the Club and stated that the earth's resources were unlimited.[2] The views of the Hudson Institute helped industries to unscrupulously exploit and exhaust natural resources for unlimited profit. This led to further disastrous consequences. After 20 years, the Club of Rome released the sequel to the earlier study, named *Beyond the Limits*[3]—sending a message of hope as well as of warning, and further supporting the results and consequences concluded in the earlier study. That message is: The future of humankind is in its own hands if it changes its lifestyle with a view to saving the earth, consequently saving itself. Humanity has been depleting the resources of the earth and that has led to an ecological crisis, which in turn has endangered world peace. *The 30-Years Update to Limits of Growth* further stressed the need for reducing humanity's total ecological footprints through integrating balance among technological advance, personal change, and longer planning horizons in the way that allows respect, caring, and sharing across political boundaries.[4] The problem is therefore an ethical one—understanding our intrinsic values, practicing co-sharing, and envisioning interrelatedness.

Recent debate suggests that "religion has the capacity to form intentional groups and communities as well as to mobilize agents to work for certain noble goals."[5] In the debate for understanding the formation of "new publics in the 21st century," "publics" may be conceived as individuals and/or groups who attempt to create knowledge and/or achieve certain actions using religious ideals, beliefs, and/or symbols. Here, some clues from the ancient Indian (Hindu) traditions are worth taking into consideration. Religion (*dharma*) plays a vital role in the Hindu quest for understanding and practicing harmony between nature and humanity, which results in the formation of a cosmological awakening, i.e., "transcending the universe." This new ecospiritual consciousness (ethical conscience) has also proved its capacity to mobilize common masses and resources. However, it also sometimes turned to superstition, fundamentalism, and has been used as a political tool for emotional blackmailing. The message of "transcendence" may be taken as a call of "deep awakening" in the 21st century, and an onward march to ecosprituality may be taken as a "way."

Ecospirituality is a manifestation of the spiritual connection between human beings and the environment. It incorporates an intuitive and embodied awareness of all life and engages a relational view of person to planet, inner to outer landscape, and soul to soil.[6] It is a process and lifestyle of thought and realization that we belong to the universe, we are home in it, and this deep experience and revelation of belongingness can make our lives profoundly meaningful—as well as make the world more humane.[7]

The question of moral duty of a human being to save community and nature is a subject involving inherently deep thought, or ethical values. According to environmental philosopher Rolston: "The prescription of an ecological morality is 'mutual coercion, mutually agreed on' in which we limit freedom to grow in order to stabilize the ecosystem to the mutual benefit of all."[8] Imposition of value appears as a human response to the world, in association with nature, in the realization to the cosmic interrelatedness. This is an issue of human duty and a wish to promote cultural interrelatedness. Another environmental philosopher Callicott, who has examined a variety of religious traditions for their ecological insights, opines that Hindu tradition entails an understanding of reality that is essentially hostile to environmental concerns. He writes: "From the Hindu perspective, the empirical world is both unimportant, because it is not ultimately real, and contemptible, because it seduces the soul into crediting appearances, pursuing false ends, and thus earning bad *Karma*."[9] The claim by Callicot has to be considered in the light of the fact that it lacks knowledge of Sanskrit philosophical literature, and in no way conforms to field experiences in India. Advaita Vedanta is similarly blamed for encouraging attitudes of devaluation and neglect of the natural universe, and for advocating that nature is to be feared, despised, and transcended.[10] One should also take note of the mosaics of culture, traditions, transitions, interdependencies, and, above all, the varying lifestyles and differing philosophies that exist in every part of India distinctively and sometimes desperately.

In spite of tremendous scientific and technological innovations and their application, humankind today faces a crisis at several levels. The main idea of "progress and development" was conceived in the light of positivistic-reductionist, empiricist, and anthropocentric enterprises introduced in Europe in the 17th century. However, the alternative worldview of interconnectedness and holism is considered more relevant today. Modern science, like new physics, is recapitulating, in many ways, the ancient spiritual worldview of integral living, where sacrality had been the prime source to realize the spirit of place or power of nature.[11] The ethical domain is based essentially on foundational values, which for Gandhi was *ahiṃsā* (nonviolence), for Albert Schweitzer *reverence for life,* and for Aldo Leopold the *sacredness of land*. Schweitzer, a Nobel laureate and humanist philosopher, rightly said: "A man is ethical only when life, as such, is sacred to him, that of plants and animals as that of his fellow men, and when he devotes himself helpfully to all life that is in need of help."[12]

Hindu thought, which has survived from the remote past (at least since 3000 BCE), subscribes to the unity of life and to psychic attachment and sympathy with nature in different forms at various levels, through a variety of rituals and sacrifices. Callicot states approvingly that, "The Hindu tradition of monism and mysticism, no less than the theism and human supremicism of the Judeo-Christian and Islamic traditions, has ambivalent implications for environmental ethics."[13] The central monistic philosophy of Hindu tradition, Vedanta, recognizes that "fundamentally all life is one, that in essence everything is reality, and that this oneness finds its natural expression in a reverence for all things."[14] In the *Bhagavad Gītā*, the world is depicted as a unified world: "This entire universe is pervaded by My subtle presence" (9.4). Additionally, the ultimate goal is to attain a state of "functional nature with deity" (14.2). This ethical message is a call for environmental sensitivity leading to the domain of sustainability. Here, an attempt is made to present some of the selected viewpoints to understand the cultural-historical roots of Indian thought, especially Hindu tradition. Hindu tradition is a congregation of several sects, groups of adherents, monastic traditions, *kathenotheism* (worshipping many gods, one at a time), and variety of belief systems and rituals. The religious tradition represents over 14 percent of the world population of 7 billion people.

ECOLOGICAL COSMOLOGY: LIFE AND FIVE GROSS ELEMENTS

According to Hindu cosmogony, the five gross elements (*pañca mahābhūtas*) are responsible for the life substance in the cosmic creation. These "elements create, nurture and sustain all forms of life, and after death or decay, they absorb what was created earlier; thus they play an important role in preserving and sustaining the environment."[15] The *Mahābhārata* (12.198.14–19) states that the Supreme God created primordial man, who first made *sky;* from sky, *water* was made and from sea of water, *fire* and *air*—these latter two together made the *earth.* Hence, in a metaphysical sense, these elements are not separated from earth other. These elements are related to one another by means of their intrinsic nature leading to a bond among creatures.[16] In the Puranic theory of creation, the Svayambhu God Brahmā (self-born creator), being desirous of progeny, created water first. The *Bhāgavata Purāṇa* (1.3.2–5) says that primordial man was lying down in the waters of the universe.

Water (*Āpaḥ*)

Water is regarded as the primary materialization of Viṣṇu's *māyā* (energy), and therefore known as a visible manifestation of the divine essence.[17] In most of the ancient cultures, it is mythologized as the primal substance, from which all forms came and to which they will return.[18] In Hindu mythology, it is considered as the first sacred fluid for purification ritual. In the *Chāndogya Upaniṣad* (7.10.1), it is described as an attribute linking subtler fire and grosser earth in different forms. The *ṚgVeda* (10.129.3) says that "in the beginning, all was water, and there was darkness which engulfed it."

The environmental ethics and crisis of water pollution have been realized in Hindu thought in the ancient period. One of the hymns of the

ṚgVeda states: "The waters in the sky, the waters of the rivers, and the waters in well whose source is ocean, may all these sacred waters protect me" (7.49.2). To maintain the sacred power of water, norms have also been suggested: "one should not cause urine, stool, or cough in the water. Anything which is mixed with these impious objects; blood and poison should not be thrown into the water" (*Manusmṛti,* 4.55). The importance of water is fully elaborated in the *Mahābhārata:* "The creator first produced water for the maintenance of life among human beings. The water enriches life and its absence destroys all creatures and plant life" (12.18.4). But in the course of time, the implications drawn from the textual ideals and practice by the masses followed antipodal paths, which produced a scarcity of drinking water and a critical level of availability of pure water. A proverb says, "*binu pani, sab sun*" (without water, everything gets deserted).

Air (*Vāyu*)

In the later Vedic mythologies, *prāṇa* (breath of life) is identified as the superior vital force represented with the wind god (*Vāyu*), who is responsible for the breath of the universe and of life, thus forming a cosmic integrity with nature. The *ṚgVeda* (10.186.1) prays to Vāyu as Vāta, who is able to prolong our life and brings well-being. A later text, *Manusmṛti* (4.77) says that the life of all creatures depends upon the air. Furthermore, it is said that the body of all organic beings can be sustained only as long as the *prāṇa* inhabits it: "All these creatures enter with the breath (into the body), and with the breath they again depart out" (*Chāndogya Upaniṣad,* 1.11.5).

Earth (*Prithvī*)

The earth is perceived as mother and upholder of all (*ṚgVeda,* 1.155.2). The narratives that feature the earth goddess describe her as being offended by immoral, unethical, or criminal activities:

> Although the idea of polluting the earth does not seem to arise in these texts, there is the idea that human beings must act in ethically suitable ways or risk the wrath or discomfiture of the earth itself. That is, there is the idea of reciprocity between humans and the earth. The earth bears and feeds human beings, and in return they are responsible for behaving in ways that are inoffensive to the earth.[19]

It has been of immense symbolic significance in Hindu mythology, particularly with respect to identification, security, and maintenance of existence and continuity of human beings. Since ancient times, Hindus have been attached to agrarian life; the sense of attachment to the earth had led to the idea of it as goddess, mother, and overall "generator of natural life."

The *Prithvī Sūkta* of the *AtharvaVeda* (12), consisting of 63 verses, integrates most of the basic thoughts of Hindu sages concerning perceiving nature, the human dependency on the earth, and the resultant care and respect required.[20]

Fire/Light (*Agni/Tejaḥ*)

Fire has played a major role in many mythologies. Agni, the fire god in the Vedic period, stood as a powerful deity and as a cosmic principle that pervades creation. It is also accepted as the source of rain. The *Śatapatha Brāhmaṇa* says: "From Agni is born steam, from steam the cloud, from the cloud rain" (5.3.5.17). In Vedic cosmology, Agni is said to exist in the three cosmic realms: the heaven, the earth, and the underworlds (*ṚgVeda,* 3.22.2). Wherever there is being, there too is Agni as the principle of life and growth. He is referred to as the ultimate being with various kinships (*ṚgVeda,* 10.7.3).

Space/Sky (*Ākāa*)

The *ṚgVeda* (1.90.7) describes sky as the father and the earth as mother. Sky and space are referred to as synonymous with one another in the Vedic texts. Space is also conceived as a dwelling place of the forces of nature (water, air, earth, and fire), where the embryo of the universe was developed (*AtharvaVeda,* 1.11.2). According to *Upaniṣadic* dialogue, it is the space out of which all beings (their souls) came from, and it is where they go back after death, because space is the final refuge of all beings (*Chāndogya Upaniṣad,* 1.9.1).

Each of the above five elements, according to Hindu mythologies, is symbolized as some part of the body of primordial man, and the divine being is the inner soul of all. The *Viṣṇu Purāṇa* describes the cosmic form of Viṣṇu: "You are everything, earth, water, fire, air and space, the subtle world, the Nature-of-All (*pradhāna*) and the Person (*puruṣa*) who stands forever aloof" (3.17.14). Additionally, the *Muṇḍaka Upaniṣad* states:

> Fire is his head, his eyes the moon and sun; the regions of space, his ears; his voice, the revealed *Vedas;* wind his breath; his heart, the whole world, out of his feet, the earth. Truly he is the inner soul of all! (2.1.4)

This verse metaphorically illustrates harmonic integration in nature, and acknowledges the importance for human peace, happiness, and tranquility with respect to the human quest for self-identity in the universe. The version has also been described with respect to the incarnation of Lord Viṣṇu, the protector god among the Hindu trinity. According to the mythology, 10 incarnations of Viṣṇu exist, the first 5 of which are considered fundamental, referring symbolically to the body and symmetrically balancing the origin of the human being with his cosmic relationship (see Table 16.1).

The five incarnations of Viṣṇu symbolize the creation and evolution process that interconnects man and nature. According to the *Śatapatha Brāhmana* (1.8.1.1–6), the first incarnation, *fish,* symbolizes the origin of life in water. In this form, Viṣṇu had saved organic life-seeds from the great cosmic flood. The *tortoise* form refers to the life form, which equally enjoys water and land. The third form of *boar,* symbolizing the life of forest and land, helped to save earth from submergence in the cosmic flood. The *man–lion* refers to the phase of cooling earth, through which human power was established over demons. The fifth form, *dwarf* (a symbol of primitive man), attempted to control over the three realms of the world. According to the Hindu timescale, the *kalpa* (initial time) of life substance started around 432 million years ago and Viṣṇu took the form of a fish. The five later incarnations (not included in the table) present the growth of vivid cognition of the human psyche, like victory over the world (*ParaŚurāma*), ideal social rule (*Rāma*), the model of karma (*Kṛṣṇa*), message of peace and synthesis (*Buddha*), and the era of falsehood (*Kalkī,* yet to be born).

The cyclical process of evolution in the Vedic and Puranic literature recognizes the fundamental interdependence of all phenomena, or ecological awareness, even in sequence. Physicist Capra believes that "ecological awareness is spiritual in its deepest sense,. . . [and] the new vision of reality is in harmony with the visions of spiritual traditions."[21] The paradigm shift in new physics concerning the unified theory projects the Earth as a "self-organizing organism"—metaphorically the Earth as Mother.

THE SPIRIT OF PLACE

In ancient Indian thought, "sacrality" (*devatva*) was described as a manifesting force to understand and to experience the deeper insights. In visiting a sacred place (*tīrthasthāna*), we are not dealing with an unending journey back and forth across a piece of territory of land solely in pursuit of experiencing awe and wonder. Instead, we are looking at a sacred journey (*tīrthayātrā*), in which each stage has sacred significance—an inherent message and in-depth meaning. We certainly need new maps for another type of geography, another worldview[22] that is rooted in and starts from emotional and spiritual connections to place (*tīrthībhūtha*)—an inherent reality of humanity. Whenever human beings feel close to the subtle and powerful force of the place or land, "spirit of place" (*genius loci*) is experienced by human sensitivity. Of course every place has some potential power, nevertheless some places have special power and possess deeper

Table 16.1
Environmental Correlations in Hinduism

Incarnation (*Avatāra*)	Gross Element Symbol	Purpose	Nature Symbol	Body Symbol	Textual Reference	Pūjā Day in Practice (Dvādaśī)	Main Item for the Pūjā
Matsya (fish)	Water	Saving organic life-seeds from the great cosmic flood	Origin of life in water	Blood	SB 1.8.1.1-6	Mārga-śīrṣa S.12	Water
Kūrma (tortoise)	Air	Providing a base for creation from water	Life in water and land	Breath	SB 7.5.1.5	Pauṣa S.12	Copper or ghee
Varāha (boar)	Earth	Getting submerged earth out of the cosmic flood	Life in forest and land	Proper substance	SB 14.1.2.11	Māgha S.12	Gold
Narasiṁha (man-lion)	Fire	Getting established human power over demons	Phase of cooling the earth	Warmth	Mbh. 12.339.77-102	Phālunga K.12	Wood
Vāmana (dwarf)	Sky/ Ether	Getting control over the three realms of world	Origin of primitive man	Mind	SB 1.2.5.1	Chaitra S.12	Icon

Notes: SB, the *Śatapatha Brāhmaṇa;* Mbh, the *Mahābhārata;* S, the *Śukla Pakṣa,* light-half; and K, the *Kṛṣṇa Pakṣa,* dark-half (both in the Hindu lunar calendar).

intensity (e.g., sacred place). By manifestation of this power (*pavitrībhū*), these places become the points of "geographical sanctity" (*bhū-pavitrika*). A sacred place is a place that symbolically represents the world, ultimately reflecting the order and wholeness like a mystic web of the cosmos. Its very own layout encloses a world, and to man it becomes, at a deeply sensual level, the cosmos.[23]

By the realization of the manifesting sacrality in the place and landscape, the associated territory converges to sacredscape (*tīrthakṣetra*). The spatial level of territorial exposition starts from kin–clan sacred ties and reaches to the higher psychic level of ethical values for mankind. There always exists a "spirit of place" that interconnects the varying niches of level and intensity. Of course, at present, perhaps due to the increasing pace of individualism, this unifying spirit is now suppressed. However, by the ethical revival of the deeply rooted old values, a healthy tradition of making a balance is being promoted. Pilgrimage (*tīrthakṣetra*) is the strongest and oldest tradition in Hindu civilization, with an aim to cross this materialistic world and experience the higher realm. The variety of a rich, vibrant, and diverse physical landscape has contributed spiritual insights to their corresponding geographies of visionary wisdom and enlightenment.[24]

According to the *AtharvaVeda* (18.4.7), one can obtain relief from all forms of suffering the moment one reaches the territory of sacredscape. In the cosmogonic frame of sanctifying environment, the whole of India is portrayed as sacredscape and symbolized as Mother (*Bhārata Mātā*) consisting of holy spots (*pīṭhas*) as represented by her body. There are 51 *Śakti Pīṭhas* in India, where some part of Satī's body (corpse-form of goddess Pārvatī, wife of Śiva) fell down. Among the 51 *Pīṭhas,* 2 are not yet identified and 9 are out of India. In fact, location of these sites refers to the concept of Greater India, *BhāratavarŚa.* These *Pīṭhas* are identical to the number of Devanāgrī/Sanskrit alphabets, i.e., "51." Each of the alphabets is associated with a *Pīṭhas* in a systematic manner.

Since ancient times, the act of pilgrimage has been the most popular way to fulfill human beings' quest for a divine connection between man and the environment—an experience of the "spirit of place." Of course, this is a hallmark of religious devotion; this is also an act of cleansing, healing, and revelation of geographical sanctity.[25] Pilgrimage is an act of crossing; to cross is to be transformed. Sacredscape is the place (and territory) of transformation. Such a place becomes holy where "wholeness" is preserved. Pilgrimage is a *spirit*—a guiding force unifying the divinity and humanity, i.e., a search for wholeness. Ultimately, the overall wholeness of landscape, and its sacred and symbolic geography, converges to a *faithscape* that encompasses sacred place, sacred time, sacred meanings, and sacred rituals, embodying both symbolic and tangible elements of the psyche in an attempt to realize man's identity in the cosmos.

Hindu tradition places a great emphasis on correct conduct and on fulfillment of duty, which often includes obligations of involving environmental preservation. That is how Hindus regard rivers as sacred, and in the concept of *līlā,* the creative play of the gods, Hindu theology engages the world as a creative manifestation of the divine.[26] In Hindu mythologies, the sacred Gaṇgā flows through the three realms of the heaven, the earth, and the underworlds (*tripathagā*)—respectively as the Mandākinī, the Gaṇgā, and the Bhogavatī. The Gaṇgā manifests the spirit of sustainability as the primordial fluid serving as the savior of life and as a divine energy interlinking the three realms. That is how the Gaṇgā is a liquid axis mundi, a pathway connecting all spheres of reality. She is also known as the Mother Ganga (Gaṇgā *Māī*), bringing life in the form of sacred water.[27] Her spatial form is manifested in five territories lying in different parts of India where the regional sacred river is known as Gaṇgā of that direction, i.e., the Mandākinī (the Gaṇgā of the north), the Mahānadī (the east), the Kāverī (the south), the Narmadā (the west), and the Godāvarī (the center). This psychic process of archetypal manifestation and acceptance in the tradition, and to be called "*Gangization,*" enhances the personality of the Gaṇgā as a "prototype of all the rivers of India."[28]

The above two examples are representative of the environmental sensitivity to the Mother Earth and her power of manifestation. This is a process and search for ecological roots through understanding the foundational value of life, i.e., the sacredness of land and spirit of place. At present, the unified way, "to approach social and cognitive environment is to encourage geography to accept salience of place as a great potentiality."[29]

THE SPIRIT OF SUSTAINABILITY

The ethics of "sustainable development," to which almost everyone subscribes today, requires this generation to use the world's environmental resources in ways that do not jeopardize the ability of future generations to meet their own needs. To be successful, this principle requires another dimension—reverence and revelation (*ecospirituality*). Development should preserve, not destroy, those assets of the natural and spiritual power of our own cultural heritage, which future generations would also wish to enjoy and cherish. The spirit of sustainability can be thought of as the ethic to behave in ways that help others and to realize the deeper nature of things—the cosmic integrity that is ultimately the sanctity of life. This involves a way of life and action determined by the deeper principle of realizing the intrinsic value one's actions serve. This is the call of the time—"Care the Earth, care ourselves," as proclaimed by Rolston: "A century ago the challenge was to know where you were geographically in a blank spot on the map, but today we are bewildered philosophically in what has long been mapped as a moral blank space. Despite our scientific and cultural taming of wild nature we will wander, confused as how to value it."[30] Obviously, "since the roots of [ecological] trouble are so largely religious, the remedy must also be essentially religious, whether that or not. We must re-think and re-feel our nature and destiny."[31] Ethical values are the moral force in the sustainable existence, progress, maintenance, and continuance for the human being.

The disappearing presence of Hindu thinking about the man–nature–cosmos relationship is one of the basic causes for the present environmental crisis that India is facing today. Mahatma Gandhi warned us that "Nature has enough for everybody's need, but not for everybody's greed."[32] During the past 700 years of foreign cultural domination—beginning with Islam and followed by European Christianity—the ancient Hindu value system has lost many of its facets. Nevertheless, the seeds of this ancient system of spiritual wisdom are still preserved in religious ethics found in ancient writings and surviving rituals. A mass awakening of awareness in context of old cultural values would promote a new spirit of sustainability. Let us raise the general consciousness and awareness to interlink the concept of sanctifying Earth and community development. If there should be a moral imperative for sustainable development, we need a sense of sanctifying about the Earth.[33]

The Gandhian view of nonviolence (*ahiṃsā*), vegetarianism, and *karma* (right action) is based on the idea of total spiritual interconnectedness of all life, of the divine within all life. One has to realize that "the living Earth has a right to life, and that right is the primary moral argument for sustainable life."[34] Gandhian thought is more relevant today and well suited to the soul and society of India. Gandhi gathered strength and inspiration to promote the sense of self-realization from the *Bhagavad Gītā:* "He whose self is harmonized by yoga seeth the Self abiding in all beings and all being in the Self; everywhere he sees the same" (7.29). We need to make development sustainable, both environmentally and culturally. The *Padma Purāṇa* prescribes punishment for the persons involved in acts of environmental pollution: "A person, who is engaged in killing creatures, polluting well, and ponds, and tanks and destroying gardens, certainly goes to hell" (*Bhūmikhaṇḍa,* 96.7–8).

The minimal core of intrinsic values for right conservation and preservation of the spirit of sustainability is formed by the following: *Reverence,* the deeper vision of the sanctity of life; *responsibility,* connecting link between ethics and rationality; *frugality,* grace without waste; and *ecojustice.*[35] The idea of reverential development is, in fact, an exposition of integration between *dharma* (moral code of conduct) and *karma* (right action). This idea, in another way, is unitary in the broadest and deepest sense, combining reverence and sanctity of life with contemporary socioeconomic, moral, cultural, and traditional premises to bring about peace and harmony with nature.[36] Peace and poise are narrated by the Vedic seers as the precondition of orderly and sustainable ecospiritual development. A hymn in the *YajurVeda* (10.17.1), a text of the 10th century BCE says:

There is peace in heavenly realm
There is peace in the environment
The water is cooling; herbs are healing
The plants are peace-giving
There is harmony in the celestial objects and perfection in knowledge;
Everything in the universe is peaceful
Peace pervades everywhere.
May that peace come to us!

In the spirit of the deeply rooted sense of attachment of inner spirit and human awakening, Rabindranath Tagore, in his *Gītāñjali* (1913), has composed a book of lyrics that preserved the essence of the Indian view of mankindness and perfection of *dharma,* and the vision of divineness that acquired universal appeal. He received the Nobel Prize for literature as a token of the recognition of his vision. He soars high among its 103 stanzas, which include the following:

Where the mind is without fear and the head is held high
Where knowledge is free
Where the world has not been broken up into fragments
By narrow domestic walls
Where words come out from the depth of truth
Where tireless striving stretches its arms towards perfection
Where the clear stream of reason has not lost its way
Into the dreary desert sand of dead habit
Where the mind is led forward by thee
Into ever-widening thought and action
Into that heaven of freedom, my Father, let my country awake![37]

The spirit of sustainability is also related to ecological identity, and refers to "all the different ways people construe themselves in relationship to the earth as manifested in personality, values, actions and sense of self."[38] Following the Vedic reflection, sustainability refers to the maintenance of a unified sensibility in search for wholeness and interrelationships among matter, life, and mind. This viewpoint is the essence of ethics behind the development and maintenance of Indian heritage—for which the Sanskrit/Hindi word "*dharohara,*" which is derived from "the mother earth" (*dharā*) and "endeavor of identity through time" (*ihara*), is explained in terms of roots—and "our" deep glories of the past.[39]

Modernization and messages contained in ancient wisdom should be allowed to coexist to help realize humanity's link with nature. This ideology should be taken as an environmental ethic having sacrality and deep attachment at the core. One may also hope for a revival of the sense of belongingness in the light of "ecoethics," preserving the age-old intangible spirit of sustainability and recognizing our ecological identity in the cosmic web of interconnectedness of all beings—a message of ecospirituality.

EPILOGUE: THE MARCH AHEAD

In the course of the acculturation process, the ideology of materialism, consumerism, and individualism, which was always negated in traditional Hindu thought, has been accepted by contemporary society.[40] At the other end, the movement to revive ancient cultural values is turning to fundamentalism as promoted by some groups. The old principle *satyameva jayate* (only truth triumphs) is now replaced by *artha eva jayate* (only wealth triumphs). The foreign cultural domination of India during the past 700 years and the influence of imported culture have played a major role in this transformation.[41]

It seems that by encouraging politicians and bureaucrats to take a more holistic view of the global ecosystem, based on self-realization and an awareness of deep human values, many of the complexities and obstacles in sustainable development may be resolved. The need of spirituality-oriented education should also be accepted as an alternative strategy. The physicist and ecophilosopher Capra feels that spirituality will ultimately lead to profound change in our social and political structures. Let us promote the attitude to humanity (say, moral ethics) by balancing and reconciling the rational-scientific and the intuitive-spiritual viewpoints in our society and ourselves. For Mahatma Gandhi, "right" comes only through the realization of truth. He says: "God is the means and Truth is the end." For him, *ahiṃsā* is linked with notions of *karma* (right act). The earliest mention of the ethical importance of *karma* in the Hindu context is found in the *Bṛhadāraṇyaka Upaniṣad* that states: "One becomes good by good action, bad by bad" (3.2.10.113). This ethic constitutes the norm of *dharma* (moral code of right conduct). The *Mahābhārata* says: "One should never do that to another which one regards as injurious to one's own self. This, in brief, is the rule of dharma" (13.113.8). Similarly, concepts such as the *dao* (underlying law of universe) of Daoism, *li* (social propriety) of Confucianism, and the Greek concepts of *dike* (the order of justice) and *logos* (the orderly principle of the universe) also suggest, in the broadest sense, that human development takes place within limits.[42] This is the prime duty of human beings to realize, that for the constant perennial flow of water (life) in the river of progress in the 21st century, a lifeway and a life philosophy that integrate ecological interconnectedness and human well-being have to be accepted as a process through deeper understanding, mass awakening, and self-realization.

Gandhi's life and work do hold possible implications for the postmodern approach to environment, mostly based on his principle of *ahiṃsā* (nonviolence) and *aparigraha* (nonpossession). He says: "I must confess that I do not draw a sharp or any distinction between economics and ethics. Economics that hurt the moral well-being of an individual or a nation are immoral and, therefore, sinful."[43] His theory of *ahiṃsā* was not strict like a sectarian rule; he says: "whoever believes in *ahimsa* will engage himself in occupations that involve the least possible violence."[44] Without any political propaganda, Acharya Tulsi's *Anuvrat movement* is promoting the process of self-purification and self-control, in many ways akin to Gandhism, since 1949. In support of this movement, Sarvepalli Radhakrishnan says: "A civilised human being must be free from greed, vanity, passion, anger. Civilisations decline if there is a coarsening of moral fibre, if there is a callousness of heart. . . . It requires strict adherence to the principles of good life."[45] Think of what Brook said: "If spiritual teaching and practice is meant to enable us to be fully aware of our own mind, yet doesn't enable us to see this 'splitting' process when it happens, maybe we need to look more deeply at the way we are applying the practice."[46]

In ancient Indian thought, we "find a way to bring our scientific understanding of nature's organic complexity an integral harmony with a spiritual understanding of reality's simplicity."[47] The *Bhagavad Gītā* (4.8) states laconically: "He who sees inaction in action and action in inaction, he is wise among men, and he does all action harmoniously."[48] Gandhi's whole life and his movement are the messages to justify the viewpoints and worldview he experienced and practiced. It is with such conviction that Gandhi always hopes for peace between religions as they all are grounded and inspired by an indwelling lure toward deeper wisdom relevant to salvation, however understood. The close connection forged with organic philosophy by Whitehead and Gandhi in terms of "ecotheology might be relevant to the larger context of the many world religions and to the better hopes of the world as a whole."[49] He further adds that the five *challenges* relative to our social locations and historical situations need serious engagement for the sake of interconnectedness and ecological cosmology: compassion (reverential/ moral concerns), repentance (cultural reconstruction/self-critical), simplicity (frugality/Geltung), ecological outlook (eternal vision/sustainability), and diversity (befriending/ pluralistic).[50] All together, they call and promote divine love as it beckons human beings to live compassionately and creatively.

Mills concludes his promises of "sociological imagination" by his future-oriented and firm exposition:

> It is now the social scientist's foremost political and intellectual task—for here the two coincide—to make clear the elements of contemporary uneasiness and indifference. It is the central demand

> made upon her by other cultural workers—by physical scientists and artists, by the intellectual community in general. It is because of this task and these demands, I believe, that the social sciences are becoming the common nominator of our cultural period, and the sociological imagination our most needed quality of mind.[51]

This is comparable to the provocative statement by Callicott: "As citizens of one planet and as denizens of its many cultural worlds, we hold the fate of the earth in our hands. And of all the means available to save it, none are so powerful or so resourceful as our collective stock of traditional ideas and ideals."[52] After all, if a mutually enhancing relationship between human civilization and the natural environment is to evolve, all our thinking and lifeways must be supplemented by environmental moral sensibility what six decades earlier American conservationist Aldo Leopold called an "ecological conscience." On the line of Gaian worldview, it is strongly argued that "we need to establish a right relationship with the planet as a living entity in which we are indissolubly embedded—and to which we all accountable."[53] Dupré's proclamation that "spirituality is of world affirmation" and there is no separate realm is a message of surrounding interconnectedness of the cosmological web, where we experience and live together with ecospiritual reality. Mazis adds rightly that "the surround, of which we are part, is the source of spiritual inspiration and the object of reverence, the gift-giver to all living and nonliving beings and the necessary focus of our care."[54]

> If I am not for myself, who will be?
> And if I am only for myself, what am I?
> And if not now, when?

So, Rabbi Hillel asks: If not now, when? Now is the time for repentance: for learning about and acknowledging the harm we have done, and for changing our views and lifestyles and our attitudes toward global, national, and local issue.[55]

Change is the law of nature. Humanity's progress is transformation. Evolution is gradual change. Revolution is accelerated change. Revelation is eternal change. We should meet to discuss moving from evolution in the roots, passing through the revolution of contemporary understanding, and reaching to the destination of revelation in creating the world of harmonious brotherhood where peace and happiness become the ultimate reality of life. One of the crucial crises that Hindu tradition faces today is misconceived idea that ritual frame of performing religion and the life philosophy and eternal quest of spirituality are complementary, and in many ways also identical. In the textual tradition, however, in course of transformation of thought-and-practice, it took an unusual turn as accepted by the masses.

As opposed to traditional intellectuals, whose concern derives from the self-enclosed realm of elite cultural life, let us cut across the disciplinary boundaries in making "civic" environmentalism and ecospirituality a way of life and concern for humanity.[56] Think *universally,* see *globally,* and act *locally* but *insightfully.* This is an appeal for cosmic vision, global humanism, and self-realization. Altogether, it promotes an ecospiritual worldview, a spirit of wholeness, and a sense of holiness grounded on an evolutionary cosmology—by the core of which lies the sanctity, the faith, and the vision of ecospirituality.

NOTES

1. Donella H. Meadows, Dennis L. Meadows, Jørgen Randers, and William W. Behrens III, *The Limits to Growth: A Report for the Club of Rome Project on Project on the Predicament of Mankind* (New York: New American Library, 1972).
2. Arun Balasubramanian, *Ecodevelopment: Towards a Philosophy of Environmental Education* (Singapore: Friedrich Naumann Stiftung, 1984), pp. 12, 13.
3. Donella Meadows, Dennis Meadows, and Jørgen Randers, *Beyond the Limits: Confronting Global Collapse, Envisioning a Sustainable Future* (Post Mills, VT: Chelsa Green Publishing, 1992).
4. Donella Meadows, Jorgen Randers, and Dennis Meadows, *The Limits to Growth: The 30-Year Update* (White River Junction, VT: Chelsea Green Publishing, 2004), p. xv.
5. Valerie Lincoln, "Ecospirituality: A Pattern that Connects," *Journal of Holistic Nursing* 18, no. 3 (2000): 227–44.
6. Ibid.
7. Fritjof Capra, *The Hidden Connection* (New Delhi: Harper Collins India, 2003), pp. 59, 60.
8. Holmes Ralston III, *Philosophy Gone Wild* (Buffalo, NY: Prometheus Books, 1989), p. 15.
9. J. Baird Callicott, *Earth's Insights: A Multicultural Survey of Ecological Ethics from the Mediterranean Basin to the Australian Outback* (Berkeley, CA: University of California, 1994), p. 48.
10. Lance E. Nelson, ed., *Purifying the Earthly Body of God: Religion and Ecology in Hindu India* (Albany, NY: State University of New York Press, 1998), p. 63.
11. Rana P. B. Singh, "Development in India: Appraising Self Retrospection," in *Geographical Thoughts in India: Snapshots and Vision for the 21st Century* (Newcastle: Cambridge Scholars Publishing, 2009), pp. 344–422.
12. Albert Schweitzer, *Out of My Life and Thought* (New York: Holt, Rinehart and Winston, 1949), pp. 158, 159.
13. Callicott, *Earth's Insights,* p. 47.
14. Eliot Deutsch, "Vedanta and Ecology," *Indian Philosophical Annual* 16 (1970): 3, –4.
15. Onkar Prasad Dwivedi, "Vedic Heritage for Environmental Stewardship," *Worldviews: Environment and Religion* 1, no. 1 (1997): 27.
16. Rana P. B. Singh, "Nature and Cosmic Integrity: A Search in Hindu Geographical Thought," *GeoJournal* 25, no. 2 (1992): 143, and also see his "Ecospirituality:

Organic Vision and Global Message," in *Uprooting Geographic Thoughts in India: Toward Ethics, Ecology and Culture in 21st Century* (Newcastle: Cambridge Scholars Publishing, 2009), p. 131.

17. Heinrich Robert Zimmer, *Myths and Symbols in Indian Art and Civilization* (Princeton, NJ: Princeton University Press, 1972), p. 34.

18. Mircea Eliade, *Patterns in Comparative Religion* (London: Sheed and Ward, 1958), p. 188.

19. David Kinsley, *Ecology and Religion: Ecological Spirituality in Cross-Cultural Perspective* (Englewood Cliffs, NJ: Prentice-Hall, Inc., 1995), p. 58.

20. Onkar Prasad Dwivedi, "Dharmic Ecology," in Christopher Key Chapple and Mary Evelyn Tucker, eds., *Hindu Tradition and Ecology: The Intersection of Earth, Sky, and Water* (Cambridge, MA: CSWR, Harvard University Press, 2000), p. 10.

21. Fritjof Capra, *The Tao of Physics,* 3rd ed. (Boston, MA: Shambhala, 1991), p. 326.

22. Paul Devereux, *Secrets of Ancient and Sacred Places* (London: Blandford, 1993), p. 7.

23. Rana P.B. Singh, ed., "Introduction: The Layout of Sacred Places," *Special Issue of Architecture and Behaviour* 9, no. 2 (1993): 162.

24. Adrian Cooper, *Sacred Mountains* (Edinburgh: Floris Books, 1997), pp. 171–74.

25. Paul Devereux, *Re-Visioning the Earth* (New York: Fireside Books, 1996), p. 128.

26. Gary T. Gardner, *Inspiring Progress: Religion's Contributions to Sustainable Development* (New York: W.W. Norton & Co., 2006), p. 146 and Thomas Berry, *The Great Work* (New York: Bell Tower, 1999), p. 70.

27. Rana P.B. Singh, "Water Symbolism and Sacred Landscape: A Study of Benares (Varanasi)," *Erdkunde* 48, no. 3 (September 1994): 210.

28. Rana P.B. Singh, "The Ganga (Ganges) River: Image and Symbol of India," in *Geographical Thoughts in India,* p. 274.

29. Rana P.B. Singh, "The Spirit and Power of Place: Human Environment and Sacrality," *The Ley Hunter,* no. 127 (Summer 1997): 32.

30. Holmes Rolston III, *Environmental Ethics* (Philadelphia, PA: Temple University, 1988), p. xiii.

31. Lynn Townshend White Jr., "The Historical Roots of Our Ecological Crisis," *Science* 155 (March 1967): 1207.

32. Onkar Prasad Dwivedi, "Satyagraha for Conservation: Awakening the Spirit of Hindu Tradition," in J. Ronald Engel and Joan Gibb Engel, eds., *Ethics of Environment and Development* (Tucson, AZ: University of Arizona Press, 1990), p. 211.

33. Rajni Kothari, "Environment, Technology and Ethics," in Engel and Engel, *Ethics of Environment and Development,* p. 33.

34. Ibid., p. 32.

35. Henryk Skolimowski, "Reverence for Life," in Engel and Engel, *Ethics of Environment and Development,* pp. 101, 102.

36. Ibid., p. 103.

37. Rabindranath Tagore, *Gitanjali: Song Offerings* (London: Macmillan Co., 1913), p. 35.

38. Mitchell Thomashow, *Ecological Identity* (Cambridge, MA: MIT Press, 1995), p. 3.

39. Rana P. B. Singh, "Sacredscape and Urban Heritage in India: Contestation and Perspective," in Brian Shaw and Roy Jones, eds., *Contested Urban Heritage* (London: Ashgate Avebury Publications, 1997), p. 101.

40. See Gardner, *Inspiring Progress*.

41. Dwivedi, "Satyagraha for Conservation," p. 210.

42. Gardner, *Inspiring Progress*, p. 92.

43. Parmeshwari Dayal, *Gandhian Theory of Social Reconstruction* (New Delhi: Atlantic Publishers & Distributers, 2006), p. 201.

44. Ibid., p. 35.

45. Christopher Key Chapple, "Nonviolence to Animals, Earth and Self," in *Asian Traditions* (Albany, NY: SUNY Press, 1993), p. 42.

46. Elaine Brook, "Gaia and the Sacred Feminine," in Mary Midgley, ed., *Earthy Realism: The Meaning of Gaia* (Exeter: Imprint Academic, 2007), pp. 106, 107.

47. Eliot Deutsch, "A Metaphysical Grounding for Natural Reverence: East-West," in J. Baird Callicott and Roger T. Ames, eds., *Nature in Asian Traditions of Thought* (Albany, NY: SUNY Press, 1989), p. 265.

48. Ibid.

49. Jay McDaniel, "Ecotheology and World Religions," in Laurel Kearns and Catherine Keller, eds., *Ecospirit: Religions and Philosophies for the Earth* (New York: Fordham University Press, 2007), p. 37.

50. Jay McDaniel, *Gandhi Hope: Learning from Other Religions as a Path to Peace* (Maryknoll, NY: Orbis Books, 2005), pp. 125, 126.

51. C. Wright Mills, *The Sociological Imagination* (New York: Oxford University Press, 1959).

52. J. Baird Callicot, *Earth's Insights: A Survey of Ecological Ethics from the Mediterranean Basin to the Australian Outback* (Berkeley, CA: University of California Press, 1997), p. 234.

53. Stephan Harding, *Animate Earth: Science, Intuition and Gaia* (Devon: Green Books, 2006).

54. Glen A. Mazis, "Ecospirituality and the Blurred Boundaries of Humans, Animals, and Machines," in Kearns and Keller, *Ecospirit*, p. 155.

55. Anne Primavesi, "Can Gaia Forgive Us?," in Midgley, *Earthy Realism*, p. 73.

56. Roger S. Gottlieb, "Religious Environmentalism: What It Is, Where It Is Heading and Why We Should Be Going in the Same Direction," *Journal for the Study of Religion, Nature and Culture (London)* 1, no. 1 (March 2007): 90.

About the Editors and Contributors

EDITORS

MADHU KHANNA is a Professor at Jamia Millia Islamia in New Delhi, India, working in the area of Indic studies with specialization in Shakta Tantra. She is also interested in goddess traditions in India, gender and religion, and ritual studies. She has published *Hindutva: Questioning the Nature of Discourse? Critical Encounters between the Ideology of the Hindu State and Traditional Theology* (2004) and contributed chapters in numerous edited volumes. She is also a founding member and President of Tantra Foundation, New Delhi.

ARVIND SHARMA is the Birks Professor of Comparative Religion in the Faculty of Religious Studies at McGill University in Montreal, Canada. He has published numerous books on a wide range of topics such as Hinduism, world religions, human rights, women in religion, and philosophy of religion. He was instrumental in organizing two global conferences on World's Religions after September 11, which met in Montreal in 2006 and 2011.

CONTRIBUTORS

RADHA MADHAV BHARADWAJ is an Associate Professor in history at Deen Dayal Upadhyaya College, University of Delhi, New Delhi, India.

I.H. AZAD FARUQI is a Professor at the Centre for the Study of Comparative Religion and Civilizations in Jamia Millia Islamia, New Delhi, India. Specializing in Islamic civilization and culture, and world religions, he has written on Sufism and Bhakti and published in both Urdu and English publications.

ANURADHA GHOSH is a lecturer at the Department of English and Modern European Languages in Jamia Millia Islamia, New Delhi, India. She specializes in film, media, and culture studies, and philosophy, and has published numerous articles and essays in the field of humanities.

GEORGE JAMES is an Associate Professor of philosophy and religion at the University of North Texas, Denton, Texas, with specialization in comparative environmental ethics, environmental issues and movements in India, and phenomenology. He has lectured at numerous symposia and had a photographic exhibition on "Waterways of India" in 2007.

BIDISHA KUMAR is a PhD candidate in the field of philosophy and religion studies at the University of North Texas, Denton, Texas.

TRAN MY-VAN is an Associate Professor and Convenor in international and Asian studies at the Division of Education, Arts and Social Sciences in School of Communication, International Studies and Languages, University of South Australia, Magill, South Australia. Her work engages the history and politics of Asia, in particular Southeast Asia, and the East–West encounter and implications. She is a member of the Order of Australia (AM) for service to the Vietnamese community and to the promotion of multiculturalism and Asian studies.

JOSEPH T. O'CONNELL taught at St. Michael's College and the Centre for the Study of Religion, University of Toronto, Toronto, Canada, from 1968 to 2000, and he made regular research visits to India and Bangladesh. His distinguished academic career includes teaching appointments at Oxford University, Visva-Bharati University, India, and more recently at the University of Dhaka, Bangladesh, where he has been instrumental in the establishment of the Department of World Religions and Culture for the past 10 years. Beyond his multifaceted scholarly contributions of teaching, writing, and curriculum development, his deep social conscience found scope in his support of various causes involving social and political injustice as they became evident to him. He passed away in May 2012, during the final preparation of this book. He will be missed.

JOSEPH PRABHU has been teaching at CSULA since 1978, and acted as visiting professor at UC Berkeley, UC Santa Barbara, Harvard, Occidental College, Boston University, and universities in India and Germany in that time as well. His interests range from metaphysics and ethics to comparative religion and social and political theory. At the moment (2012), he is working on three books, in various stages of completion: *Liberating Gandhi: Community, Empire and a Culture of Peace, Human Rights in Cross-Cultural Perspective,* and *Hegel, India and the Dark Face of Modernity.* He has published widely on the topics of Gandhi, Panikkar, human rights, and postcolonialism.

MALINI SARAN is the coauthor with Vinod C. Khanna of *The Ramayana in Indonesia,* published in 2004. She had lived for 12 years in Southeast Asia, where she did the research for this book. She has had several publications on the subject, and is currently collaborating on a translation from Hindi into English of *Rāmakathā and Other Essays* (2010), by Rev. Father Camille Bulcke.

RANA P.B. SINGH is a Professor of cultural geography and heritage studies at Banaras Hindu University, Varanasi, India. He is the founding president of several organizations, including Society of Pilgrimage Studies, Society of Heritage Planning and Environmental Health, and Indo-Nordic Cultural Association. He has been involved in studying, performing, and promoting heritage planning, ecotourism, and rural studies and development in the Varanasi region for the last three decades. He has given lectures at various centers in America, Europe, East Asia, and Australia on these topics. He also serves as activist, collaborator, organizer, cultural analyst, and writer on Indian culture, Hinduism, and the Varanasi region.

AHMAD SOHAIB is an Assistant Professor at the Centre for the Study of Comparative Religion and Civilizations in Jamia Millia Islamia, New Delhi, India. His research is in the field of social history of early Buddhism, particularly the problem of early Buddhist identity, and Buddhism and caste. He is currently completing his doctoral thesis "Going into the Tiśarana: In Quest of Identity among the Followers of Buddhadhamma in the Majjhimadeśa: From the Time of the Buddha to Pre-Gupta Period" at the Centre for Historical Studies, Jawaharlal Nehru University, New Delhi, India.

ASHOK VOHRA is a Professor and Head of the Department of Philosophy at the University of Delhi, New Delhi, India. His research interests include Wittgenstein, philosophy of religion, contemporary Indian philosophy, philosophy of mind, and cognitive sciences. He was awarded Swami Pranavananda Darshan Puruskar for best book in philosophy by Akhil Bhartiya Darshan Parishad in 1987, 1996, and 1998.

GERRIT DE VYLDER is an Associate Professor at Department of Business Studies in Lessius Hogeschool, Antwerp, Belgium, as well as an affiliated researcher at Leuven University, Leuven, Belgium. He has given lectures on globalization, economics of religion, and problems of economic growth at a number of institutions and has presented papers at international conferences and workshops in Belgium, India, China, Colombia, Poland, the Netherlands, and Norway. He is currently working on the history of globalization (an Asia-centric point of view), and as a member of the Advisory Board of Spirituality in Economics and Society; he is also working on the relationship between religion (Hinduism, Buddhism, Islam, and Christianity) and economics, and between Orientalist literature and economics.

ALBERT WELTER has established a reputation as a leading expert in the academic study of Chan (Zen) Buddhist texts and Chinese Buddhism during the transition from the Tang (late medieval) to the Song (early modern) dynasties (9th–11th centuries). While popular images of Zen and Buddhism emphasize exotic ideas and eccentric characteristics, he interprets these as textual representations embedded in a particular East-Asian intellectual and cultural context. His research has been supported since 1999 by the Social Sciences and Humanities Research Council of Canada. In 2006–2007, he was awarded a China–Canada Scholars' Exchange grant, and was a visiting professor at Renmin University in Beijing. In 2009, he sponsored a workshop, "Exploring Diversity: Human Rights in China," and in 2010, he initiated the university's East Asian Language and Culture program.

GHULAM-SARWAR YOUSOF is one of Malaysia's most distinguished scholars and one of the world's leading specialists of traditional Southeast Asian theater. He was responsible for setting up Malaysia's first performing arts program at the Science University of Malaysia in Penang in 1970. He served at that university as lecturer and Associate Professor. He joined the Cultural Centre, University of Malaya, Kuala Lumpur, Malaysia as Professor in 2002. Currently, he is an Adjunct Professor at the center, and also Director of The Asian Cultural Heritage Centre Berhad, a private research initiative set up by him to promote research in traditional Asian cultures. He has carved a unique niche for himself in the area of Southeast Asian theater, with meticulous fieldwork and research, in some previously unexplored genres, resulting in the most important existing publication, his *Dictionary of Traditional South-East Asian Theatre*. His vast collection of fieldwork materials and documentation is currently held by the Asian Cultural Heritage Centre Berhad.

Index

Edwards Brothers Malloy
Thorofare, NJ USA
February 18, 2013